Biscuit 365

(Biscuit - Volume 1)

Enjoy 365 Days with Amazing Biscuit Recipes in Your Own Biscuit Cookbook!

Emma Kim

Contents

8

Introduction

***

Eating bread that's freshly baked at home makes us appreciate the value of superior-quality ingredients. Compared to other cooking methods, baking bread is well-loved by experienced bakers, while it causes anxiety to beginners. To bake successfully, you need a combination of high-quality ingredients, the right equipment, a balanced recipe, skilled hands, and of course, creativity.

Long years of training people how to bake bread have made me see how home bakers take honing their baking skills seriously. They're enthusiastic about improving their baking skills and putting a personal touch to each bread they make. But they also have to innovate and experiment. I aimed to come up with a book series for serious home bakers. This will also be a great material for casual holiday bakers who are building their technical skills gradually to find the best recipe. I wished to produce something that's not only easy to read but also reflects my own passion for baking

Somehow, I have gotten back to where I came from through this bread series. This bread baking series is indeed my best—from the traditional white bread that's the staple in America to quick doughs made using a food processor; top homemade croissants; best-known flatbreads and pizza; simplest breads to bake; and details about sour starters. You are handling "Biscuit 365 Volume 1"

This series also features information on breakfast rolls; lavish celebration breads; tasty breads for main dishes; and a wide range of healthy and delicious everyday loaves. Many American-style breads are baked in the commonly-known rectangular-loaf shape, which tend to be a richer and little sweeter than their crusty and free-form European predecessors. A lot of excellent breads are easy to make, almost similar to cakes in the sense that they require accurate amounts of flour, liquid, flavorings, fat, and leavening. However, these breads provide something of value to today's bakers: quick and easy preparation.

Baking a homemade bread is an easy way to achieve a well-balanced and healthy diet.

You won't find confusing and complex techniques or trick recipes in this book. Instead, you'll get many simple tips that are usually left out in other baking books just because they're simple. You'll also find here details on dough makeup and assembly, a broad variety of baking and mixing techniques, and useful stuff about ingredients. Understanding the craft of baking bread is just as important as the discipline and skills needed to get a bread loaf in and out of the oven. To be a skillful baker, you don't have to know a lot of recipes. A simple and unassuming but well-executed bread recipe serves as a good foundation for everything when it comes to baking.

As a reader, I want you to shake off the feeling that you need to bake. Browse this baking book or find pleasure in reading it. Then go to your favorite market or bakery to search for a delicious bread, flatbread, muffin, croissant, or biscuit to indulge in. Breads that are as yummy and healthy as any homemade loaf are made by big commercial companies and small artisanal bakeries. Baking with anxiety or under pressure defeats the very purpose of this book. However, you need to bake at home to enjoy immediately your own crusty country loaf, an aromatic coffee cake or breakfast bread, baby brioche hot from the oven, or the perfect biscuit.

A good bread baker has a sense of innocence, peacefulness, creativity, and life-giving. To be one, you also need scientific techniques, good observation skills, and a talent for infusing precious flavors—all without compromising quality. Baking bread is a skill that links the baker with the rich tradition of bread and all the baking communities in the world.

You also see more different types of bread recipes such as:

- ✓ *Holiday Bread*
- ✓ *Pastries*

- ✓ *Bread Machine*
- ✓ *Muffin*
- ✓ *Yeast Bread*
- ✓ *...*

Thank you for choosing "Biscuit 365 Volume 1". I really hope that each book in the series will be always your best friend in your little kitchen.

Let's live happily and bake more bread every day!

Enjoy the book,

365 Amazing Biscuit Recipes

***

1. 7Up Biscuits

"You'd never believe that these biscuits have only four ingredients and one of them is soda! They can be whipped up in no time and come out light and fluffy with a decadent flavor."

Serving: 8 | Prep: 10 m | Cook: 15 m | Ready in: 30 m

Ingredients

- 2 cups all-purpose biscuit baking mix
- 1/2 cup lemon-lime soda
- 1/2 cup sour cream
- 1/4 cup butter, melted

Direction

- Preheat oven to 425 degrees F (220 degrees C). Grease a large baking sheet.
- Whisk baking mix, lemon-lime soda, sour cream, and melted butter in a bowl until batter is smooth. Drop biscuits by large spoonful onto the prepared baking sheet.
- Bake in the preheated oven until biscuits are golden brown, 12 to 15 minutes. Let biscuits rest for about 5 minutes before serving.

Nutrition Information

- Calories: 211 calories
- Total Fat: 13.3 g
- Cholesterol: 22 mg
- Sodium: 428 mg
- Total Carbohydrate: 20.8 g
- Protein: 2.6 g

2. 7Up Buttermilk Biscuits

"Incredibly simple yet outrageously tasty; sour cream makes them super moist and tender. Reminiscent of the original Kentucky Fried Chicken® biscuits, but much better! Great with all kinds of meals but they make an especially fantastic biscuits and gravy breakfast (or lunch or dinner)."

Serving: 15 | Prep: 15 m | Cook: 15 m | Ready in: 30 m

Ingredients

- 1/4 cup butter, melted
- 5 cups all-purpose buttermilk baking mix
- 1 cup lemon-lime soda (such as 7Up®)
- 1 cup sour cream
- 1/4 cup butter, softened

Direction

- Preheat oven to 425 degrees F (220 degrees C). Spread melted butter all over a 9x13-inch baking dish.
- Stir baking mix, lemon-lime soda, sour cream, and softened butter together in a bowl until dough is well-mixed; knead with your hands, adding more baking mix as necessary, until dough is smooth but still sticky.
- Roll dough into 15 equal-size balls and place dough balls in prepared baking dish, turning to coat each completely in melted butter.
- Bake in the preheated oven until biscuits are golden brown, 15 to 20 minutes. Let rest for 5 minutes before serving.

Nutrition Information

- Calories: 222 calories
- Total Fat: 13.6 g
- Cholesterol: 23 mg
- Sodium: 381 mg
- Total Carbohydrate: 21 g
- Protein: 3.4 g

3. After-Holiday Ham on Biscuits

Billie George of Saskatoon, Saskatchewan puts leftover ham and hard-cooked eggs to good use by making tasty After-Holiday Ham on Biscuits with a creamy white sauce. "When my children were young, they loved to color lots of Easter eggs, so this recipe was a great way to use them up," she writes.

Serving: 4 servings. | Prep: 20 m | Cook: 10 m | Ready in: 30 m

Ingredients

- 1 cup all-purpose flour
- 2 teaspoons baking powder
- 1/4 teaspoon salt
- 3 tablespoons cold butter
- 1/2 cup milk
- CREAM SAUCE:
- 1 cup cubed fully cooked ham
- 1/4 cup chopped onion
- 3 tablespoons butter
- 1/2 teaspoon chicken bouillon granules
- 1/2 teaspoon Worcestershire sauce
- 1/8 teaspoon pepper
- 3 tablespoons all-purpose flour
- 1-3/4 cups milk
- 3 hard-boiled large eggs, chopped
- 1 tablespoon minced fresh parsley

Direction

- In a large bowl, combine the flour, baking powder and salt. Cut in butter until mixture resembles coarse crumbs. Stir in milk just until moistened. Turn onto a lightly floured surface; knead 8-10 times.
- Pat or roll out to 1/2-in. thickness; cut with a floured 2-1/2-in. biscuit cutter. Place 2 in. apart on a greased baking sheet. Bake at 425 degrees for 10-12 minutes or until golden brown.
- Meanwhile, in a large skillet, sauté ham and onion in butter for 3-4 minutes or until onion is crisp-tender. Stir in the bouillon, Worcestershire sauce and pepper. Combine flour and milk until smooth; gradually stir into pan. Bring to a boil; cook and stir for 2 minutes or until thickened. Gently stir in eggs and parsley.
- Split warm biscuits in half horizontally; top with ham mixture.

Nutrition Information

- Calories: 196 calories
- Total Fat: 12g
- Cholesterol: 97mg
- Sodium: 478mg
- Total Carbohydrate: 15g
- Protein: 8g
- Fiber: 0 g

4. Angel Biscuits

I first received a sample of these light, wonderful biscuits, along with the recipe, from an elderly gentleman friend. I now bake them often as a Saturday-morning treat, served with butter and honey. They're perfect with sausage gravy, too! --Faye Hintz, Springfield, Missouri

Serving: 2-1/2 dozen. | Prep: 20 m | Cook: 10 m | Ready in: 30 m

Ingredients

- 2 packages (1/4 ounce each) active dry yeast
- 1/4 cup warm water (110° to 115°)
- 2 cups warm buttermilk (110° to 115°)
- 5 to 5-1/2 cups all-purpose flour
- 1/3 cup sugar
- 2 teaspoons salt
- 2 teaspoons baking powder
- 1 teaspoon baking soda
- 1 cup shortening
- Melted butter

Direction

- In a small bowl, dissolve yeast in warm water. Let stand 5 minutes. Stir in warm buttermilk; set aside.
- In a large bowl, combine the flour, sugar, salt, baking powder and baking soda. Cut in

shortening with a pastry blender until mixture resembles coarse crumbs. Stir in yeast mixture.

- Turn onto a lightly floured surface; knead lightly 3-4 times. Roll out to 1/2-in. thickness; cut with a 2-1/2-in. round biscuit cutter or pumpkin-shaped cookie cutter. Place 2 in. apart on lightly greased baking sheets. Cover with kitchen towels and let rise in a warm place until almost doubled, about 1 hour.
- Bake at 450 degrees for 8-10 minutes or until golden brown. Lightly brush tops with melted butter. Serve warm.

Nutrition Information

- Calories: 150 calories
- Total Fat: 7g
- Cholesterol: 1mg
- Sodium: 244mg
- Total Carbohydrate: 19g
- Protein: 3g
- Fiber: 1g

5. Angel Yeast Biscuits

These versatile yeast biscuits are so light, they almost melt in your mouth. They can be served with a sweet topping like jelly or a savory scoop of sausage gravy.

Serving: 1 dozen. | Prep: 25 m | Cook: 15 m | Ready in: 40 m

Ingredients

- 1 package (1/4 ounce) active dry yeast
- 1/4 cup warm water (110 degrees to 115 degrees)
- 1 tablespoon sugar
- 3/4 cup warm buttermilk (110 degrees to 115 degrees)
- 3 cups all-purpose flour
- 2 teaspoons baking powder
- 3/4 teaspoon salt
- 1/2 teaspoon baking soda
- 1/2 cup cold butter

Direction

- In a large bowl, dissolve yeast in warm water. Add sugar; let stand for 5 minutes. Stir in buttermilk; set aside. In a bowl, combine the flour, baking powder, salt and baking soda. Cut in butter until mixture resembles coarse crumbs. Stir in yeast mixture; mix well.
- Turn onto a floured surface; gently knead for 1 minute. Place in a greased bowl, turning once to grease top. Cover and let rise in a warm place until doubled, about 30 minutes.
- Punch dough down. Turn onto a lightly floured surface; roll to 3/4-in. thickness. Cut with a floured 2-1/2-in. round biscuit cutter. Place 2 in. apart on a greased baking sheet. Prick tops with a fork. Cover and let rise until doubled, about 45 minutes.
- Bake at 375 degrees for 15-18 minutes or until golden brown. Remove from pan to cool on a wire rack. Serve warm.

Nutrition Information

- Calories: 193 calories
- Total Fat: 8g
- Cholesterol: 21mg
- Sodium: 361mg
- Total Carbohydrate: 26g
- Protein: 4g
- Fiber: 1g

6. Apple Cider Biscuits

In Milford, Indiana, Harriet Stichter's family enjoys these tender, flaky biscuits warm from the oven. "We have a lot of apple trees, so we're always looking for apple recipes," she says. "This is a tasty way to use some of our cider."

Serving: about 1 dozen. | Prep: 15 m | Cook: 15 m | Ready in: 30 m

Ingredients

- 2 cups all-purpose flour
- 1 tablespoon baking powder
- 2 teaspoons sugar
- 1/2 teaspoon salt

- 1/3 cup cold butter
- 3/4 cup apple cider
- 1/8 teaspoon ground cinnamon

Direction

- In a bowl, combine the flour, baking powder, sugar and salt. Cut in butter until mixture resembles coarse crumbs. Stir in cider just until moistened. Turn onto a lightly floured surface and knead 8-10 times.
- Roll out to 1/2-in. thickness; cut with a 2-1/2-in. biscuit cutter. Place on ungreased baking sheets. Sprinkle with cinnamon; pierce tops of biscuits with a fork.
- Bake at 425 degrees for 12-14 minutes or until golden brown. Serve warm.

Nutrition Information

- Calories: 131 calories
- Total Fat: 5g
- Cholesterol: 14mg
- Sodium: 252mg
- Total Carbohydrate: 18g
- Protein: 2g
- Fiber: 1g

7. AppleTopped Biscuits

Sharon Rose Ristich of Rochester, New York creates a tasty fruit topping for convenient refrigerated biscuits. "I usually double this recipe and put it in two pie plates to serve a crowd," she says. "It really isn't hard to make the topping, but in a pinch, you can substitute canned apple pie filling instead," she suggests.

Serving: 8 servings. | Prep: 15 m | Cook: 20 m | Ready in: 35 m

Ingredients

- 3 cups sliced peeled tart apples
- 1/3 cup sugar
- 1 tablespoon quick-cooking tapioca
- 1-1/2 teaspoons lemon juice
- 1/2 teaspoon ground cinnamon
- 1/8 teaspoon salt
- 1/8 teaspoon ground nutmeg

- 1 tube (16.3 ounces) large refrigerated buttermilk biscuits

Direction

- In a large saucepan, combine the apples, sugar, tapioca, lemon juice, cinnamon, salt and nutmeg. Let stand for 15 minutes. Cook over medium heat for 8-10 minutes or until apples are tender.
- Transfer apple mixture to a greased 9-in. pie plate. Place biscuits over apples. Bake at 375 degrees for 18-20 minutes or until biscuits are browned. Immediately invert onto a serving plate.

Nutrition Information

- Calories: 247 calories
- Total Fat: 8g
- Cholesterol: 0 mg
- Sodium: 610mg
- Total Carbohydrate: 40g
- Protein: 4g
- Fiber: 1g

8. Apricot Cream Biscuits

Melt-in-your-mouth good when warm, these shortcut biscuits with a hint of orange prove that the right mix really can offer homemade taste. – Betty Saint Turner, Attalla, Alabama

Serving: 1 dozen. | Prep: 20 m | Cook: 10 m | Ready in: 30 m

Ingredients

- 3 cups biscuit/baking mix
- 2 teaspoons grated orange zest
- 1 cup heavy whipping cream
- 1/4 cup apricot preserves
- 2 tablespoons cream cheese, softened
- 2 teaspoons sugar

Direction

- In a large bowl, combine baking mix and orange zest. Stir in cream just until moistened. Turn onto a lightly floured surface; knead 8-10 times. Roll out to 1/2-in. thickness; cut with a floured 2-1/2-in. biscuit cutter.
- Place 2 in. apart on an ungreased baking sheet. Using the end of a wooden spoon handle, make a 1-1/4-in.-wide and 1/4-in.-deep indentation in the center of each biscuit.
- In a small bowl, beat apricot preserves and cream cheese until blended. Drop by teaspoonfuls into the center of each biscuit. Sprinkle with sugar.
- Bake at 400 degrees for 10-15 minutes or until golden brown. Serve warm.

Nutrition Information

- Calories: 218 calories
- Total Fat: 13g
- Cholesterol: 30mg
- Sodium: 395mg
- Total Carbohydrate: 24g
- Protein: 3g
- Fiber: 1g

9. Awesome Yogurt Biscuits

"With only 2 ingredients, you can't miss! These taste like old-fashioned buttermilk or sourdough biscuits. The easiest recipe for biscuits, and so very good! Enjoy with butter, honey, or jelly."

Serving: 6 | Prep: 7 m | Cook: 8 m | Ready in: 15 m

Ingredients

- 2 cups all-purpose biscuit baking mix
- 1 (8 ounce) container plain yogurt

Direction

- Preheat an oven to 450 degrees F (230 degrees C).

- Place the biscuit mix into a bowl and lightly stir in the yogurt just until barely combined. Mixture will seem dry. Knead to mix a few times, but don't overknead. Roll the dough out lightly onto a floured work surface about 1/2-inch thick; cut into rounds with a biscuit cutter.
- Bake in the preheated oven until lightly golden brown, about 8 minutes.

Nutrition Information

- Calories: 187 calories
- Total Fat: 6.6 g
- Cholesterol: 2 mg
- Sodium: 530 mg
- Total Carbohydrate: 27.3 g
- Protein: 4.8 g

10. Bacon Cheese Biscuits

In Douglas, Georgia, Kimberly Harrell can stir up a golden batch of these simple savory biscuits in no time. With bacon and cheese throughout, they make a nice accompaniment to soup or chili.

Serving: 9 biscuits. | Prep: 15 m | Cook: 15 m | Ready in: 30 m

Ingredients

- 2 cups self-rising flour
- 1 tablespoon sugar
- 1/2 teaspoon baking soda
- 1/2 cup shortening
- 1 cup buttermilk
- 3/4 pound sliced bacon, cooked and crumbled
- 1 cup shredded cheddar cheese

Direction

- In a large bowl, combine the flour, sugar and baking soda. Cut in shortening until mixture resembles coarse crumbs. Stir in buttermilk just until combined. Fold in the bacon and cheese.

- Turn onto a lightly floured surface; knead 4-5 times. Roll out to 1/2-in. thickness. Cut with a floured 2-1/2-in. biscuit cutter. Place 1 in. apart on a greased baking sheet. Bake at 425 degrees for 12-15 minutes or until golden brown. Remove from pan to a wire rack. Serve warm.

Nutrition Information

- Calories: 319 calories
- Total Fat: 21g
- Cholesterol: 25mg
- Sodium: 693mg
- Total Carbohydrate: 23g
- Protein: 10g
- Fiber: 0 g

11. Bacon Monkey Bread

My daughters made this ring when they were in 4-H, and we've enjoyed it for many years. Handy refrigerated biscuits get a holiday spin combined with other tasty, colorful ingredients.

Serving: 12 servings. | Prep: 15 m | Cook: 30 m | Ready in: 45 m

Ingredients

- 1/2 pound bacon strips, diced
- 1/4 cup grated Parmesan cheese
- 1/4 cup chopped onion, optional
- 1/4 cup chopped green pepper, optional
- 1 tube (16.3 ounces) large refrigerated flaky biscuits
- 1/3 cup butter, melted

Direction

- Preheat oven to 350 degrees. In a large skillet, cook bacon until crisp; drain. Combine bacon with cheese and, if desired, onion and green pepper. Cut biscuits into quarters; add to bacon mixture. Stir in butter and toss to coat. Transfer to a greased 10-in. tube pan.
- Bake until browned, about 30 minutes. Cool 10 minutes before inverting onto a serving platter. Refrigerate leftovers.

Nutrition Information

- Calories: 214 calories
- Total Fat: 14g
- Cholesterol: 22mg
- Sodium: 557mg
- Total Carbohydrate: 17g
- Protein: 6g
- Fiber: 1g

12. Bacon n Egg Biscuits

On busy mornings, Katie can fix these tasty sandwiches in about 15 minutes. "While the flaky biscuits bake, cook the eggs and warm up precooked bacon," she suggests. "Then add cheese for a homemade in-hand breakfast."

Serving: 8 servings. | Prep: 5 m | Cook: 10 m | Ready in: 15 m

Ingredients

- 2 cups Buttermilk Biscuit Baking Mix
- 7 tablespoons water
- 8 eggs
- 8 slices process American cheese
- 8 bacon strips, halved and cooked

Direction

- In a large bowl, combine biscuit mix and water just until blended. Turn onto a lightly floured surface and knead 5 times. Roll out to 1/2-in. thickness; cut with a lightly floured 3-in. biscuit cutter.
- Place on an ungreased baking sheet. Bake at 425 degrees for 9-10 minutes or until golden brown. Meanwhile, scramble the eggs. Split the biscuits; fill each with a slice of cheese, scrambled egg and two bacon pieces.

Nutrition Information

- Calories:
- Total Fat: g
- Cholesterol: mg
- Sodium: mg

- Total Carbohydrate: g
- Protein: g
- Fiber: g

- Total Carbohydrate: 28g
- Protein: 5g
- Fiber: 1g

13. BaconApple Cider Biscuits

The sweet and salty flavors of apple and bacon make these special biscuits stand out. Be prepared to make more-- they're gonna go fast!

Serving: 8 biscuits. | Prep: 20 m | Cook: 15 m | Ready in: 35 m

Ingredients

- 2 cups all-purpose flour
- 2 teaspoons baking powder
- 2 teaspoons brown sugar
- 1/2 teaspoon salt
- 1/4 teaspoon baking soda
- 1/4 teaspoon apple pie spice
- 8 tablespoons cold butter, cubed, divided
- 5 bacon strips, cooked and crumbled
- 3/4 cup apple cider or juice
- 1/8 teaspoon ground cinnamon

Direction

- In a large bowl, combine the first six ingredients. Cut in 7 tablespoons butter until mixture resembles coarse crumbs. Add bacon. Stir in cider just until combined.
- Turn onto a lightly floured surface; knead 8-10 times. Roll into a 10-in. x 6-in. rectangle. Melt remaining butter; brush over dough. Sprinkle with cinnamon.
- Cut into eight rectangles. Place 1 in. apart on an ungreased baking sheet. Bake at 450 degrees for 12-15 minutes or until golden brown. Serve warm.

Nutrition Information

- Calories: 251 calories
- Total Fat: 13g
- Cholesterol: 34mg
- Sodium: 462mg

14. BakedPotato Buttermilk Biscuits

I have a love of potatoes that is unlike any other love. I grew up eating them often as a kid – almost every day – so now I'm always looking for new ways to incorporate this versatile vegetable into my everyday life. There's just something so special about biscuits loaded with shredded potatoes, cheddar cheese, and chives. I can't put it into words, but I feel like I don't have to because you get it. It's the baked potato you never knew you wanted... in biscuit form.

Serving: Makes 20 biscuits | Prep: 30 m | Cook: 50 m

Ingredients

- 1 medium baking potato, rinsed and dried
- 2 cups all-purpose flour
- 1 tablespoon baking powder
- 1/4 teaspoon baking soda
- 1 teaspoon salt
- 1/2 teaspoon coarsely ground black pepper
- 6 tablespoons very cold unsalted butter, diced, plus 2 tablespoons, melted
- 1/4 cup shredded white Cheddar cheese
- 2 tablespoons chopped chives
- 1 cup buttermilk

Direction

- Preheat the oven to 425°F. Line a baking sheet with parchment paper, and set aside.
- Cook the potato in a microwave, an oven, or in boiling water until almost fork-tender (see Cooks' Note :). Let cool completely. Using a paring knife, peel the potato, and then shred with a box grater.
- In a large mixing bowl, combine the flour, baking powder, baking soda, salt, and pepper. Add the cold butter and cut in using 2 knives, a pastry blender, potato masher, or your

hands, until the dough resembles coarse crumbs the size of peas. Fold in the cheese, chives, and shredded potato.

- Add the buttermilk and stir with a wooden spoon until the dough just comes together. It'll be sticky, but don't panic. Transfer to a well-floured work surface and knead a few times to smooth it out. Fold the dough onto itself about 4 times, turning clockwise after each fold. Pat the dough with your hands until it's about 3/4 inch thick.
- Use a 2-inch round cookie or biscuit cutter to cut into rounds. Place the biscuits on the prepared baking pan just barely touching each other. Gather scraps and repeat patting and cutting (you should have 20).
- Brush the biscuits with the melted butter, and bake until golden brown, 18 to 20 minutes. Let cool before serving. Store any leftovers in an airtight container in the refrigerator for up to 4 days.
- Cooks' Note: If you cook the potato all the way, it'll be really difficult to peel and grate later on, so make sure to cook it just a bit shy of almost done. I use the microwave to make it easy and fast.

Nutrition Information

- Calories: 106
- Total Fat: 5 g (8%)
- Saturated Fat: 3 g (16%)
- Cholesterol: 14 mg (5%)
- Sodium: 104 mg (4%)
- Total Carbohydrate: 12 g (4%)
- Protein: 2 g (5%)
- Fiber: 0 g (2%)

15. Baking Powder Biscuits

When I was growing up, mother made these wonderful baking powder biscuits often. Some time ago, I consulted her box of old recipes and was delighted to find this childhood favorite. Now these warm and tender biscuits are a special treat for my family, too. --Catherine Yoder, Bertha, Minnesota

Serving: 10 biscuits. | Prep: 15 m | Cook: 10 m | Ready in: 25 m

Ingredients

- 2 cups all-purpose flour
- 2 tablespoons sugar
- 3 teaspoons baking powder
- 1/2 teaspoon salt
- 1/2 cup shortening
- 1 egg
- 2/3 cup milk

Direction

- In a large bowl, combine the flour, sugar, baking powder, and salt. Cut in shortening until mixture resembles coarse crumbs. Beat egg and milk; stir into dry ingredients just until moistened.
- Turn onto a lightly floured surface; roll to 1/2-in. thickness. Cut with a 2-1/2-in. floured biscuit cutter. Place 1 in. apart on an ungreased baking sheet. Bake at 450 degrees for 10-12 minutes or until golden brown. Serve warm.

Nutrition Information

- Calories: 206 calories
- Total Fat: 11g
- Cholesterol: 23mg
- Sodium: 253mg
- Total Carbohydrate: 22g
- Protein: 4g
- Fiber: 1g

16. Baking Powder Biscuits I

"A drop biscuit is great for people with small kitchens. So simple, but oh so good!"

Serving: 12 | Prep: 30 m | Cook: 15 m | Ready in: 45 m

Ingredients

- 2 cups all-purpose flour
- 1 tablespoon baking powder
- 1/2 teaspoon salt
- 1/4 cup shortening
- 1 cup milk

Direction

- Preheat oven to 450 degrees F (230 degrees C). Lightly grease a baking sheet.
- In a bowl mix the flour, baking powder, and salt. Cut in the shortening until the mixture has only pea sized lumps. Add milk and mix until dry mixture is absorbed. Drop dough by heaping spoonfuls onto the prepared baking sheet.
- Bake for 12 to 15 minutes in the preheated oven, until golden brown.

Nutrition Information

- Calories: 124 calories
- Total Fat: 4.9 g
- Cholesterol: 2 mg
- Sodium: 190 mg
- Total Carbohydrate: 17.1 g
- Protein: 2.8 g

17. Baking Powder Biscuits II

"Tender biscuits with less fat than most."

Serving: 12 | Prep: 20 m | Cook: 20 m | Ready in: 40 m

Ingredients

- 2 cups all-purpose flour
- 1 tablespoon baking powder
- 1 teaspoon salt
- 1/3 cup vegetable oil
- 2/3 cup buttermilk

Direction

- Preheat oven to 375 degrees F (190 degrees C). Lightly grease a baking sheet.
- In a large bowl, mix together flour, baking powder and salt. Use a fork to blend in the oil. Add buttermilk and stir until the dough comes together.
- Roll dough out on a lightly floured surface. Cut dough into biscuits.
- Bake in preheated oven for 15 minutes, or until golden brown.

Nutrition Information

- Calories: 136 calories
- Total Fat: 6.4 g
- Cholesterol: < 1 mg
- Sodium: 292 mg
- Total Carbohydrate: 16.8 g
- Protein: 2.6 g

18. Baking Powder Drop Biscuits

One day I had company coming and realized I had run out of biscuit mix. I'd never made biscuits from scratch before, but I decided to give this recipe a try. Now this is the only way I make them!

Serving: 1 dozen. | Prep: 10 m | Cook: 10 m | Ready in: 20 m

Ingredients

- 2 cups all-purpose flour
- 2 tablespoons sugar
- 4 teaspoons baking powder
- 1/2 teaspoon cream of tartar
- 1/2 teaspoon salt
- 1/2 cup shortening
- 2/3 cup milk
- 1 egg

Direction

- In a large bowl, combine the first five ingredients. Cut in shortening until the mixture resembles coarse crumbs. In a small bowl, whisk milk and egg. Stir into crumb mixture just until moistened.
- Drop by heaping spoonfuls 2 in. apart onto an ungreased baking sheet. Bake at 450 degrees for 10-12 minutes or until golden brown. Serve warm.

Nutrition Information

- Calories: 172 calories
- Total Fat: 9g
- Cholesterol: 20mg
- Sodium: 244mg
- Total Carbohydrate: 19g
- Protein: 3g
- Fiber: 1g

19. Bannock Two Ways

While researching bannock (a pan-fried, biscuit- or scone-like quick bread), we came across a fantastic online resource called Bannock Awareness. Put together by Michael Blackstock of the Kamloops Forest Region, it describes a history of bannock within First Nations' pre-contact culture, offering a different story than that which suggests bannock arrived exclusively with Scottish traders. Before wheat flour arrived, wild plants, corn, and nuts were ground into a sort of flour and then cooked in ways that could be considered an early form of the bread-like staple. Here we've provided two recipes for our favourite kinds of bannock. The first (our go-to while camping) comes from Greg Mazur and is more of a drop biscuit style. The second is a rolled version and comes from Doreen Crowe, a restaurant owner in the Alderville First Nation in Ontario. Our friend Chris went to her restaurant almost daily with his parents, and grew up with this bannock.

Serving: Each recipe serves 4–6

Ingredients

- 2 cups (500 mL) all-purpose flour
- 1 Tbsp (15 mL) baking powder
- 1 Tbsp (15 mL) white sugar
- 1/8 tsp salt
- 2 Tbsp (30 mL) unsalted butter
- 1 egg
- 1/4 to 1/2 cup (60 to 125 mL) whole milk
- Oil, for frying
- For serving: Maple syrup, flaky sea salt
- 2 cups (500 mL) all-purpose flour, plus extra for rolling
- 2 1/2 tsp (12 mL) baking powder
- 1/2 tsp (2 mL) salt
- 3/4 to 1 cup (185 to 250 mL) water, to start
- Oil, for frying

Direction

- For Greg's Bella Coola Bannock: Combine the flour, baking powder, sugar, and salt. Using a pastry cutter or knife, cut in the butter until the pieces are pea-sized. Mix in the egg, then pour in about 1/4 cup (60 mL) of milk. Mix together just until a dough forms, adding more milk if needed. Divide the dough into 10 to 12 biscuit-sized pieces. In a large frying pan, pour in about 1/4 inch (6 mm) of oil and heat over medium-high. When the oil is hot, fry the bannock—being careful not to crowd them—until golden brown. Serve immediately with maple syrup and flaky sea salt.
- For Doreen Crowe's Bannock: In a large bowl, mix the flour, baking powder, salt, and water together to form a dough. If the dough is a bit dry, add more water 1 Tbsp (15 mL) at a time. Turn the dough out onto a floured surface and roll out into a 9×12-inch (23×30-cm) rectangle about 1/4-inch (6-mm) thick. Cut into approximately 3×3-inch (8×8-cm) squares. Heat about 1/4 inch (6 mm) of oil in a large frying pan over medium-high heat, and fry the bannock—being careful not to crowd them—until golden brown, about 2 minutes on each side. Serve warm.

Nutrition Information

- Calories: 812
- Total Fat: 35 g (55%)
- Saturated Fat: 7 g (33%)
- Cholesterol: 58 mg (19%)

- Sodium: 615 mg (26%)
- Total Carbohydrate: 107 g (36%)
- Protein: 16 g (32%)
- Fiber: 4 g (14%)

20. BAs Best Strawberry Shortcake

You're looking at the quintessential June dessert, perfected by the BA Test Kitchen.

Serving: 6 servings

Ingredients

- 2 hard-boiled egg yolks, cooled
- 1 1/3 cups all-purpose flour
- 3 tablespoons semolina flour or fine-grind cornmeal
- 1 tablespoon baking powder
- 1/4 teaspoon kosher salt
- 3 tablespoons granulated sugar
- 6 tablespoons chilled unsalted butter, cut into pieces
- 2/3 cup plus 2 tablespoons heavy cream
- Sanding or granulated sugar (for sprinkling)
- 1 1/2 pounds strawberries (about 1 quart), hulled, halved, quartered if large
- 1/4 cup granulated sugar
- 1 teaspoon finely grated lemon zest
- Kosher salt
- 2 teaspoons fresh lemon juice, divided
- 1 cup heavy cream
- 2 tablespoons powdered sugar
- 1/2 vanilla bean, halved lengthwise

Direction

- Make the shortcakes: Pulse egg yolks, both flours, baking powder, salt, and granulated sugar in a food processor to combine. Add butter and pulse until only pea-size pieces remain. Drizzle in 2/3 cup cream, then pulse 2–3 times to barely incorporate. Transfer dough to a work surface and gently fold on top of itself several times just to bring it together and work in any dry spots.
- Using a 2-oz. ice cream scoop, make 6 balls and place on a parchment-lined baking sheet. Do not flatten. (Or measure out mounded scoops with a 1/4-cup measuring cup.) Cover and chill until cold, 20–25 minutes.
- Preheat oven to 350°F. Brush tops of shortcakes with remaining 2 Tbsp. cream and sprinkle with sanding sugar. Bake until golden and sides are firm to the touch, 28–32 minutes. Let cool.
- To assemble: Toss strawberries, granulated sugar, lemon zest, and a pinch of salt in a medium bowl to combine. Transfer half of strawberries to a large saucepan and add 1 Tbsp. water; let remaining strawberries macerate while you bring strawberries in saucepan to a gentle simmer over medium-low. Cook, stirring occasionally and reducing heat if needed to keep at a low simmer, until strawberries are starting to break down and become jammy and liquid is syrupy, 12–18 minutes. Let cool, then stir in 1 tsp. lemon juice. Stir remaining 1 tsp. lemon juice into macerated strawberries.
- Combine heavy cream, powdered sugar, and a pinch of salt in a medium bowl. Scrape in seeds from vanilla bean; reserve pod for another use. Beat cream until soft peaks form.
- Split shortcakes and divide strawberry compote, macerated strawberries, and whipped cream among bottoms. Close with shortcake tops.
- Do Ahead Shortcakes can be baked 1 day ahead. Store airtight at room temperature. Reheat before serving.

Nutrition Information

- Calories: 601
- Total Fat: 40 g (61%)
- Saturated Fat: 24 g (121%)
- Cholesterol: 177 mg (59%)
- Sodium: 620 mg (26%)
- Total Carbohydrate: 58 g (19%)
- Protein: 6 g (13%)

- Fiber: 3 g (13%)

21. Basic Biscuits

"This is a basic biscuit recipe with baking powder used as the leavening. They're easy to make and go with almost any meal."

Serving: 10 | Prep: 15 m | Cook: 10 m | Ready in: 25 m

Ingredients

- 2 cups all-purpose flour
- 1 tablespoon baking powder
- 1/2 teaspoon salt
- 1/2 cup shortening
- 3/4 cup milk

Direction

- Preheat oven to 450 degrees F (230 degrees C).
- In a large mixing bowl sift together flour, baking powder and salt. Cut in shortening with fork or pastry blender until mixture resembles coarse crumbs.
- Pour milk into flour mixture while stirring with a fork. Mix in milk until dough is soft, moist and pulls away from the side of the bowl.
- Turn dough out onto a lightly floured surface and toss with flour until no longer sticky. Roll dough out into a 1/2 inch thick sheet and cut with a floured biscuit or cookie cutter. Press together unused dough and repeat rolling and cutting procedure.
- Place biscuits on ungreased baking sheets and bake in preheated oven until golden brown, about 10 minutes.

Nutrition Information

- Calories: 191 calories
- Total Fat: 10.9 g
- Cholesterol: 1 mg
- Sodium: 225 mg
- Total Carbohydrate: 20.2 g
- Protein: 3.2 g

22. Beaten Biscuits

"This is the traditional biscuit of the ham-loving South. In days gone by, these were made by beating the dough until it blistered (about 15-30 minutes). It was then baked, and each biscuit sliced in half to receive a paper-thin slice of incredible salt cured ham. Today, you could use the food processor or a biscuit brake (usually nothing more than a converted washing wringer) to make the dough "snap.""

Serving: 24 | Prep: 25 m | Cook: 15 m | Ready in: 40 m

Ingredients

- 2 cups all-purpose flour
- 1/4 teaspoon salt
- 1/4 teaspoon baking powder
- 1 1/2 tablespoons white sugar
- 1/4 cup lard, chilled and cut into small pieces
- 1/3 cup light cream
- 2 tablespoons cold water (optional)

Direction

- Preheat the oven to 450 degrees F (230 degrees C).
- Sift flour, salt, baking powder, and sugar together. Use a fork to "cut" the lard into the flour until it looks like coarse meal. Using a standing mixer, or a wooden spoon, mix the dough as you slowly add the cream. Mix well to form the dough into a ball, adding water if needed.
- Place the dough onto a tabletop, and knead slightly. With a mallet or a one-piece rolling pin, beat the dough a few times to form it into a rough rectangle. Fold the dough over, and then beat it out again. Repeat this process until the dough becomes white and blisters form on the surface, about 15 minutes.
- Roll out the dough to about 1/4 inch thick. Cut into 2 inch rounds, and prick the top a few times with the tines of a fork. Place on greased baking sheets.
- Bake for 15 minutes, or until golden.

Nutrition Information

- Calories: 67 calories
- Total Fat: 2.9 g
- Cholesterol: 4 mg
- Sodium: 31 mg
- Total Carbohydrate: 8.9 g
- Protein: 1.2 g

23. Beer Biscuits

"The beer adds flavor and leavening to these biscuits."

Serving: 12

Ingredients

- 2 cups all-purpose flour
- 3 teaspoons baking powder
- 1 teaspoon salt
- 1/4 cup shortening
- 3/4 cup beer

Direction

- Preheat oven to 450 degrees F (230 degrees C).
- Sift together flour, baking powder, and salt. Cut in shortening until it has cornmeal consistency. Stir in beer, and knead lightly.
- Roll dough out to 1/2 inch thickness. Cut with biscuit cutter.
- Bake 10 to 12 minutes, or until golden brown.

Nutrition Information

- Calories: 121 calories
- Total Fat: 4.5 g
- Cholesterol: 0 mg
- Sodium: 317 mg
- Total Carbohydrate: 16.8 g
- Protein: 2.2 g

24. Beer n Brat Biscuits

"My husband, our three girls and I all love to cook, so we're always coming up with something new to try," explains Nancy Bourget of Round Rock, Texas. These yummy biscuits require just four ingredients, including leftover brats. TIP: "Serve them with mustard and a big bowl of rice and beans or bean soup." recommends Nancy.

Serving: 16 biscuits. | Prep: 10 m | Cook: 20 m | Ready in: 30 m

Ingredients

- 2 fully cooked bratwurst links
- 4 cups biscuit/baking mix
- 2 to 3 teaspoons caraway seeds
- 1 can (12 ounces) beer or nonalcoholic beer

Direction

- Cut bratwurst into bite-size pieces. In a large bowl, combine the biscuit mix, caraway seeds and bratwurst; stir in beer just until moistened. Fill greased muffin cups two-thirds full.
- Bake at 400 degrees for 18-20 minutes or until golden brown. Cool for 5 minutes before removing from pans to wire racks. Serve warm. Refrigerate leftovers.

Nutrition Information

- Calories: 164 calories
- Total Fat: 7g
- Cholesterol: 6mg
- Sodium: 438mg
- Total Carbohydrate: 20g
- Protein: 4g
- Fiber: 1g

25. Best Biscuits

Rich buttermilk biscuits baking in the oven will bring back warm memories of your own mom's kitchen. These have a classic old-fashioned flavor that's stood the test of time. You can make them with little effort.

Serving: 1 dozen. | Prep: 20 m | Cook: 10 m | Ready in: 30 m

Ingredients

- 2 cups all-purpose flour
- 2-1/4 teaspoons baking powder
- 3/4 teaspoon salt
- 1/4 teaspoon baking soda
- 1/3 cup shortening
- 3/4 cup buttermilk

Direction

- In a large bowl, combine the dry ingredients. Cut in shortening until mixture resembles coarse crumbs. Stir in buttermilk just until moistened.
- Turn onto a lightly floured surface. Roll to 1/2-in. thickness; cut with a floured 2-1/2-in. biscuit cutter. Place 1 in. apart on an ungreased baking sheet. Bake at 450 degrees for 8-10 minutes or until golden brown. Serve warm.

Nutrition Information

- Calories: 131 calories
- Total Fat: 6g
- Cholesterol: 1mg
- Sodium: 265mg
- Total Carbohydrate: 17g
- Protein: 3g
- Fiber: 1g

26. Big as a Cathead Biscuits

"This is my mom's biscuit recipe, passed down from her mom and grandma who lived their entire lives on the Mississippi Delta. Of course it took a lot of trial and error to get it right because she was from the 'handful of this and a pinch of that' school of cooking. You can use milk or plain yogurt in place of the buttermilk. Shortening or butter can stand in for the lard. Serve with butter, jelly, honey, gravy, or whatever your favorite biscuit topping is."

Serving: 8 | Prep: 20 m | Cook: 15 m | Ready in: 35 m

Ingredients

- butter-flavored cooking spray
- 2 1/4 cups all-purpose flour
- 1 teaspoon baking powder
- 3/4 teaspoon salt
- 1/2 teaspoon baking soda
- 4 1/2 tablespoons lard
- 1 cup buttermilk

Direction

- Preheat oven to 450 degrees F (230 degrees C). Prepare a 9-inch cake pan with cooking spray.
- Mix flour, baking powder, salt, and baking soda together in a mixing bowl.
- Mash small chunks of lard into the flour mixture with a pastry cutter or with your fingers, letting each addition integrate fully before adding the next, until all the lard has been added and the mixture resembles coarse-ground cornmeal.
- Make a well in the center of the flour mixture. Pour milk into the well. Stir the mixture with a spoon, making sure to scrape the edges of the bowl so that the dry flour there gets wet, just until the milk is incorporated into the dry mix and there are no large areas of powdery flour remaining, leaving lumpy dough which is sticky in some places and even a bit grainy in the driest areas. From here, use your hands to carefully mix to ensure even consistency.
- Divide dough into 8 equal chunks and shape each into a thick biscuit. Put the shaped biscuits into the prepared cake pan with the sides touching.

- Bake in preheated oven until the tops are light golden brown, about 15 minutes.

Nutrition Information

- Calories: 206 calories
- Total Fat: 7.8 g
- Cholesterol: 8 mg
- Sodium: 390 mg
- Total Carbohydrate: 28.5 g
- Protein: 4.6 g

27. Biscones

"This is part biscuit, part scone, and all delicious! Brush with milk before baking, if desired."

Serving: 8 | Prep: 15 m | Cook: 20 m | Ready in: 35 m

Ingredients

- 2 cups unbleached all-purpose flour
- 4 teaspoons baking powder
- 1 tablespoon white sugar, or more to taste
- 1/2 teaspoon salt
- 6 tablespoons butter
- 3/4 cup buttermilk

Direction

- Preheat oven to 400 degrees F (200 degrees C). Grease a baking sheet.
- Combine flour, baking powder, sugar, and salt together in a bowl. Cut butter into flour mixture using a fork, your hands, or a pastry blender until mixture resembles coarse crumbs. Mix buttermilk into flour mixture until dough starts to stick together.
- Turn dough onto a floured work surface and shape into a 1/2-inch-thick circle. Cut dough into 4 wedges and then into 8 wedges using a sharp knife. Arrange wedges on the prepared baking sheet.
- Bake in the preheated oven until biscones are lightly browned, about 20 minutes.

Nutrition Information

- Calories: 207 calories
- Total Fat: 9.1 g
- Cholesterol: 24 mg
- Sodium: 475 mg
- Total Carbohydrate: 27.2 g
- Protein: 4.1 g

28. Biscuits

"I saw these being made on a cooking show on PBS they are very tender and buttery. You can freeze in muffin tins and pop in oven when needed."

Serving: 16 | Prep: 15 m | Cook: 20 m | Ready in: 35 m

Ingredients

- 4 cups all-purpose flour
- 1/4 cup baking powder
- 1 1/2 cups butter, cut into large chunks
- 1 3/4 cups buttermilk
- 8 ounces crumbled cooked bacon

Direction

- Preheat oven to 350 degrees F (175 degrees C). Lightly butter 2 muffin tins.
- Mix flour and baking powder together in a large bowl; cut in butter until mixture resembles coarse crumbs. Stir buttermilk and bacon into flour mixture just until dough holds together.
- Turn dough onto a floured surface and roll into an even thickness. Fold dough over itself a few times. Cut dough into circles using a cookie or biscuit cutter and arrange circles in the prepared muffin tins.
- Bake in the preheated oven on the top rack until biscuits are lightly browned, 20 to 25 minutes.

Nutrition Information

- Calories: 355 calories
- Total Fat: 23.7 g

- Cholesterol: 62 mg
- Sodium: 747 mg
- Total Carbohydrate: 26 g
- Protein: 9.6 g

- Fiber: 1g

29. Biscuits for 2

I created this recipe in a larger quantity to enter in the Kentucky State Fair. It won first place! Since biscuits are best fresh out of the oven, I sized my recipe down to yield four--perfect for two. I make them whenever biscuits fit into the menu. --Bessie Hulett, Shively, Kentucky

Serving: 4 biscuits. | Prep: 15 m | Cook: 10 m | Ready in: 25 m

Ingredients

- 1/2 cup all-purpose flour
- 1 teaspoon baking powder
- 1/8 teaspoon salt
- 2 tablespoons shortening
- 3 tablespoons milk
- 2 tablespoons butter, melted, divided

Direction

- In a small bowl, combine the flour, baking powder and salt; cut in shortening until mixture resembles coarse crumbs. Add milk, tossing with a fork until a ball forms.
- Turn onto a lightly floured surface; knead 5-6 times. Roll or pat to 1/2-in. thickness; cut with a 2-1/2-in. biscuit cutter. Place on a greased baking sheet. Brush tops with 1 tablespoon butter. Bake at 450 degrees for 9-11 minutes or until golden brown. Brush with remaining butter. Serve warm.

Nutrition Information

- Calories: 338 calories
- Total Fat: 24g
- Cholesterol: 34mg
- Sodium: 475mg
- Total Carbohydrate: 25g
- Protein: 4g

30. Biscuits For Two

"A friend shared this recipe with me," writes Sylvia McCoy from Lees Summit, Missouri. "I think the biscuits taste wonderful warm from the oven."

Serving: 4 biscuits. | Prep: 10 m | Cook: 10 m | Ready in: 20 m

Ingredients

- 1 cup all-purpose flour
- 2-1/2 teaspoons baking powder
- 1 teaspoon sugar
- 1/2 teaspoon salt
- 1/8 teaspoon cream of tartar
- 1/4 cup shortening
- 1/2 cup 2% milk

Direction

- In a small bowl, combine dry ingredients. Cut in shortening until mixture resembles coarse crumbs. Stir in milk just until moistened. Turn onto a lightly floured surface; knead 8-10 times.
- Pat or roll out to 1/2-in. thickness; cut with a floured 2-1/2-in. biscuit cutter.
- Place on a greased baking sheet. Bake at 450 degrees for 10-12 minutes or until golden brown. Serve warm.

Nutrition Information

- Calories: 494 calories
- Total Fat: 27g
- Cholesterol: 8mg
- Sodium: 1121mg
- Total Carbohydrate: 53g
- Protein: 8g
- Fiber: 2g

31. Biscuits with Blue Cheese Butter

"This is a unique twist on your standard biscuits that is absolutely delectable. I serve these every Thanksgiving to rave reviews."

Serving: 8 | Prep: 5 m | Cook: 15 m | Ready in: 20 m

Ingredients

- 1 (7.5 ounce) package refrigerated biscuit dough
- 1/2 cup unsalted butter, melted
- 2 tablespoons crumbled blue cheese

Direction

- Preheat the oven to 375 degrees F (190 degrees C). Grease a 9x13-inch baking dish.
- Separate biscuits and cut into quarters; place biscuit pieces into prepared baking dish. Mix unsalted butter and blue cheese together in a bowl until thoroughly combined and brush the butter mixture over the biscuits.
- Bake in the preheated oven until biscuits are golden brown, 10 to 15 minutes. Pull apart to serve.

Nutrition Information

- Calories: 195 calories
- Total Fat: 15.7 g
- Cholesterol: 32 mg
- Sodium: 297 mg
- Total Carbohydrate: 11.6 g
- Protein: 2.3 g

32. Biscuits with Ham Butter

"Whether as a finger food or brunch dish, these are a great way to use leftover ham," advises Andrea Bolden of Unionville, Tennessee.

Serving: 10 servings. | Prep: 15 m | Cook: 10 m | Ready in: 25 m

Ingredients

- 1-1/2 cups all-purpose flour
- 2 teaspoons baking powder
- 1/2 teaspoon salt
- 3/4 cup sour cream
- 1 egg, lightly beaten
- 1 cup cubed fully cooked ham
- 1/2 cup butter, softened

Direction

- In a bowl, combine flour, baking powder and salt; set aside. Combine sour cream and egg; mix well. Stir into dry ingredients just until moistened. Turn onto a lightly floured surface; knead gently 4 to 5 times. Roll to 1/2-in. thickness; cut with a 2-1/2-in. biscuit cutter. Place on a greased baking sheet. Bake at 425 degrees for 10-12 minutes or until lightly browned.
- Meanwhile, in a blender or food processor, process ham until finely minced. Add butter and continue processing until well mixed. Spread over warm biscuits.

Nutrition Information

- Calories: 215 calories
- Total Fat: 14g
- Cholesterol: 65mg
- Sodium: 485mg
- Total Carbohydrate: 15g
- Protein: 6g
- Fiber: 1g

33. Black Pepper Rings

"For Italian families, pepper rings are a type of biscuit eaten in place of bread. In our family, they are traditionally served at Easter, but are delicious any time of year. They taste extra special if heated before serving. Try them with black coffee or espresso."

Serving: 12 | Prep: 20 m | Cook: 20 m | Ready in: 40 m

Ingredients

- 12 eggs
- 1/2 cup butter, melted
- 1/3 cup vegetable oil
- 6 cups all-purpose flour
- 1 tablespoon salt
- 2 tablespoons coarsely ground black pepper
- 3 tablespoons baking powder

Direction

- Bring a large pot of water to boil over medium-high heat. Preheat oven to 450 degrees F (230 degrees C).
- In a large bowl, beat eggs. Stir in melted butter and oil. In a separate bowl, mix together flour, salt, pepper and baking powder.
- Make a well in the center of the flour mixture and pour in the egg mixture. Mix until dough pulls together. Turn dough out onto a lightly floured surface and knead briefly. Divide dough into 12 equal pieces. Roll each piece into an 8 inch long cylinder. Bend each cylinder into a ring shape and pinch ends together. With a sharp knife, score each ring around its outside edge.
- Drop rings two at a time into boiling water and boil for 1 minute. Remove rings from water and place on lightly greased cookie sheets.
- Bake in preheated oven for 20 minutes, until golden brown.

Nutrition Information

- Calories: 432 calories
- Total Fat: 19.8 g
- Cholesterol: 232 mg
- Sodium: 951 mg
- Total Carbohydrate: 49.6 g
- Protein: 12.9 g

34. Blue Cheese Biscuits

THIS simple addition to prepared biscuits is impressive. I have served them often for luncheons and they disappear fast. I don't remember where or when I found the recipe, but the card in my recipe box tells me I have been preparing them for a long time.

Serving: 2 servings. | Prep: 5 m | Cook: 25 m | Ready in: 30 m

Ingredients

- 2 individually frozen biscuits
- 1 tablespoon butter
- 1 tablespoon crumbled blue cheese
- 2 teaspoons minced fresh parsley

Direction

- Place biscuits in an ungreased 9-in. round baking pan. In a small microwave-safe dish, combine butter and blue cheese. Microwave, uncovered, on high until butter is melted; spoon mixture over biscuits.
- Bake according to package directions. Sprinkle with parsley.

Nutrition Information

- Calories: 266 calories
- Total Fat: 18g
- Cholesterol: 18mg
- Sodium: 750mg
- Total Carbohydrate: 23g
- Protein: 5g
- Fiber: 1g

35. Brown Bears

"My kids love making these brown bear biscuits for breakfast whenever we go camping. They're super simple and no prep for mom!"

Serving: 8 | Prep: 15 m | Cook: 15 m | Ready in: 30 m

Ingredients

- 1/4 cup ground cinnamon
- 1 cup white sugar
- 1/2 cup butter, melted
- 1 (10 ounce) can refrigerated biscuit dough

Direction

- Mix cinnamon and sugar together in a bowl. Pour melted butter into another bowl. Separate biscuits and form each piece of dough into a rope 4 to 5 inches long. Wrap the dough pieces around sticks.
- Hold sticks over campfire and slowly turn until the biscuit dough is browned and set, 8 to 10 minutes. Dip biscuits into melted butter and then into cinnamon sugar. Eat biscuits from sticks.

Nutrition Information

- Calories: 320 calories
- Total Fat: 16.3 g
- Cholesterol: 31 mg
- Sodium: 432 mg
- Total Carbohydrate: 42.9 g
- Protein: 2.6 g

36. Brown Sugar Biscuits

"These yummy rolls aren't really biscuits, but they're named after rolls I used to get at my local bakery. My family thinks they're sweet enough without icing, but a simple powdered sugar one would be nice."

Serving: 12 | Prep: 20 m | Cook: 15 m | Ready in: 35 m

Ingredients

- 2 cups all-purpose flour
- 1/4 cup brown sugar
- 1 tablespoon baking powder
- 1/4 teaspoon salt
- 1/4 teaspoon cream of tartar
- 1/2 cup butter flavored shortening
- 2/3 cup milk
- 1 teaspoon vanilla extract
- 1/4 cup butter, softened
- 1/4 cup brown sugar
- 5 1/2 teaspoons ground cinnamon

Direction

- Preheat oven to 375 degrees F (190 degrees C). Lightly grease a baking sheet, or use parchment paper.
- In a large bowl, combine flour, brown sugar, baking powder, salt and cream of tartar. Cut in shortening until mixture resembles coarse crumbs. Mix in milk and vanilla. Knead briefly on a floured surface. Roll out into a large rectangle, 1/2 inch thick. Spread softened butter onto surface of dough. Mix together brown sugar and cinnamon; sprinkle evenly over butter. Roll tightly, and cut into 12 equal slices. Place on prepared baking sheet.
- Bake in preheated oven for 15 to 20 minutes, or until golden brown.

Nutrition Information

- Calories: 223 calories
- Total Fat: 13.2 g
- Cholesterol: 11 mg
- Sodium: 167 mg
- Total Carbohydrate: 23.6 g
- Protein: 2.7 g

37. Buckwheat Sour Cream Biscuits

"Delicious and easy gluten-free biscuits with the healthy twist of buckwheat flour."

Serving: 12 | Prep: 20 m | Cook: 15 m | Ready in: 35 m

Ingredients

- 2 cups buckwheat flour
- 1 teaspoon gluten-free baking powder
- 1 teaspoon baking soda
- 1/2 teaspoon salt
- 1/3 cup unsalted butter, at room temperature
- 3/4 cup light sour cream
- 1/4 cup milk

Direction

- Preheat the oven to 400 degrees F (200 degrees C).
- Stir buckwheat flour, baking powder, baking soda, and salt together in a bowl. Cut in butter until mixture resembles coarse crumbs. Stir in sour cream and milk with a fork until dough forms a ball.
- Turn dough out on a lightly floured surface and knead about 5 times. Pat out to 3/4-inch thickness. Cut into rounds with a 2- or 3-inch cutter. Transfer biscuits to a nonstick baking sheet.
- Bake in the preheated oven until bottoms are nicely browned, about 15 minutes.

Nutrition Information

- Calories: 137 calories
- Total Fat: 7.2 g
- Cholesterol: 19 mg
- Sodium: 263 mg
- Total Carbohydrate: 15.6 g
- Protein: 3.8 g

38. Bunny Biscuits

When our granddaughter Amanda was younger, she wanted to cook every time she visited. These biscuits are nice for snacking with a glass of juice or milk or a cup of hot chocolate.--Flo Burtnett, Gage, Oklahoma

Serving: 5 servings. | Prep: 10 m | Cook: 10 m | Ready in: 20 m

Ingredients

- 1 tube (7-1/2 ounces) refrigerated buttermilk biscuits
- 10 raisins
- 20 slivered almonds
- 1 tube pink decorating icing
- 5 red-hot candies or red candied cherries

Direction

- Gently shape five biscuits into oval shapes; place on a greased baking sheet about 2 in. apart. Cut remaining biscuits in half. Shape biscuit halves to form ears; press firmly to attach to whole biscuits. On each biscuit, press on two raisin eyes and four slivered almond whiskers.
- Bake at 375 degrees for 8-10 minutes or until biscuits are browned. Cool slightly; use icing to frost ears and attach candy noses.

Nutrition Information

- Calories:
- Total Fat: g
- Cholesterol: mg
- Sodium: mg
- Total Carbohydrate: g
- Protein: g
- Fiber: g

39. Butter Dips

"Biscuits dipped in butter and cinnamon-sugar."

Serving: 16 | Prep: 10 m | Cook: 12 m | Ready in: 22 m

Ingredients

- 2 teaspoons white sugar, or to taste
- 1 teaspoon ground cinnamon, or to taste
- 1 (8 count) can refrigerated biscuit dough, separated and halved
- 1/4 cup butter, melted, or as needed

Direction

- Preheat oven to 350 degrees F (175 degrees C).
- Mix sugar and cinnamon together in a bowl. Dip biscuit halves in butter and roll in cinnamon-sugar. Arrange coated biscuits on a baking sheet.
- Bake in the preheated oven until golden brown, 12 to 14 minutes.

Nutrition Information

- Calories: 119 calories
- Total Fat: 6.7 g
- Cholesterol: 8 mg
- Sodium: 304 mg
- Total Carbohydrate: 12.9 g
- Protein: 1.9 g

40. Buttered Biscuits

"These biscuits are very easy to make and are very good."

Serving: 12 | Prep: 15 m | Cook: 10 m | Ready in: 25 m

Ingredients

- 2 cups self-rising flour
- 1/2 cup butter or margarine
- 2/3 cup buttermilk

Direction

- Preheat an oven to 450 degrees F (230 degrees C). Grease a baking sheet or line it with parchment paper.
- Cut butter into flour until the size of small peas. Pour in the buttermilk and stir just until combined.
- Drop by rounded tablespoonfuls on prepared baking sheet. Bake until golden brown, about 10 minutes.

Nutrition Information

- Calories: 147 calories
- Total Fat: 8 g
- Cholesterol: 21 mg
- Sodium: 333 mg
- Total Carbohydrate: 16.1 g
- Protein: 2.6 g

41. Buttermilk Angel Biscuits

When I make these slightly sweet biscuits, sometimes I cut them and fold over one side about a third of the way for a more traditional look. --Carol Holladay, Danville, Alabama

Serving: 2 dozen. | Prep: 30 m | Cook: 10 m | Ready in: 40 m

Ingredients

- 2 packages (1/4 ounce each) active dry yeast
- 1/4 cup warm water (110 degrees to 115 degrees)
- 5-1/4 to 5-1/2 cups self-rising flour
- 1/3 cup sugar
- 1 teaspoon baking soda
- 1 cup shortening
- 1-3/4 cups buttermilk

Direction

- In a small bowl, dissolve yeast in warm water. In a large bowl, whisk 5-1/4 cups flour, sugar and baking soda. Cut in shortening until mixture resembles coarse crumbs. Stir in buttermilk and yeast mixture to form a soft dough (dough will be sticky).

- Turn onto a floured surface; knead gently 8-10 times, adding flour if needed. Roll dough to 3/4-in. thickness; cut with a floured 2-1/2-in. biscuit cutter. Place 2 in. apart on greased baking sheets. Let stand at room temperature 20 minutes.
- Preheat oven to 450 degrees. Bake 8-12 minutes or until golden brown. Serve warm.

Nutrition Information

- Calories: 180 calories
- Total Fat: 8g
- Cholesterol: 1mg
- Sodium: 386mg
- Total Carbohydrate: 23g
- Protein: 3g
- Fiber: 1g

42. Buttermilk Biscuits

"Make a great big batch of buttermilk biscuits with this no-nonsense recipe. Serves a crowd!"

Serving: 60 | Prep: 20 m | Cook: 12 m | Ready in: 32 m

Ingredients

- 5 pounds self-rising flour
- 2 tablespoons baking powder
- 1 cup lard, melted
- 2 quarts buttermilk
- 1 cup 2% milk
- 1/4 cup bacon drippings

Direction

- Preheat the oven to 375 degrees F (190 degrees C).
- In a large bowl, stir together the self-rising flour and baking powder. Pour in the melted lard and mix until blended. Stir in the buttermilk and milk just until the dough comes together.

- Pat the dough out on a lightly floured surface and roll to 3/4 inch thickness. Cut into biscuits using a biscuit cutter or round cookie cutter. Place on baking sheets, spacing about 1 inch apart. Brush the tops with bacon drippings.
- Bake for 10 to 12 minutes in the preheated oven, until the bottoms and tops are lightly browned.

Nutrition Information

- Calories: 189 calories
- Total Fat: 5.1 g
- Cholesterol: 6 mg
- Sodium: 552 mg
- Total Carbohydrate: 29.9 g
- Protein: 5 g

43. Buttermilk Biscuits I

"This recipe was sent to me by a friend, the biscuits are delicious and very easy to make!"

Serving: 12 | Prep: 10 m | Cook: 15 m | Ready in: 25 m

Ingredients

- 4 cups self-rising flour
- 1 tablespoon white sugar
- 1 tablespoon baking powder
- 2/3 cup shortening
- 2 cups buttermilk
- 1/4 cup buttermilk

Direction

- Preheat oven to 400 degrees F (200 degrees C). Lightly grease two baking sheets.
- In a large mixing bowl, combine flour, sugar and baking powder; stir well. Cut in shortening until mixture resembles coarse cornmeal. Add 2 cups buttermilk and mix just to moisten.
- Roll out dough to 1 inch thick and cut into biscuits. Place biscuits on prepared baking sheets; brush tops with remaining 1/4 cup buttermilk.

- Bake in preheated oven for 15 minutes, or until golden.

Nutrition Information

- Calories: 271 calories
- Total Fat: 12.2 g
- Cholesterol: 2 mg
- Sodium: 661 mg
- Total Carbohydrate: 34.4 g
- Protein: 5.6 g

44.Buttermilk Biscuits II

"These biscuits are moist and crumbly and rich. Their delicate texture comes from the lack of handling and the wetness of the dough."

Serving: 4 | Prep: 20 m | Cook: 25 m | Ready in: 45 m

Ingredients

- 2 cups self-rising flour
- 1/4 cup white sugar
- 1/2 teaspoon salt
- 1/4 cup shortening
- 2/3 cup heavy cream
- 1 cup buttermilk
- 1 tablespoon butter, melted

Direction

- Preheat oven to 425 degrees F (220 degrees C). Lightly grease one baking sheet.
- In a large bowl, mix together flour, sugar and salt. Cut in shortening until mixture resembles coarse meal. Stir in cream and buttermilk until dough resembles cottage cheese.
- Generously sprinkle a smooth surface with flour. Spoon out batter into four lumps spaced well apart on the floured surface. Flour the top of the dough and your hands. Turn dough balls in the flour, shake off excess flour and place on prepared pan.
- Bake in preheated oven for 20 to 25 minutes, or until lightly browned. Remove from oven, brush with melted butter and serve.

Nutrition Information

- Calories: 570 calories
- Total Fat: 31.5 g
- Cholesterol: 64 mg
- Sodium: 1184 mg
- Total Carbohydrate: 62.9 g
- Protein: 9.1 g

45.Buttermilk Biscuits III

"This is a taste alike recipe for buttermilk biscuits from a Southern fast food chain."

Serving: 8 | Prep: 5 m | Cook: 15 m | Ready in: 20 m

Ingredients

- 4 cups self-rising flour
- 1 teaspoon white sugar
- 1 teaspoon baking powder
- 2/3 cup shortening
- 2 cups buttermilk
- 2 tablespoons buttermilk, for brushing

Direction

- Preheat oven to 400 degrees F (200 degrees C). Lightly grease a baking sheet.
- In a large bowl, stir together flour, sugar and baking powder. Cut in shortening until mixture resembles coarse crumbs. Stir in 2 cups buttermilk, mixing just enough for dough to come together.
- Roll dough out until 1 inch thick. Cut into rounds with a biscuit cutter. Place biscuits on prepared baking pan. Brush biscuits with 2 tablespoons buttermilk.
- Bake in preheated oven for 15 minutes, until golden.

Nutrition Information

- Calories: 400 calories
- Total Fat: 18.2 g
- Cholesterol: 3 mg
- Sodium: 907 mg

- Total Carbohydrate: 50.1 g
- Protein: 8.3 g

46.Buttermilk Biscuits With Honey Butter

Sweet honey butter, seasoned with a kiss of flaky sea salt, is the ultimate topping for these light-as-air biscuits.

Serving: Makes 14 biscuits | Prep: 25 m | Cook: 1 h

Ingredients

- 1 tablespoon plus 1 1/2 teaspoons sugar
- 4 teaspoons baking powder
- 1 1/2 teaspoons kosher salt
- 1/2 teaspoon baking soda
- 3 cups all-purpose flour, plus more for surface
- 3/4 cup plus 2 Tbsp. (1 3/4 sticks) chilled unsalted butter, cut into small cubes
- 1 1/4 cups buttermilk
- 1/2 cup (1 stick) unsalted butter, softened
- 2 tablespoons honey
- 2 teaspoons flaky sea salt, plus more for serving
- A 2 1/2-inch-diameter round cutter or glass

Direction

- For the biscuits: Position rack in middle of oven and preheat to 425°F. Whisk sugar, baking powder, kosher salt, baking soda, and 3 cups flour in a large bowl. Cut in butter using a pastry cutter or 2 butter knives until pea-sized lumps form. Stir in buttermilk until a shaggy dough forms.
- Gather dough into a ball. On a lightly floured surface, press into an 8" square. Fold sides over like a letter. Turn 90° and fold sides again, forming a small square. Press or roll to an 8" square and repeat once, adding flour as needed to prevent sticking.
- Pat dough into a scant 3/4" round. Cut out rounds with 2 1/2" cutter; transfer to a parchment-lined rimmed baking sheet. Gather scraps and repeat patting and cutting (you

should have 14). Freeze until chilled, about 15 minutes.
- Bake biscuits, rotating sheet halfway through, until golden brown, 22–24 minutes.
- For the Honey Butter: Stir butter, honey, and 2 tsp. sea salt in a medium bowl until well combined.
- Top biscuits with Honey Butter and sprinkle with sea salt; serve warm or at room temperature.

Nutrition Information

- Calories: 281
- Total Fat: 19 g (29%)
- Saturated Fat: 12 g (58%)
- Cholesterol: 49 mg (16%)
- Sodium: 193 mg (8%)
- Total Carbohydrate: 26 g (9%)
- Protein: 4 g (7%)
- Fiber: 1 g (3%)

47. Buttery Apple Biscuits

What better way to start the day than with warm biscuits filled with apple and the homey sweetness of molasses? Make a double batch and freeze half for a sensible snack. -- Athena Russell, Florence, South Carolina

Serving: 6 biscuits. | Prep: 20 m | Cook: 10 m | Ready in: 30 m

Ingredients

- 1 cup self-rising flour
- 1-1/2 teaspoons sugar
- Pinch salt
- 3 tablespoons cold butter
- 1 egg, lightly beaten
- 2 tablespoons fat-free milk
- 1 tablespoon molasses
- 1/2 cup chopped peeled tart apple

Direction

- In a small bowl, combine the flour, sugar and salt. Cut in butter until mixture resembles coarse crumbs. Combine the egg, milk and molasses; stir into flour mixture just until moistened. Stir in apple. Turn onto a lightly floured surface; knead 8-10 times.

- Pat or roll out to 1/2-in. thickness; cut with a floured 2-1/2-in. biscuit cutter. Place 2 in. apart on a baking sheet coated with cooking spray. Bake at 425 degrees for 6-8 minutes or until golden brown. Serve warm.

Nutrition Information

- Calories: 149 calories
- Total Fat: 7g
- Cholesterol: 50mg
- Sodium: 320mg
- Total Carbohydrate: 20g
- Protein: 3g
- Fiber: 0 g

48. Buttery Buttermilk Biscuits

"Flaky, croissant-like biscuits with delicious buttery layers achieved through the dough laminating process."

Serving: 12 | Prep: 1 h | Cook: 15 m | Ready in: 1 h 15 m

Ingredients

- 3 1/2 cups all-purpose flour
- 1 teaspoon salt
- 2 teaspoons baking powder
- 1/4 teaspoon baking soda
- 1 1/2 cups cold LAND O LAKES® Butter
- 1 1/2 cups cold buttermilk

Direction

- Sift flour, salt, baking powder, and baking soda together in a mixing bowl.
- Slice the butter into 1/8-inch to 1/4-inch pieces. Put the butter pieces in the flour and mix with your hands, gently rubbing the flour and butter together between your fingers without directly touching the butter to avoid melting it. Mix until the butter pieces are dime-size and covered by the flour mixture.

- Stir buttermilk into the flour mixture; mix just until ingredients are combined and form into a ball.
- Line a baking sheet with parchment paper.
- Dust work surface and top of dough with flour. Roll out dough into a 3/4-inch-thick rectangle. Fold into thirds (like a letter) using a bench scraper, if needed. Turn dough a half turn, and roll back into a 3/4 inch thick rectangle. Repeat twice more, folding and rolling dough a total of three times.
- Fold the dough into thirds once more and transfer the dough to the prepared pan. Cover with plastic wrap and refrigerate 20 minutes.
- Place the dough on the work surface and roll it out again to 3/4 inch thickness. Use a cookie or biscuit cutter to cut the dough into rounds.
- Place the biscuits about 1 inch apart on parchment-lined sheet pan. Cover biscuits and refrigerate for at least 20 minutes.
- Preheat oven to 500 degrees F (260 degrees C).
- Brush the tops of the biscuits with buttermilk. Place biscuits in preheated oven.
- Immediately reduce oven temperature to 375 degrees F (190 degrees C).
- Bake until biscuits are lightly browned and golden all around (any lighter and they will be doughy inside), 12 to 15 minutes. Allow biscuits to cool for 5 minutes; serve warm.

Nutrition Information

- Calories: 349 calories
- Total Fat: 23.6 g
- Cholesterol: 62 mg
- Sodium: 337 mg
- Total Carbohydrate: 29.5 g
- Protein: 5 g

49. Buttery Sweet Potato Biscuits

These biscuits taste buttery and are simple to make. Cut them into jack-o'-lantern shapes for autumn but different shapes for other seasons. They are especially delicious when eaten warm!

Serving: 13 biscuits. | Prep: 15 m | Cook: 20 m | Ready in: 35 m

Ingredients

- 2-1/4 cups all-purpose flour
- 3 teaspoons baking powder
- 1 teaspoon salt
- 3/4 cup cold butter, cubed
- 1 can (15-3/4 ounces) sweet potatoes, drained and mashed
- 1/2 cup half-and-half cream

Direction

- In a large bowl, combine the flour, baking powder and salt. Cut in butter until mixture resembles coarse crumbs. In a small bowl, combine sweet potatoes and cream until smooth; add to dry ingredients just until moistened.
- Turn onto a lightly floured surface; knead 8-10 times. Pat or roll to 1/2-in. thickness; cut with a floured 2-in. pumpkin-shaped cookie cutter. Place 2 in. apart on lightly greased baking sheets.
- Bake at 425 degrees for 16-20 minutes or until edges are browned. Remove from pans to wire racks. Serve warm.

Nutrition Information

- Calories: 214 calories
- Total Fat: 12g
- Cholesterol: 32mg
- Sodium: 368mg
- Total Carbohydrate: 24g
- Protein: 3g
- Fiber: 1g

50. Canadian Bacon and Cheese Biscuits

My husband and I own and operate a fishing lodge here in northwestern Ontario. We're always looking for new sandwiches to serve our guests. These have met with raves for years.

Serving: 5 servings. | Prep: 25 m | Cook: 15 m | Ready in: 40 m

Ingredients

- 2 cups all-purpose flour
- 4 teaspoons baking powder
- 1 teaspoon Italian seasoning
- 1/2 teaspoon salt
- 1/4 cup shortening
- 3/4 cup milk
- 2 tablespoons prepared mustard
- 5 slices Swiss cheese (1/8 inch thick)
- 5 thin slices red onion (about 2-1/2-in. round)
- 5 round slices fully cooked Jones Canadian Bacon

Direction

- In a large bowl, combine the flour, baking powder, Italian seasoning and salt. Cut in shortening until mixture resembles coarse crumbs. Stir in milk just until moistened.
- Turn dough onto a lightly floured surface; knead 6-8 times. Pat or roll out to 1/4-in. thickness; cut 10 biscuits with a 2-1/2-in. floured biscuit cutter. Spread each with about 1/2 teaspoon mustard.
- Cut cheese with a 2-1/2-in. round cutter; place a slice on five of the biscuits. Top with onion and bacon. Cover with remaining biscuits, mustard side down.
- Place on a 1-in. apart on greased baking sheet. Bake at 425 degrees for 15-18 minutes or until golden browned. Serve warm.

Nutrition Information

- Calories: 433 calories
- Total Fat: 20g
- Cholesterol: 43mg
- Sodium: 1042mg

- Total Carbohydrate: 42g
- Protein: 18g
- Fiber: 2g

---

51. Canadian Tea Biscuits

"A delicious recipe with a mingling of melt-in-your-mouth flavor!"

Serving: 6 | Prep: 15 m | Cook: 15 m | Ready in: 30 m

Ingredients

- 2 cups all-purpose flour
- 1 tablespoon baking powder
- 1 teaspoon salt
- 1/3 cup shortening
- 1/2 cup shredded Cheddar cheese
- 2 tablespoons chopped fresh chives
- 1 cup milk, or as needed

Direction

- Preheat oven to 425 degrees F (220 degrees C).
- Whisk together flour, baking powder, and salt in a bowl. Cut in shortening with a knife or pastry blender until the mixture resembles coarse crumbs. Stir Cheddar cheese and chives into flour mixture; gradually stir in milk to form a soft dough.
- Turn dough out onto a lightly floured surface and with floured hands, knead until smooth, about 15 times. Roll dough out to a 1-inch thickness with a floured rolling pin. Cut biscuits with a 2 1/2-inch round cookie cutter; place onto an ungreased baking sheet. Press dough trimmings together, roll out again, and cut remaining dough into rounds.
- Bake in the preheated oven until golden brown, about 15 minutes.

Nutrition Information

- Calories: 312 calories
- Total Fat: 15.7 g
- Cholesterol: 13 mg
- Sodium: 707 mg
- Total Carbohydrate: 34.5 g

- Protein: 8 g

---

52. Cape Cod Biscuits

"This is a different change of pace from ordinary biscuits, colorful for the holidays, and so easy to make."

Serving: 16 | Prep: 15 m | Cook: 10 m | Ready in: 25 m

Ingredients

- 4 cups biscuit baking mix
- 1 1/2 cups milk
- 1/3 cup whole berry cranberry sauce

Direction

- Preheat an oven to 450 degrees F (230 degrees C). Lightly grease a baking sheet.
- Use a fork to lightly blend the biscuit mix and milk in a large bowl. With spoon, drop 16 biscuits onto prepared baking sheet. Make a small depression in the center of each biscuit.
- Bake in preheated oven until golden brown, 10 to 15 minutes. Just before serving, evenly fill the depression in each biscuit with cranberry sauce.

Nutrition Information

- Calories: 142 calories
- Total Fat: 5 g
- Cholesterol: 2 mg
- Sodium: 389 mg
- Total Carbohydrate: 21.7 g
- Protein: 2.9 g

53. Caraway Cheese Biscuits

My grandchildren are always happy when I pull a pan of my cheese biscuits from the oven. The golden-brown goodies are perfect for dipping into chili or stew. -- Lorraine Caland, Shuniah, Ontario

Serving: 10 biscuits. | Prep: 10 m | Cook: 15 m | Ready in: 25 m

Ingredients

- 2 cups all-purpose flour
- 3 teaspoons baking powder
- 3/4 teaspoon salt
- 6 tablespoons cold butter, cubed
- 1 cup (4 ounces) finely shredded cheddar cheese, divided
- 1-1/2 teaspoons caraway seeds
- 3/4 cup 2% milk

Direction

- Preheat oven to 425 degrees. In a large bowl, whisk flour, baking powder and salt. Cut in butter until mixture resembles coarse crumbs. Stir in 3/4 cup cheese and caraway seeds. Add milk; stir just until moistened.
- Drop by 1/4 cupfuls onto ungreased baking sheets. Sprinkle with remaining cheese. Bake 12-15 minutes or until golden brown. Serve warm.

Nutrition Information

- Calories:
- Total Fat: g
- Cholesterol: mg
- Sodium: mg
- Total Carbohydrate: g
- Protein: g
- Fiber: g

54. Caraway Wheat Biscuits

My family can't eat just one of these fresh-from-the-oven biscuits. Onions make them moist and savory.--Nancy Messmore, Silver Lake Village, Ohio

Serving: about 1 dozen. | Prep: 20 m | Cook: 10 m | Ready in: 30 m

Ingredients

- 2-1/2 cups whole wheat flour
- 2 tablespoons caraway seeds
- 1 tablespoon baking powder
- 1/8 teaspoon salt
- 1-1/3 cups grated onions (about 3 medium)
- 2 eggs, beaten
- 1/2 cup vegetable oil

Direction

- In a large bowl, combine the flour, caraway seeds, baking powder and salt. In a small bowl, combine the onions, eggs and oil; add to dry ingredients just until moistened.
- Turn onto a floured surface. Roll dough to 3/4-in. thickness; cut with a floured 2-in. biscuit cutter. Place 1 in. apart on a greased baking sheet. Bake at 425 degrees for 10-15 minutes or until golden brown. Serve warm.

Nutrition Information

- Calories: 188 calories
- Total Fat: 11g
- Cholesterol: 35mg
- Sodium: 137mg
- Total Carbohydrate: 20g
- Protein: 5g
- Fiber: 4g

55. Cardamom Biscuits

"These biscuits taste great with fruit jam or nut butter."

Serving: 6 | Prep: 15 m | Cook: 15 m | Ready in: 40 m

Ingredients

- 1 1/2 cups all-purpose flour

- 1/2 cup nonfat dry milk powder
- 2 teaspoons baking powder
- 1 teaspoon ground cardamom
- 1/8 teaspoon salt
- 1/3 cup warm milk
- 1/3 cup honey
- 3 tablespoons canola oil
- 1/2 teaspoon vanilla extract
- 1 tablespoon turbinado sugar

Direction

- Preheat oven to 425 degrees F (220 degrees C). Spray a baking sheet with cooking spray, and set aside.
- Combine the flour, dry milk powder, baking powder, cardamom, and salt in a bowl. In another bowl, stir together warm milk, honey, oil, and vanilla extract. Pour the milk mixture into the flour mixture, and stir a few times, until just combined.
- Gather the dough together and turn out onto a floured surface. Gently pat the dough into a 9x3 inch rectangle, and cut the dough into 3 3-inch squares with a sharp knife. Cut each square on the diagonal to make 6 triangles, and place the triangles onto the prepared baking sheet.
- Bake for 6 minutes in the preheated oven, remove from oven, and sprinkle the tops of the biscuits with turbinado sugar. Return the biscuits to the oven, and bake for 8 more minutes. Let cool on rack before serving.

Nutrition Information

- Calories: 286 calories
- Total Fat: 7.7 g
- Cholesterol: 3 mg
- Sodium: 272 mg
- Total Carbohydrate: 47.9 g
- Protein: 7.4 g

56. Cheddar and Roasted Garlic Biscuits

"Simply stir Swanson® Seasoned Chicken Broth with Roasted Garlic into baking mix along with shredded Cheddar cheese for flavorful, flaky biscuits every time."

Serving: 24 | Cook: 25 m | Ready in: 25 m

Ingredients

- 5 cups all-purpose baking mix
- 1 cup shredded Cheddar cheese
- 1 (14 ounce) can Swanson® Seasoned Chicken Broth with Roasted Garlic

Direction

- Preheat oven to 450 degrees F.
- Mix baking mix, cheese and broth to form a soft dough. Drop by spoonfuls onto ungreased baking sheets, making 24.
- Bake for 10 minutes or until golden. Serve hot.

Nutrition Information

- Calories: 122 calories
- Total Fat: 5.4 g
- Cholesterol: 5 mg
- Sodium: 410 mg
- Total Carbohydrate: 15.6 g
- Protein: 3 g

57. Cheddar Bay Biscuits

"These biscuits are cheesy and rich, and fairly close to the ones a famous seafood restaurant chain serves."

Serving: 20

Ingredients

- 4 cups baking mix
- 3 ounces Cheddar cheese, shredded
- 1 1/3 cups water
- 1/2 cup melted butter
- 1 teaspoon garlic powder
- 1/4 teaspoon salt

- 1/8 teaspoon onion powder
- 1/8 teaspoon dried parsley

Direction

- Preheat oven to 375 degrees F (190 degrees C). Line a baking sheet with parchment paper.
- In a mixing bowl, combine the baking mix, cheese, and water. Mix until dough is firm. Using a small scoop, place dough on the prepared pan.
- Bake at 375 degrees F (190 degrees C) for 10 to 12 minutes, or until golden brown.
- Combine the melted butter, garlic powder, salt, onion powder and parsley. Brush over baked biscuits immediately upon removing from oven.

Nutrition Information

- Calories: 139 calories
- Total Fat: 6.3 g
- Cholesterol: 17 mg
- Sodium: 550 mg
- Total Carbohydrate: 17.5 g
- Protein: 3.2 g

58. Cheddar Beer Triangles

"These are yummy, flaky, and quick."

Serving: 10 | Prep: 10 m | Cook: 10 m | Ready in: 20 m

Ingredients

- 2 cups baking mix
- 1/2 cup shredded Cheddar cheese
- 1/2 cup beer

Direction

- Preheat an oven to 450 degrees F (230 degrees C). Grease a baking sheet.
- Stir the baking mix, Cheddar cheese, and beer in a bowl until the mixture clings together. Knead briefly on a lightly-floured surface until the dough just holds together. Pat the dough

into a 6-inch circle and cut into 10 wedges; place the wedges onto the prepared baking sheet.
- Bake in the preheated oven until browned on the bottom and golden brown on top, 8 to 10 minutes.

Nutrition Information

- Calories: 109 calories
- Total Fat: 2.2 g
- Cholesterol: 6 mg
- Sodium: 497 mg
- Total Carbohydrate: 17.9 g
- Protein: 3.5 g

59. Cheddar Biscuits

"This is a very tasty, easy bread to make. It goes great with things like spaghetti and lasagna."

Serving: 8 | Prep: 15 m | Cook: 20 m | Ready in: 35 m

Ingredients

- 2 cups biscuit baking mix
- 1 cup shredded Cheddar cheese
- 2/3 cup milk
- 1/2 teaspoon garlic powder
- 2 tablespoons margarine, melted
- 2 teaspoons dried parsley
- 1 teaspoon garlic salt

Direction

- Preheat oven to 400 degrees F (205 degrees C). Grease a cookie sheet, or line with parchment paper.
- In a large bowl, combine baking mix, Cheddar cheese, and garlic powder. Stir in milk. Drop batter by heaping tablespoonfuls onto prepared cookie sheet.
- Bake in preheated oven for 10 minutes. Brush biscuits with melted margarine, and sprinkle with parsley and garlic salt. Bake for 5 more minutes, or until lightly browned on the bottom.

Nutrition Information

- Calories: 214 calories
- Total Fat: 12.3 g
- Cholesterol: 16 mg
- Sodium: 732 mg
- Total Carbohydrate: 19.9 g
- Protein: 6.4 g

60. Cheddar Biscuits with Chive Butter

"Chives are the first herb to come up in the spring, and their delicate flavor pairs well with these biscuits. A little bit of Parmesan cheese makes the flavor of Cheddar cheese really pop; try it next time you make mac and cheese!"

Serving: 12 | Prep: 20 m | Cook: 15 m | Ready in: 35 m

Ingredients

- Chive Butter:
- 1/4 cup butter, softened
- 3 tablespoons chopped fresh chives
- 1/4 teaspoon cayenne pepper
- Cheddar Biscuits:
- 2 cups flour
- 2 teaspoons baking powder
- 1/2 teaspoon baking soda
- 1/4 teaspoon salt
- 6 tablespoons cold butter
- 1 1/4 cups shredded extra-sharp Cheddar cheese
- 1/4 cup grated Parmesan cheese
- 1 cup buttermilk
- 1 egg, lightly beaten

Direction

- Beat softened butter, chives, and cayenne pepper together in a bowl until well-combined and smooth.
- Preheat oven to 450 degrees F (230 degrees C).
- Stir flour, baking powder, baking soda, and salt together in a bowl. Cut cold butter into flour mixture with a pastry blender or two knives until mixture resembles oatmeal. Add Cheddar cheese and Parmesan cheese; toss to coat. Stir buttermilk into flour mixture until dough is just-moistened.
- Turn dough out onto a floured work surface and gently knead until dough comes together, about 6 to 8 times. Roll dough into a 9-inch square (1/2 inch thick) with a floured rolling pin. Cut dough lengthwise into 4 strips and crosswise into 6 strips. Place biscuits on a baking sheet and brush tops with beaten egg.
- Bake biscuits in the preheated oven until golden, about 15 minutes. Transfer to a rack and cool until warm, at least 15 minutes. Serve with chive butter.

Nutrition Information

- Calories: 228 calories
- Total Fat: 14.6 g
- Cholesterol: 56 mg
- Sodium: 378 mg
- Total Carbohydrate: 17.7 g
- Protein: 7 g

61. Cheddar Buttermilk Biscuits

Every bite of these flaky biscuits get a little kick from cayenne pepper and sharp cheddar cheese. They're a nice accompaniment to soup and stew. --Kimberley Nuttall, San Marco, California

Serving: 6-8 biscuits. | Prep: 20 m | Cook: 15 m | Ready in: 35 m

Ingredients

- 2 cups all-purpose flour
- 2 tablespoons sugar
- 4 teaspoons baking powder
- 1/2 teaspoon salt
- 1/4 to 1/2 teaspoon cayenne pepper
- 1/2 cup cold butter. cubed
- 1/2 cup shredded sharp cheddar cheese
- 3/4 cup buttermilk

Direction

- In a large bowl, combine the flour, sugar, baking powder, salt and cayenne. Cut in butter until mixture resembles coarse crumbs. Add the cheese and toss. Stir in buttermilk just until moistened.
- Turn onto a lightly floured surface; knead 8-10 times. Pat or roll to 1 in. thickness; cut with a floured 2-1/2-in. biscuit cutter. Place 1 in. apart on an ungreased baking sheet. Bake at 425 degrees for 15-18 minutes or until golden brown. Serve warm.

Nutrition Information

- Calories: 261 calories
- Total Fat: 14g
- Cholesterol: 39mg
- Sodium: 530mg
- Total Carbohydrate: 28g
- Protein: 6g
- Fiber: 1g

Direction

- Preheat oven to 425 degrees. In a large bowl, whisk flour, baking powder, mustard and salt. Cut in butter until mixture resembles coarse crumbs. Add corn, cheese and eggs; stir just until moistened.
- Turn onto a lightly floured surface; knead gently 8-10 times. Pat or roll dough to 1-in. thickness; cut with a floured 2-1/2-in. biscuit cutter. Place 2 in. apart on ungreased baking sheets; brush with milk. Bake 18-22 minutes or until golden brown. Serve warm.

Nutrition Information

- Calories: 270 calories
- Total Fat: 13g
- Cholesterol: 57mg
- Sodium: 476mg
- Total Carbohydrate: 30g
- Protein: 7g
- Fiber: 1g

62. Cheddar Corn Biscuits

Skip standard bake-and-serve dinner rolls this year and try my fast-to-fix biscuits studded with cheddar and corn. It's almost impossible to resist eating one right from the oven! --Susan Braun, Swift Current, Saskatchewan

Serving: 16 biscuits. | Prep: 20 m | Cook: 20 m | Ready in: 40 m

Ingredients

- 4-1/4 cups all-purpose flour
- 2 tablespoons baking powder
- 1 teaspoon ground mustard
- 3/4 teaspoon salt
- 3/4 cup cold butter, cubed
- 1 can (14-3/4 ounces) cream-style corn
- 1-1/2 cups shredded cheddar cheese
- 2 large eggs, lightly beaten
- 2 tablespoons 2% milk

63. Cheddar Cornmeal Biscuits with Chives

These chive-flecked cornmeal biscuits taste best made with extra-sharp Cheddar, but any type of Cheddar will work.

Serving: 12 | Cook: 20 m | Ready in: 35 m

Ingredients

- 1½ cups all-purpose flour
- ½ cup cornmeal, preferably stone-ground (see Shopping Tip)
- 1 tablespoon baking powder
- ½ teaspoon baking soda
- ½ teaspoon salt
- ¼ teaspoon freshly ground pepper
- ½ cup shredded extra-sharp Cheddar cheese
- 2 tablespoons cold butter, cut into ½-inch cubes
- ¾ cup reduced-fat sour cream
- ¼ cup finely chopped fresh chives

- 1 tablespoon honey, (optional)
- 3-5 tablespoons low-fat milk

Direction

- Preheat oven to 400°F.
- Combine flour, cornmeal, baking powder, baking soda, salt and pepper in a food processor. Pulse a few times to mix. Add cheese and butter and pulse again until the mixture looks pebbly with small oat-size lumps. Transfer the mixture to a large bowl.
- Add sour cream, chives and honey (if using) and stir with a rubber spatula until almost combined. Add 3 tablespoons milk, stirring, just until the dough comes together; add more milk as needed until the dough holds together in a shaggy mass. Don't overmix.
- On a lightly floured surface, lightly pat the dough into a rectangle about 9 by 5 inches and just over ½ inch thick. Using a large chef's knife, divide the dough evenly into 12 biscuits. Place on an ungreased baking sheet.
- Bake the biscuits until lightly browned on top, 14 to 16 minutes. Serve warm or at room temperature.

Nutrition Information

- Calories: 132 calories
- Total Fat: 5 g
- Saturated Fat: 3 g
- Cholesterol: 15 mg
- Sodium: 327 mg
- Total Carbohydrate: 17 g
- Protein: 3 g
- Fiber: 1 g
- Sugar: 0 g

64. Cheddar Dill Biscuits

"My husband and I try to eat in a healthful way, decreasing fat and calories wherever possible," writes Carol Braly of South Fork, Colorado. "These homemade biscuits are one of our favorite weekend breakfasts."

Serving: 1 dozen. | Prep: 15 m | Cook: 15 m | Ready in: 30 m

Ingredients

- 2 cups all-purpose flour
- 2 teaspoons sugar
- 1 teaspoon dill weed
- 1/2 teaspoon baking soda
- 1/2 teaspoon cream of tartar
- 1/2 teaspoon salt
- 1/4 cup cold butter, cubed
- 2/3 cup buttermilk
- 1/4 cup egg substitute
- 1/2 cup shredded reduced-fat cheddar cheese

Direction

- In a large bowl, combine the first six ingredients. Cut in butter until mixture resembles coarse crumbs. Combine buttermilk and egg substitute; stir into flour mixture just until moistened. Stir in cheese.
- Turn onto a lightly floured surface; knead 8-10 times. Pat to 3/4-in. thickness; cut with a floured 2-1/2-in. biscuit cutter.
- Place 1 in. apart on an ungreased baking sheet. Bake at 400 degrees for 12-16 minutes or until golden brown. Serve warm.

Nutrition Information

- Calories: 134 calories
- Total Fat: 5g
- Cholesterol: 14mg
- Sodium: 245mg
- Total Carbohydrate: 18g
- Protein: 4g
- Fiber: 1g

65. Cheddar Drop Biscuits

Bakers of any skill level can make these savory biscuits because there's no rolling and cutting. The heavenly biscuits are filled with the fabulous flavor of cheese, butter and garlic.--Marlana Barousse, Carriere, Mississippi

Serving: 1-1/2 dozen. | Prep: 20 m | Cook: 10 m | Ready in: 30 m

Ingredients

- 1-1/4 cups self-rising flour
- 3/4 cup cake flour
- 1 tablespoon sugar
- 3/4 teaspoon baking powder
- 1/2 teaspoon salt
- 1/4 teaspoon garlic powder
- 1/8 teaspoon baking soda
- 1/4 cup cold butter
- 1-1/4 cups heavy whipping cream
- 1 cup shredded sharp cheddar cheese
- OIL MIXTURE:
- 1/3 cup olive oil
- 1 teaspoon garlic powder
- 1 teaspoon dried parsley flakes
- 1/4 teaspoon salt

Direction

- In a small bowl, combine the first seven ingredients. Cut in butter until mixture resembles coarse crumbs. Stir in cream and cheese just until moistened.
- Drop dough by 1/8 cupfuls 2 in. apart onto a greased 15x10x1-in. baking pan. In a small bowl, combine the remaining ingredients. Brush half of oil mixture over biscuits.
- Bake at 450 degrees for 8-10 minutes or until golden brown. Brush with remaining oil mixture. Serve warm.

Nutrition Information

- Calories: 189 calories
- Total Fat: 14g
- Cholesterol: 36mg
- Sodium: 286mg
- Total Carbohydrate: 12g
- Protein: 3g

- Fiber: 0 g

66. Cheddar Keto Biscuits

"Almond flour makes these cheesy, garlicky biscuits perfect for anyone following the keto diet."

Serving: 8 | Prep: 20 m | Cook: 10 m | Ready in: 1 h 5 m

Ingredients

- 1 1/2 cups shredded mozzarella cheese
- 1/2 (8 ounce) package cream cheese, softened
- 2/3 cup almond flour
- 2 large eggs
- 4 teaspoons baking powder
- 1/2 teaspoon garlic powder
- 1 cup shredded Cheddar cheese
- 1 teaspoon butter, or as needed

Direction

- Combine mozzarella cheese and cream cheese in a large microwave-safe bowl. Heat in the microwave on high power until slightly melted, about 45 seconds. Remove from microwave and stir. Repeat, heating for about 20 seconds more. Remove from microwave again and stir; consistency should be very sticky and cheese should be completely melted. Return to microwave, if necessary, until all cheese is melted.
- Mix almond flour, eggs, baking powder, and garlic powder together in a bowl. Add mixture to the large bowl with the melted cheeses and mix well. Add Cheddar cheese and stir into the dough.
- Lay a sheet of plastic wrap on a flat surface and dust lightly with almond flour. Pour dough onto the middle of the plastic wrap and roll up to form a ball. Place in the refrigerator until slightly hardened, 20 to 30 minutes.
- Preheat the oven to 425 degrees F (220 degrees C). Grease a dark baking sheet with butter.
- Remove dough from the refrigerator and cut into 8 equal-sized pieces. Roll each into a ball and place on the prepared baking sheet,

- spacing equally and avoiding the sides, as biscuits will spread while cooking.
- Bake in the preheated oven until golden brown, checking at 10 minutes. Remove from oven immediately and cool completely before serving, about 15 minutes.

Nutrition Information

- Calories: 244 calories
- Total Fat: 19.8 g
- Cholesterol: 92 mg
- Sodium: 525 mg
- Total Carbohydrate: 4.2 g
- Protein: 13.5 g

67. Cheddar Onion Drop Biscuits

"These tasty biscuits have a savory Cheddar and onion flavor. Perfect with a bowl of chili or hearty soup in the winter or a main dish salad in the summer."

Serving: 12 | Prep: 10 m | Cook: 15 m | Ready in: 25 m

Ingredients

- 2 1/4 cups all-purpose flour
- 1/2 teaspoon baking powder
- 1/2 teaspoon baking soda
- 1/2 teaspoon salt
- 3 tablespoons butter
- 1 tablespoon dried minced onion
- 1/2 cup shredded Parmesan cheese
- 1 1/2 cups shredded sharp Cheddar cheese
- 1 cup 1% buttermilk

Direction

- Preheat an oven to 450 degrees F (230 degrees C). Line a baking sheet with parchment paper.
- Whisk the flour, baking powder, baking soda, and salt together in a bowl. Cut the butter into the flour mixture until the mixture resembles course crumbs. Stir the onion, Parmesan cheese, and Cheddar cheese into the flour mixture. Pour the buttermilk into the bowl; stir until evenly combined. Drop by 1/4-cupfuls

onto prepared baking sheet, about 2 inches apart.
- Bake in the preheated oven until the tops of the biscuits are lightly browned, 12 to 15 minutes. Serve warm.

Nutrition Information

- Calories: 191 calories
- Total Fat: 8.9 g
- Cholesterol: 26 mg
- Sodium: 351 mg
- Total Carbohydrate: 19.5 g
- Protein: 8 g

68. Cheddar Puff Biscuits

This is one of my favorite biscuit recipes because it's fast, simple and doesn't require any special ingredients. I sometimes freeze some baked puffs, then reheat in foil.

Serving: about 2 dozen. | Prep: 20 m | Cook: 25 m | Ready in: 45 m

Ingredients

- 1/2 cup milk
- 2 tablespoons butter
- 1/2 cup all-purpose flour
- 2 eggs
- 1/2 cup shredded cheddar cheese
- 1/4 cup chopped onion
- 1/4 teaspoon garlic powder
- 1/4 teaspoon pepper

Direction

- In a small saucepan, bring milk and butter to a boil. Add flour all at once and stir until a smooth ball forms. Remove from the heat; let stand for 5 minutes. Add eggs, one at a time, beating well after each addition. Add the cheese, onion, garlic powder and pepper; beat until mixture is smooth and shiny.
- Drop by rounded teaspoonfuls 2 in. apart onto greased baking sheets. Bake at 350 degrees for

25-30 minutes or until golden brown. Serve warm. Refrigerate leftovers.

Nutrition Information

- Calories: 36 calories
- Total Fat: 2g
- Cholesterol: 23mg
- Sodium: 32mg
- Total Carbohydrate: 3g
- Protein: 1g
- Fiber: 0 g

69. CheddarThyme Flaky Biscuits

"Anxious to utilize my herb garden, I took advantage of my favorite biscuit recipe -- excellent with chicken and salad!"

Serving: 10 | Prep: 15 m | Cook: 10 m | Ready in: 25 m

Ingredients

- 2 cups flour
- 4 teaspoons baking powder
- 3 tablespoons white sugar
- 1/2 teaspoon salt
- 1/2 teaspoon cream of tartar
- 1/2 cup butter or margarine
- 3/4 cup milk
- 1/2 cup shredded Cheddar cheese
- 1 tablespoon chopped fresh thyme

Direction

- Preheat the oven to 425 degrees F (220 degrees C).
- In a medium bowl, stir together the flour, baking powder, sugar, salt and cream of tartar. Cut in butter using a pastry cutter or a fork until it is the size of peas. Make a well in the center of the mixture and measure the milk, cheese and thyme into the bowl. Gently mix until a soft dough forms.
- Roll or pat out on a floured surface to 3/4 inch thick. Cut into circles and place on a baking sheet.

- Bake for 10 minutes in the preheated oven, or until the bottoms of the biscuits are golden brown.

Nutrition Information

- Calories: 220 calories
- Total Fat: 11.7 g
- Cholesterol: 32 mg
- Sodium: 420 mg
- Total Carbohydrate: 24.4 g
- Protein: 4.7 g

70. Cheese Garlic Biscuits

My biscuits won the division Best Quick Bread at my county fair. One of the judges liked it so much, she asked for the recipe! These buttery, savory biscuits go with just about anything.—Tall Pines Farm, Gloria Jarrett, Loveland, Ohio

Serving: 2-1/2 dozen. | Prep: 10 m | Cook: 10 m | Ready in: 20 m

Ingredients

- 2-1/2 cups biscuit/baking mix
- 3/4 cup shredded sharp cheddar cheese
- 1 teaspoon garlic powder
- 1 teaspoon ranch salad dressing mix
- 1 cup buttermilk
- TOPPING:
- 1/2 cup butter, melted
- 1 tablespoon minced chives
- 1/2 teaspoon garlic powder
- 1/2 teaspoon ranch salad dressing mix
- 1/4 teaspoon pepper

Direction

- In a large bowl, combine the baking mix, cheese, garlic powder and salad dressing mix. Stir in buttermilk just until moistened. Drop by tablespoonfuls onto greased baking sheets.
- Bake at 450 degrees for 6-8 minutes or until golden brown. Meanwhile, combine topping ingredients. Brush over biscuits. Serve warm.

Nutrition Information

- Calories: 81 calories
- Total Fat: 5g
- Cholesterol: 11mg
- Sodium: 176mg
- Total Carbohydrate: 7g
- Protein: 2g
- Fiber: 0 g

71. Cheese Pesto Biscuits

Biscuits always liven up a meal, especially when they're golden brown and filled with pesto, garlic and cheese for extra zip. --Liz Bellville, Jacksonville, North Carolina

Serving: 1 dozen. | Prep: 15 m | Cook: 10 m | Ready in: 25 m

Ingredients

- 2 cups all-purpose flour
- 2 teaspoons baking powder
- 1/2 teaspoon salt
- 1/4 teaspoon baking soda
- 1/3 cup cold butter, cubed
- 1 cup shredded Italian cheese blend
- 1-1/4 cups buttermilk
- 1 tablespoon prepared pesto
- 1 tablespoon butter, melted
- 1 garlic clove, minced

Direction

- Preheat oven to 450 degrees. In a large bowl, whisk flour, baking powder, salt and baking soda. Cut in butter until mixture resembles coarse crumbs. Stir in cheese. In a small bowl, whisk buttermilk and pesto until blended; stir into flour mixture just until moistened.
- Drop dough by 1/4 cupfuls 2 in. apart onto an ungreased baking sheet. Bake 10-12 minutes or until golden brown.
- Mix melted butter and garlic; brush over biscuits. Serve warm.

Nutrition Information

- Calories: 175 calories
- Total Fat: 9g
- Cholesterol: 24mg
- Sodium: 357mg
- Total Carbohydrate: 18g
- Protein: 5g
- Fiber: 1g

72. Cheese Biscuits

"THE BREAD at this meal sometimes varied, but we loved Mother's cheese biscuits best. Although the biscuit bowl was always filled to the top, there never seemed to be enough. The cheese gives these biscuits an unforgettable flavor, and buttermilk makes them especially light."

Serving: 8 biscuits. | Prep: 20 m | Cook: 15 m | Ready in: 35 m

Ingredients

- 1-2/3 cups all-purpose flour
- 2 teaspoons baking powder
- 1/2 teaspoon salt
- 1/4 teaspoon baking soda
- 1/4 cup shortening
- 1 cup shredded cheddar cheese
- 3/4 cup buttermilk

Direction

- In a bowl, combine flour, baking powder, salt and baking soda. Cut in shortening until the mixture resembles coarse crumbs. Stir in cheese. Add buttermilk; stir just until dough clings together. On a lightly floured surface, knead dough lightly until easy to handle. Roll into a 12-in. circle. Cut into eight wedges. Begin at wide end of wedge and roll toward point. Place biscuits, point side down, on a greased baking sheet. Bake at 450 degrees for 12-14 minutes or until golden brown. Serve warm.

Nutrition Information

- Calories: 209 calories
- Total Fat: 10g
- Cholesterol: 16mg
- Sodium: 396mg
- Total Carbohydrate: 21g
- Protein: 6g
- Fiber: 1g

73. Cheese Biscuits I

"I got this recipe from a friend. Best if eaten warm!!!"

Serving: 10 | Prep: 10 m | Cook: 10 m | Ready in: 20 m

Ingredients

- 2 cups baking mix
- 2/3 cup milk
- 1/2 cup shredded Cheddar cheese
- 1/4 cup Parmesan cheese
- 1/4 cup butter
- 1/2 teaspoon garlic powder
- 1 teaspoon dried parsley

Direction

- Preheat oven to 450 degrees F (230 degrees C).
- Stir together baking mix, milk and cheeses until soft dough forms. Drop by spoonfuls onto an ungreased cookie sheet.
- Bake for 10 to 12 minutes, or until bottoms are lightly browned.
- Melt butter, and stir in garlic powder and parsley flakes. Brush over warm biscuits.

Nutrition Information

- Calories: 161 calories
- Total Fat: 7.7 g
- Cholesterol: 21 mg
- Sodium: 567 mg
- Total Carbohydrate: 18.4 g
- Protein: 4.8 g

74. Cheese Biscuits II

"A tasty biscuit with a flavor kick courtesy of bell pepper and pimentos."

Serving: 6 | Prep: 10 m | Cook: 15 m | Ready in: 25 m

Ingredients

- 2 cups all-purpose flour
- 2 teaspoons white sugar
- 4 teaspoons baking powder
- 1/2 teaspoon salt
- 1/2 teaspoon cream of tartar
- 1/2 cup shortening
- 2/3 cup shredded Cheddar cheese
- 1/4 cup chopped green bell pepper
- 2 tablespoons chopped pimento peppers
- 2/3 cup milk

Direction

- Preheat oven to 425 degrees F (220 degrees C).
- In a large mixing bowl, combine the flour, sugar, baking powder, salt, and cream of tartar. Cut in the shortening with a pastry blender. Add the grated cheese, green bell pepper, and pimento; mix with a fork. Stir in milk and mix well.
- Turn the dough out onto a floured surface and knead 5 times. Roll out to a rectangular shape and cut into squares using a knife or pizza cutter. Place onto an ungreased baking sheet.
- Bake for 15 minutes, or until browned.

Nutrition Information

- Calories: 376 calories
- Total Fat: 22.2 g
- Cholesterol: 15 mg
- Sodium: 524 mg
- Total Carbohydrate: 35.9 g
- Protein: 8.4 g

75. Cheese Drop Biscuits

"These are easy, fast, and very tasty. Great for a little extra for supper or camping trips."

Serving: 12 | Prep: 15 m | Cook: 15 m | Ready in: 30 m

Ingredients

- 2 cups all-purpose flour
- 1 tablespoon baking powder
- 1 teaspoon dried chives
- 1/2 teaspoon garlic salt
- 1/2 teaspoon salt
- 1/4 cup shortening
- 3/4 cup milk
- 1/4 cup shredded sharp Cheddar cheese

Direction

- Preheat oven to 450 degrees F (230 degrees C). Lightly grease a baking sheet.
- In a large bowl, mix together flour, baking powder, chives, garlic salt and salt. Cut in the shortening until the mixture has only small lumps. Add milk and cheese and stir until moistened. Drop dough by heaping spoonfuls onto prepared baking sheet.
- Bake in preheated oven for 12 to 15 minutes, until golden.

Nutrition Information

- Calories: 131 calories
- Total Fat: 5.6 g
- Cholesterol: 4 mg
- Sodium: 278 mg
- Total Carbohydrate: 16.9 g
- Protein: 3.2 g

76. Cheese Garlic Biscuits I

"These delicious cheese and garlic biscuits are just like the ones at our favorite seafood restaurant. They're easy to make and sure to please."

Serving: 9 | Prep: 5 m | Cook: 10 m | Ready in: 15 m

Ingredients

- 2 cups biscuit mix
- 2/3 cup milk
- 1/2 cup shredded Cheddar cheese
- 2 tablespoons butter, melted
- 1/8 teaspoon garlic powder

Direction

- Preheat oven to 450 degrees F (230 degrees C). Lightly grease a baking sheet.
- Measure biscuit mix into a large bowl. Stir in milk and cheese until a soft dough forms. Drop 9 spoonfuls of the dough onto prepared baking sheet.
- Bake in preheated oven for 8 to 10 minutes, until golden brown. While biscuits bake stir together butter and garlic powder. Remove biscuits from oven and brush with butter mixture.

Nutrition Information

- Calories: 162 calories
- Total Fat: 8.1 g
- Cholesterol: 15 mg
- Sodium: 422 mg
- Total Carbohydrate: 17.8 g
- Protein: 4.6 g

77. Cheese Garlic Biscuits II

"Cheese garlic biscuits like those served at a certain famous seafood restaurant."

Serving: 12 | Prep: 10 m | Cook: 15 m | Ready in: 25 m

Ingredients

- 1 3/4 cups all-purpose flour

- 1/2 teaspoon salt
- 1/2 teaspoon baking powder
- 5 tablespoons butter
- 1 cup milk
- 1 cup shredded Cheddar cheese
- 1/4 cup butter, melted
- 1 clove garlic, minced

Direction

- Preheat oven to 450 degrees F (230 degrees C).
- In a large bowl, sift together flour, salt and baking powder. Cut in butter until mixture resembles coarse crumbs. Make a well in the center of flour mixture. Add the milk and cheddar cheese; stir to combine. Drop batter by spoonfuls onto an ungreased baking sheet.
- Bake in preheated oven for 12 to 15 minutes, until lightly browned. While biscuits are baking mix melted butter and minced garlic. Brush garlic butter over hot baked biscuits.

Nutrition Information

- Calories: 191 calories
- Total Fat: 12.3 g
- Cholesterol: 34 mg
- Sodium: 240 mg
- Total Carbohydrate: 15.1 g
- Protein: 5 g

78. CheeseGarlic Biscuits

"Do you have 15 minutes to spare? Surprise your family by baking a batch of these restaurant-style biscuits!"

Serving: 9 | Prep: 5 m | Ready in: 15 m

Ingredients

- 2 cups Original Bisquick® mix
- 2/3 cup milk
- 1/2 cup shredded Cheddar cheese
- 2 tablespoons butter or margarine
- 1/8 teaspoon garlic powder

Direction

- Heat oven to 450 degrees F.
- Stir Bisquick mix, milk and cheese until soft dough forms. Drop dough by 9 spoonfuls onto ungreased cookie sheet.
- Bake 8 to 10 minutes or until golden brown. Stir together butter and garlic powder; brush over warm biscuits.

Nutrition Information

- Calories: 166 calories
- Total Fat: 9 g
- Cholesterol: 15 mg
- Sodium: 400 mg
- Total Carbohydrate: 17.4 g
- Protein: 4.1 g

79. Cheesy Drop Biscuits

I wanted to capture the flavor of cheese biscuits from a popular restaurant. So I took my favorite buttermilk biscuit recipe and added to it.

Serving: 10 biscuits. | Prep: 10 m | Cook: 10 m | Ready in: 20 m

Ingredients

- 2 cups all-purpose flour
- 2 teaspoons baking powder
- 1 teaspoon salt
- 1/4 teaspoon baking soda
- 1/4 teaspoon garlic powder
- 1 cup shredded cheddar cheese
- 1/4 cup grated Parmesan cheese
- 2/3 cup buttermilk
- 1/3 cup canola oil
- Additional Parmesan cheese, optional

Direction

- In a large bowl, combine the first five ingredients. Add cheeses.
- In a small bowl, combine buttermilk and oil. Stir into dry ingredients just until moistened.

Drop by 1/4 cupfuls 2 in. apart onto a greased baking sheet. Sprinkle with additional Parmesan cheese if desired.

- Bake at 450 degrees for 10-12 minutes or until golden brown. Serve warm.

Nutrition Information

- Calories: 176 calories
- Total Fat: 10g
- Cholesterol: 12mg
- Sodium: 392mg
- Total Carbohydrate: 17g
- Protein: 5g
- Fiber: 1g

80. Cheesy Keto Biscuits

"Large keto biscuits that are very substantial and filling."

Serving: 9 | Prep: 20 m | Cook: 20 m | Ready in: 40 m

Ingredients

- 2 cups almond flour
- 1 tablespoon baking powder
- 2 1/2 cups shredded Cheddar cheese
- 4 eggs
- 1/4 cup half-and-half

Direction

- Preheat the oven to 350 degrees F (175 degrees C). Line a baking sheet with parchment paper.
- Combine almond flour and baking powder in a large bowl. Mix in Cheddar cheese by hand. Create a small well in the middle of the bowl; add eggs and half-and-half to the center. Use a large fork, spoon, or your hands to blend in the flour mixture until a sticky batter forms.
- Drop 9 portions of batter onto the prepared baking sheet.
- Bake in the preheated oven until golden, about 20 minutes.

Nutrition Information

- Calories: 329 calories
- Total Fat: 27.1 g
- Cholesterol: 118 mg
- Sodium: 391 mg
- Total Carbohydrate: 7.2 g
- Protein: 16.7 g

81. Cheesy Onion Biscuits

Fresh from our Test Kitchen, these scone-shaped biscuits have a savory onion-and-cheddar flavor and a golden shell. Serve them with a pat of butter alongside your favorite soup.

Serving: 4 biscuits. | Prep: 15 m | Cook: 10 m | Ready in: 25 m

Ingredients

- 1/4 cup chopped onion
- 3/4 cup all-purpose flour
- 1/8 teaspoon baking powder
- 1/8 teaspoon baking soda
- 1/8 teaspoon salt
- 1 tablespoon shortening
- 1/4 cup shredded cheddar cheese
- 1/3 cup buttermilk

Direction

- Place onion in a small microwave-safe bowl; cover and microwave on high for 1-2 minutes or until tender. In a small bowl, combine the flour, baking powder, baking soda and salt. Cut in shortening until mixture resembles coarse crumbs. Stir in cheese and onion. Stir in buttermilk just until moistened.
- Turn onto a lightly floured surface; knead 8-10 times. Pat or roll out into a 4-in. circle; cut into four wedges. Place 2 in. apart on a baking sheet coated with cooking spray. Bake at 450 degrees for 8-12 minutes or until golden brown. Serve warm.

Nutrition Information

- Calories: 150 calories
- Total Fat: 5g
- Cholesterol: 8mg
- Sodium: 190mg
- Total Carbohydrate: 20g
- Protein: 5g
- Fiber: 1g

82. Cheesy PHILLY Biscuits

"Fluffy, savoury biscuits incorporate both delicious cream cheese and shredded double Cheddar cheese."

Serving: 14 | Prep: 15 m | Cook: 15 m | Ready in: 30 m

Ingredients

- 2 cups all-purpose flour
- 1 tablespoon Magic Baking Powder
- 1 (250 g) package Philadelphia Brick Cream Cheese, cubed
- 1 cup Kraft Double Cheddar Shredded Cheese
- 1/2 cup milk

Direction

- Heat oven to 425 degrees F.
- Mix flour and baking powder in large bowl. Cut in cream cheese with pastry blender or 2 knives until mixture resembles coarse crumbs. Stir in shredded cheese. Add milk; stir until mixture forms soft dough.
- Pat dough to 3/4-inch thickness on floured surface. Cut into 14 rounds with 2-inch fluted biscuit cutter, rerolling scraps as necessary. Place, 2 inches apart, on baking sheet.
- Bake 12 to 15 minutes or until golden brown.

Nutrition Information

- Calories: 153 calories
- Total Fat: 8.2 g
- Cholesterol: 29 mg
- Sodium: 235 mg
- Total Carbohydrate: 15.2 g

- Protein: 5.2 g

83. Chef Johns Butter Puff Biscuit Dough

"This biscuit dough is similar to puff pastry but uses a much less fussy procedure. It works great for fruit tarts, ham and cheese turnovers, and chocolate croissants--and of course, plain biscuits served with butter and jam."

Serving: 6 | Prep: 30 m | Ready in: 1 h 30 m

Ingredients

- 2 cups self-rising flour
- 3/4 cup cold water, or as needed
- 7 tablespoons frozen unsalted butter

Direction

- Place self-rising flour and cold water in the bowl of a stand mixer. Using dough hook attachment knead to form a soft, slightly elastic, but not too sticky dough, about 2 minutes. Form dough into a ball and wrap in plastic wrap. Refrigerate at least 30 minutes.
- Place chilled dough on a floured surface and roll out to a 1/2-inch thick rectangle using just enough flour to keep it from sticking. Grate about 4 tablespoons of frozen butter onto the surface of the dough to within about 1/2 inch of the edge. Lightly flour a sheet of plastic wrap. Spread the plastic wrap, floured side down, onto the butter and gently press the butter into the dough. Carefully remove the plastic wrap.
- Fold 1/3 of the dough over the middle third; then fold the other 1/3 over the middle into a tri-fold with 2 layers of butter. Roll dough again into a rectangle, brush off excess flour, and create another tri-fold. Roll again to about a 1-inch thickness. Wrap dough in plastic wrap and refrigerate for another 30 minutes.
- Place chilled dough again on a floured surface, roll into a rectangle, and make another tri-fold. Roll back out again into a 1/2-inch thick

rectangle. Grate about 3 tablespoons butter onto the surface of the dough. Cover with floured plastic wrap and press butter into dough. Remove plastic wrap. Give dough another tri-fold and press layers together. Roll out dough and fold in half. Roll out again, and fold in half. Roll out dough one more time. Wrap in plastic wrap and chill until ready to use.

- Bake at 400 degrees F (200 degrees C).

Nutrition Information

- Calories: 266 calories
- Total Fat: 13.8 g
- Cholesterol: 36 mg
- Sodium: 532 mg
- Total Carbohydrate: 30.9 g
- Protein: 4.3 g

84. Chef Johns Buttermilk Biscuits

"This deceptively simple recipe can come out a million different ways with some very minor variations on the ingredients and amounts. This one's my favorite - flaky, but not dry; chewy, but not tough; crisp in just the right spots."

Serving: 12 | Prep: 20 m | Cook: 15 m | Ready in: 35 m

Ingredients

- 2 cups all-purpose flour
- 2 teaspoons baking powder
- 1 teaspoon salt
- 1/4 teaspoon baking soda
- 7 tablespoons unsalted butter, chilled in freezer and cut into thin slices
- 3/4 cup cold buttermilk
- 2 tablespoons buttermilk for brushing

Direction

- Preheat oven to 425 degrees F (220 degrees C).
- Line a baking sheet with a silicone baking mat or parchment paper.

- Whisk flour, baking powder, salt, and baking soda together in a large bowl.
- Cut butter into flour mixture with a pastry blender until the mixture resembles coarse crumbs, about 5 minutes.
- Make a well in the center of butter and flour mixture. Pour in 3/4 cup buttermilk; stir until just combined.
- Turn dough onto a floured work surface, pat together into a rectangle.
- Fold the rectangle in thirds. Turn dough a half turn, gather any crumbs, and flatten back into a rectangle. Repeat twice more, folding and pressing dough a total of three times.
- Roll dough on a floured surface to about 1/2 inch thick.
- Cut out 12 biscuits using a 2 1/2-inch round biscuit cutter.
- Transfer biscuits to the prepared baking sheet. Press an indent into the top of each biscuit with your thumb.
- Brush the tops of biscuits with 2 tablespoons buttermilk.
- Bake in the preheated oven until browned, about 15 minutes.

Nutrition Information

- Calories: 143 calories
- Total Fat: 7.1 g
- Cholesterol: 19 mg
- Sodium: 321 mg
- Total Carbohydrate: 17 g
- Protein: 2.8 g

85. Chef Johns Sweet Potato Biscuits

"This would be a great way to use leftover Thanksgiving sweet potatoes, but they're even better right on that holiday table with the rest of the feast. By forming and folding dough, we develop beautifully buttery layers and avoid overmixing. These were delicious with the pomegranate spread."

Serving: 8 | Prep: 20 m | Cook: 20 m | Ready in: 40 m

Ingredients

- Biscuits:
- 1 large orange-fleshed sweet potato, peeled
- 1 teaspoon salt
- 1 tablespoon brown sugar
- 1/2 cup buttermilk
- 3 1/4 cups self-rising flour
- 1 1/2 sticks unsalted butter, frozen
- 1 tablespoon melted butter
- Pomegranate Spread:
- 4 tablespoons butter, room temperature
- 1 teaspoon pomegranate molasses
- 1 teaspoon pomegranate juice
- Fresh pomegranate seeds for garnish

Direction

- Cut sweet potato in half lengthwise. Cut each in half again lengthwise, then in half cross-wise. Cut each piece in half to make about 16 evenly sized chunks. Transfer into pot; cover with water and add salt. Bring to a simmer on high heat; reduce heat to medium-low and cook until potatoes are tender, about 17 minutes. Drain thoroughly; return to pot and mash potatoes. You will need 1 1/2 cups mashed sweet potatoes. Cool thoroughly.
- Transfer cooled mashed potatoes to a mixing bowl. Add brown sugar and buttermilk. Mix together until well combined.
- Place self-rising flour in a separate mixing bowl. Grate frozen butter into flour, tossing with a fork to coat with flour after each addition of about 1/3 to 1/2 stick. This will prevent butter from clumping. Mixture should look like floury pieces of butter. Add sweet potato mixture. Toss with a fork until evenly distributed, but don't overmix.
- Transfer mixture onto a lightly floured work surface. Push and press mixture together into a rectangular shape, about 1 1/2 inches thick. Dough will be floury and a bit crumbly. Fold rectangle into thirds, lifting up one-third and folding onto the middle and doing the same with the other side. Dust with a bit of flour if sticking.
- Preheat oven to 425 degrees F (220 degrees C). Line a rimmed baking sheet with a silicone mat.
- Press dough into a rectangle again, about 1 inch thick. Repeat the tri-fold step. Press out into a rectangle, about 1 inch thick. Trim off the rough edges to square off the sides; this will maximize rising. Cut into 8 equal portions. Transfer to prepared baking pan, spacing biscuits evenly. Brush tops lightly with 1 tablespoon melted butter.
- Bake in preheated oven until browned, 20 to 25 minutes. Cool slightly before serving.
- Mix 4 tablespoons butter (room temperature), pomegranate syrup, and pomegranate juice together in a small bowl. Spread on warm biscuits. Sprinkle with a few pomegranate seeds for garnish.

Nutrition Information

- Calories: 459 calories
- Total Fat: 25.1 g
- Cholesterol: 65 mg
- Sodium: 1037 mg
- Total Carbohydrate: 51.9 g
- Protein: 6.7 g

86. Chili Cheddar Biscuits

Chili powder lends a little kick to these flaky, buttery biscuits. "I like to serve them with steaming bowls of chili or hearty beef soup," writes Kim Marie Van Rheenen of Mendota, Illinois.

Serving: 15 biscuits. | Prep: 20 m | Cook: 10 m | Ready in: 30 m

Ingredients

- 1-1/3 cups all-purpose flour
- 3 teaspoons baking powder
- 3 teaspoons dried parsley flakes
- 1 teaspoon chili powder
- 1/4 teaspoon salt
- 1/2 cup cold butter, cubed
- 1/2 cup whole milk
- 1 large egg, lightly beaten
- 1-1/2 cups shredded cheddar cheese

Direction

- In a large bowl, combine the dry ingredients. Cut in butter until mixture resembles coarse crumbs. Stir in milk and egg just until moistened. Add cheese.
- Turn onto a lightly floured surface. Roll to 1/2-in. thickness; cut with a 2-1/2-in. biscuit cutter. Place 1 in. apart on an ungreased baking sheet. Bake at 450 degrees for 8-10 minutes or until golden brown. Serve warm.

Nutrition Information

- Calories: 145 calories
- Total Fat: 10g
- Cholesterol: 44mg
- Sodium: 259mg
- Total Carbohydrate: 9g
- Protein: 4g
- Fiber: 0 g

87. Chive Lemon Biscuits

These tender, browned biscuits have a subtle lemon and chive flavor that delightfully complements Very Veggie Soup. – Jim Gales, Glendale, Wisconsin

Serving: 9 biscuits. | Prep: 15 m | Cook: 15 m | Ready in: 30 m

Ingredients

- 2 cups all-purpose flour
- 3 teaspoons baking powder
- 1 teaspoon sugar
- 1 teaspoon salt
- 1/2 cup cold butter
- 3/4 cup half-and-half cream
- 1/2 cup minced chives
- 1-1/2 teaspoons grated lemon peel
- 1 egg
- 1 tablespoon water

Direction

- In a large bowl, combine the flour, baking powder, sugar and salt. Cut in butter until mixture resembles coarse crumbs. Stir in cream just until moistened. Stir in chives and lemon peel. Turn onto a lightly floured surface; knead 8-10 times.
- Pat or roll out to 3/4-in. thickness; cut with a floured 2-1/2-in. biscuit cutter.
- Place 2 in. apart on a greased baking sheet. In a small bowl, whisk egg and water; brush over biscuits. Bake at 400 degrees for 15-20 minutes or until golden brown. Serve warm.

Nutrition Information

- Calories: 222 calories
- Total Fat: 13g
- Cholesterol: 43mg
- Sodium: 480mg
- Total Carbohydrate: 23g
- Protein: 4g
- Fiber: 1g

88. Chive Biscuits

I like to serve these light moist biscuits with my soups, stews and roasts during fall and winter. Sometimes I substitute other herbs for a change.--Norma Erne, Albuquerque, New Mexico

Serving: 1 dozen. | Prep: 15 m | Cook: 10 m | Ready in: 25 m

Ingredients

- 2 cups all-purpose flour
- 3 teaspoons baking powder
- 1/2 teaspoon salt
- 1/4 teaspoon baking soda
- 1/3 cup butter-flavored shortening
- 1 cup buttermilk
- 2 tablespoons minced chives

Direction

- In a small bowl, combine the flour, baking powder, salt and baking soda. Cut in shortening until mixture resembles coarse crumbs. Stir in buttermilk and chives just until moistened.
- Drop by tablespoonfuls 2 in. apart onto a greased baking sheet. Bake at 450 degrees for 10-12 minutes or until lightly browned. Serve warm.

Nutrition Information

- Calories: 133 calories
- Total Fat: 6g
- Cholesterol: 1mg
- Sodium: 246mg
- Total Carbohydrate: 17g
- Protein: 3g
- Fiber: 1g

89. Chive Cheese Biscuits

From Black Creek, British Columbia, Joan Baskin writes, "These are the lightest biscuits I've ever baked. My husband loves them with a meal of macaroni and cheese and coleslaw." Flecks of fresh chives and golden bits of cheddar cheese make the biscuits a savory standout.

Serving: 1 dozen. | Prep: 20 m | Cook: 15 m | Ready in: 35 m

Ingredients

- 2 cups all-purpose flour
- 3 teaspoons baking powder
- 1/2 teaspoon cream of tartar
- 1/2 teaspoon salt
- 3/4 cup shredded cheddar cheese
- 1/2 cup shortening
- 3/4 cup milk
- 1/3 cup minced chives

Direction

- In a large bowl, combine the flour, baking powder, cream of tartar and salt. Cut in cheese and shortening until mixture resembles coarse crumbs. Stir in milk and chives until moistened.
- Turn onto a lightly floured surface; gently knead 8-10 times. Roll to 3/4-in. thickness; cut with a 2-1/2-in. biscuit cutter. Place on an ungreased baking sheet.
- Bake at 400 degrees for 13-15 minutes or until golden brown. Serve warm.

Nutrition Information

- Calories: 184 calories
- Total Fat: 11g
- Cholesterol: 10mg
- Sodium: 249mg
- Total Carbohydrate: 17g
- Protein: 4g
- Fiber: 1g

90. Cinnamon Biscuits

"A cinnamon and raisin biscuit, but made in a traditional cinnamon roll shape!"

Serving: 8 | Prep: 15 m | Cook: 12 m | Ready in: 30 m

Ingredients

- 1 1/4 cups Reduced Fat Bisquick®
- 1 cup whole wheat baking mix
- 2/3 cup buttermilk
- 2 cups HERSHEY®'S Cinnamon Chips
- 1 cup cinnamon coated raisins
- 3 tablespoons melted butter
- 1/2 cup confectioners' sugar
- 1 tablespoon melted butter
- 1 tablespoon water

Direction

- Preheat oven to 425 degrees F (220 degrees C).
- In a food processor, process cinnamon chips until coarsely ground. Remove 1/2 of the chips, and continue to process the remaining chips until finely ground.
- In a large bowl, whisk together baking mixes, 1 cup coarsely ground cinnamon chips, and raisins. Make a well in center, add buttermilk, and stir just until dough comes together.
- Turn dough out onto a lightly floured, flat surface. Knead gently for 1 minute. Flatten dough to an 8x10 inch rectangle. Brush with melted butter, and sprinkle with finely ground cinnamon chips. Starting from one long side, roll up the dough. Pinch seams and ends to seal. Slice roll crosswise into 8 equal slices, and arrange in a 9x13 ungreased baking pan.
- Bake 12 minutes, until lightly golden. In a separate bowl, stir confectioners' sugar, 1 tablespoon melted butter, and water until smooth. Drizzle glaze over hot biscuits.

Nutrition Information

- Calories: 560 calories
- Total Fat: 27.7 g
- Cholesterol: 19 mg
- Sodium: 609 mg
- Total Carbohydrate: 86.3 g
- Protein: 8.7 g

91. Cinnamon Fruit Biscuits

Because these sweet treats are so easy, I'm almost embarrassed when people ask me for the recipe. They're a snap to make with refrigerated buttermilk biscuits, sugar, cinnamon and your favorite fruit preserves. --Ione Burham, Washington, Iowa

Serving: 10 servings. | Prep: 15 m | Cook: 15 m | Ready in: 30 m

Ingredients

- 1/2 cup sugar
- 1/2 teaspoon ground cinnamon
- 1 tube (12 ounces) refrigerated buttermilk biscuits, separated into 10 biscuits
- 1/4 cup butter, melted
- 10 teaspoons strawberry preserves

Direction

- In a small bowl, combine sugar and cinnamon. Dip top and sides of biscuits in butter, then in cinnamon-sugar.
- Place on ungreased baking sheets. With the end of a wooden spoon handle, make a deep indentation in the center of each biscuit; fill with 1 teaspoon preserves.
- Bake at 375 degrees for 15-18 minutes or until golden brown. Cool for 15 minutes before serving (preserves will be hot).

Nutrition Information

- Calories: 178 calories
- Total Fat: 5g
- Cholesterol: 12mg
- Sodium: 323mg
- Total Carbohydrate: 31g
- Protein: 3g
- Fiber: 0 g

- Fiber: 1g

92. Cinnamon Raisin Biscuits

My husband, children, in-laws and grandchildren really enjoy these biscuits! They're especially good for breakfast, but can be served at any meal.

Serving: 8-10 biscuits. | Prep: 20 m | Cook: 15 m | Ready in: 35 m

Ingredients

- 2 cups all-purpose flour
- 3 teaspoons baking powder
- 1 tablespoon sugar
- 1 teaspoon ground cinnamon
- 1/2 teaspoon salt
- 1/2 cup shortening
- 2/3 cup milk
- 1/3 cup raisins
- ICING:
- 1 cup confectioners' sugar
- 4-1/2 teaspoons milk
- 1/2 teaspoon vanilla extract

Direction

- In a large bowl, combine flour, baking powder, sugar, cinnamon and salt. Cut in shortening until mixture resembles coarse crumbs. Add milk and raisins; stir just until combined.
- Turn dough onto a floured surface. Knead just until smooth, about 2 minutes. Roll to 1/2-in. thickness. Cut with a floured 2-1/2-in. round biscuit cutter; place on an ungreased baking sheet. Bake at 450 degrees for 12-15 minutes or until golden.
- Meanwhile, combine icing ingredients. Drizzle over warm biscuits.

Nutrition Information

- Calories: 257 calories
- Total Fat: 11g
- Cholesterol: 3mg
- Sodium: 248mg
- Total Carbohydrate: 37g
- Protein: 3g

93. Cinnamon Roll Biscuits

When my grandchildren visit, this is their favorite "Breakfast at Grammy's House" treat. If you're not a nut lover, these biscuits are also delicious without the pecans.
— Joyce Conway, Westerville, Ohio

Serving: 14 biscuits. | Prep: 25 m | Cook: 20 m | Ready in: 45 m

Ingredients

- 2 cups all-purpose flour
- 3 teaspoons baking powder
- 1 teaspoon salt
- 1/4 teaspoon baking soda
- 1 cup buttermilk
- 1/4 cup canola oil
- 1 teaspoon vanilla extract
- 1/2 cup butter, softened
- 1/2 cup sugar
- 3/4 teaspoon ground cinnamon
- 1/4 teaspoon ground cardamom
- 1/2 cup chopped pecans, optional
- GLAZE:
- 1 cup confectioners' sugar
- 1 teaspoon vanilla extract
- 3 to 4 teaspoons 2% milk

Direction

- In a large bowl, combine the flour, baking powder, salt and baking soda. Combine the buttermilk, oil and vanilla; stir into dry ingredients just until moistened (dough will be sticky).
- Turn onto a well-floured surface; knead 8-10 times. Roll out dough into a 15x9-in. rectangle. Spread butter to within 1/2 in. of edges. Combine the sugar, cinnamon, cardamom and pecans if desired; sprinkle over butter. Roll up jelly-roll style, starting with a long side; pinch seam to seal. Cut into 1-1/2-in. slices.

- Place 1 in. apart on a parchment paper-lined baking sheet. Bake at 400 degrees for 20-25 minutes until lightly browned.
- Meanwhile, in small bowl, combine the confectioners' sugar, vanilla and enough milk to achieve a drizzling consistency. Drizzle over warm biscuits. Serve immediately.

Nutrition Information

- Calories: 228 calories
- Total Fat: 11g
- Cholesterol: 18mg
- Sodium: 342mg
- Total Carbohydrate: 30g
- Protein: 3g
- Fiber: 1g

94. Cinnamon Sour Cream Biscuits

"I received a champion ribbon at the county fair with these biscuits. They're good warm or cooled. They're great for breakfast or anytime."

Serving: 12 | Prep: 15 m | Cook: 15 m | Ready in: 30 m

Ingredients

- 2 cups all-purpose flour
- 2 tablespoons white sugar
- 1/2 teaspoon ground cinnamon
- 2 teaspoons baking powder
- 1/4 teaspoon baking soda
- 1/4 teaspoon salt
- 1/2 cup margarine
- 1 cup sour cream
- 2 tablespoons milk
- 1/2 cup raisins
- 1/2 cup confectioners' sugar
- 2 teaspoons milk

Direction

- Preheat oven to 450 degrees F (230 degrees C).
- In a large mixing bowl, combine flour, sugar, cinnamon, baking powder, soda, and salt. Cut in margarine. Make a well in center. Add sour cream, 2 tablespoons milk, and raisins, stirring

till just combined (add a bit more milk, if needed).
- On floured surface, gently knead 8-10 stokes. Pat dough to 1/2" thickness. Cut with biscuit cutter, dipping in flour between cuts. Place on baking sheet.
- Bake at 450 degrees F (230 degrees C) for 10-12 minutes. Cool slightly on wire racks.
- Stir together confectioners' sugar and 2 teaspoons milk. Drizzle over biscuits. Sprinkle with additional cinnamon and sugar, if desired.

Nutrition Information

- Calories: 232 calories
- Total Fat: 11.8 g
- Cholesterol: 9 mg
- Sodium: 256 mg
- Total Carbohydrate: 29.1 g
- Protein: 3.1 g

95. Cinnamon Sweet Puffs

"Easy, VERY sweet, cheap and fun for cooks of all ages!"

Serving: 12 | Prep: 15 m | Cook: 15 m | Ready in: 30 m

Ingredients

- cooking spray
- 1/2 cup white sugar
- 1 tablespoon ground cinnamon
- 2 (10 ounce) cans refrigerated biscuit dough (such as Pillsbury Grands! ®)
- 12 large marshmallows
- 1/2 cup butter, melted

Direction

- Preheat oven to 350 degrees F (175 degrees C). Spray 12 muffin cups with cooking spray.
- Combine sugar and cinnamon in a bowl. Separate biscuits. Place a marshmallow in the center of each biscuit and wrap biscuit dough around marshmallow. Press dough to seal marshmallow completely. Roll dough ball in

melted butter, then roll in cinnamon-sugar mixture. Arrange each dough ball in the prepared muffin cups.

- Bake in the preheated oven until golden brown, about 15 minutes.

Nutrition Information

- Calories: 275 calories
- Total Fat: 14.1 g
- Cholesterol: 21 mg
- Sodium: 526 mg
- Total Carbohydrate: 34.8 g
- Protein: 3.3 g

96. CinnamonRaisin Buttermilk Biscuits

"I modeled this recipe after a favorite restaurant treat," explains Myrna Itterman from Aberdeen, South Dakota. *"They're excellent at brunch with a steaming cup of tea or coffee."*

Serving: 4 biscuits. | Prep: 15 m | Cook: 15 m | Ready in: 30 m

Ingredients

- 1 cup all-purpose flour
- 1 tablespoon sugar
- 2 teaspoons baking powder
- 1/2 teaspoon ground cinnamon
- 1/3 cup butter-flavored shortening
- 1/3 cup buttermilk
- 1/4 cup golden raisins
- GLAZE:
- 1/2 cup confectioners' sugar
- 1 tablespoon milk
- 1/4 teaspoon vanilla extract

Direction

- In a bowl, combine the flour, sugar, baking powder and cinnamon; cut in shortening until crumbly. Stir in buttermilk just until moistened. Turn onto a lightly floured surface.

Sprinkle raisins over dough; knead 2 or 3 times. Pat to 3/4-in. thickness. Cut with a floured 2-1/2-in. biscuit cutter.

- Place on an ungreased baking sheet. Bake at 400 degrees for 12-15 minutes or until golden brown. Combine glaze ingredients; drizzle over biscuits. Serve warm.

Nutrition Information

- Calories: 370 calories
- Total Fat: 17g
- Cholesterol: 1mg
- Sodium: 225mg
- Total Carbohydrate: 51g
- Protein: 4g
- Fiber: 1g

97. CinnamonRaisin Yogurt Biscuits

"This recipe was given to me by a friend and they are amazing! Think half cinnamon roll, half biscuit, and wholly delicious!"

Serving: 10 | Prep: 20 m | Cook: 10 m | Ready in: 30 m

Ingredients

- 1/4 cup white sugar
- 1 teaspoon ground cinnamon
- 2 cups all-purpose flour
- 2 teaspoons baking powder
- 1/4 teaspoon baking soda
- 1/4 teaspoon salt
- 1/4 cup butter
- 1 (8 ounce) container plain yogurt
- 1/2 cup raisins
- 1/2 cup confectioners' sugar (optional)
- 1 teaspoon orange juice (optional)

Direction

- Preheat an oven to 450 degrees F (230 degrees C).

- Stir white sugar and cinnamon together in a bowl. Combine half the sugar mixture, flour, baking powder, baking soda, and salt together in a separate bowl. Cut butter into flour mixture using a pastry blender until mixture resembles coarse crumbs. Make a well in the center of the crumbly mixture; add yogurt and raisins to the well. Stir just until dough clings together.
- Turn dough onto a lightly floured surface and gently knead 8 to 10 times. Roll dough into 1/2-inch thickness and cut with a 2 1/2-inch biscuit cutter. Arrange biscuits on a baking sheet; sprinkle with remaining sugar mixture.
- Bake in the preheated oven until lightly browned, 10 to 12 minutes.
- Whisk confectioners' sugar and orange juice together in a bowl until icing is smooth; drizzle over warm biscuits.

Nutrition Information

- Calories: 213 calories
- Total Fat: 5.2 g
- Cholesterol: 14 mg
- Sodium: 237 mg
- Total Carbohydrate: 38.2 g
- Protein: 4.1 g

98. CinnamonSugar Fan Biscuits

"I love to bake," says Doris Heath from Franklin, North Carolina. "The recipe for these layered homemade biscuits came from a lady in Florida years ago. They're so easy when you need a breakfast treat for company."

Serving: 6 biscuits, 6 servings, 1 per serving. | Prep: 20 m | Cook: 15 m | Ready in: 35 m

Ingredients

- 2 cups all-purpose flour
- 3 tablespoons sugar
- 4 teaspoons baking powder
- 1/2 teaspoon salt
- 1/2 teaspoon cream of tartar

- 1/2 cup shortening
- 2/3 cup milk
- FILLING:
- 3 tablespoons butter, softened
- 3 tablespoons sugar
- 1 teaspoon ground cinnamon

Direction

- In a bowl, combine the flour, sugar, baking powder, salt and cream of tartar. Cut in shortening until mixture resembles coarse crumbs. Stir in milk just until moistened.
- Turn onto a lightly floured surface; knead 8-10 times. Roll or pat into a 12-in. x 10-in. rectangle. Spread with butter. Combine sugar and cinnamon; sprinkle over butter.
- Cut into five 2-in. strips; stack strips on top of each other. Cut into six 2-in. pieces; place cut side down in six greased muffin cups. Bake at 425 degrees for 11-14 minutes or until golden brown. Remove from pan to wire racks. Serve warm.

Nutrition Information

- Calories: 415 calories
- Total Fat: 23g
- Cholesterol: 19mg
- Sodium: 536mg
- Total Carbohydrate: 46g
- Protein: 5g
- Fiber: 1g

99. Coconut Biscuits

These sweet biscuits are wonderful with coffee in the morning.,,or alongside chicken for dinner. "Sometimes I even top them with fresh pineapple or mango chunks and whipped cream for a delicious dessert," suggests Howie Wiener of Spring Hill, Florida. "it's my grandmother's recipe."

Serving: about 1-1/2 dozen. | Prep: 15 m | Cook: 10 m | Ready in: 25 m

Ingredients

- 2 cups all-purpose flour

- 2 tablespoons sugar
- 2-1/2 teaspoons baking powder
- 1/2 teaspoon salt
- 1/3 cup shortening
- 1 cup milk
- 1/2 teaspoon vanilla extract
- 3/4 cup sweetened shredded coconut, toasted

Direction

- In a large bowl, combine the flour, sugar, baking powder and salt; cut in shortening until crumbly. Combine milk and vanilla; stir into dry ingredients just until moistened. Fold in coconut. Drop by 2 tablespoonfuls 2 in. apart onto greased baking sheets. Bake at 425 degrees for 8-10 minutes or until golden brown. Serve warm.

Nutrition Information

- Calories: 116 calories
- Total Fat: 6g
- Cholesterol: 2mg
- Sodium: 138mg
- Total Carbohydrate: 14g
- Protein: 2g
- Fiber: 1g

100. Colorful Sweet Potato Biscuits

Even people who don't like sweet potatoes will enjoy these colorful biscuits from Andrea Bolden. "They are good served with butter and maple syrup," points out the baker from Unionville, Tennessee.

Serving: 9 biscuits. | Prep: 10 m | Cook: 20 m | Ready in: 30 m

Ingredients

- 3/4 cup mashed cooked sweet potatoes
- 2/3 cup milk
- 1/4 cup butter, melted
- 1-2/3 cups self-rising flour
- 1 tablespoon sugar

Direction

- In a bowl, combine the sweet potatoes, milk and butter. Combine the flour and sugar; stir in the sweet potato mixture just until moistened.
- On a lightly floured surface, knead dough slightly or until no longer sticky. Roll to 1/2-in. thickness; cut with a floured 2-1/2-in. biscuit cutter. Place on a lightly greased baking sheet. Bake at 425 degrees for 10-15 minutes or until golden brown. Serve warm.

Nutrition Information

- Calories: 164 calories
- Total Fat: 6g
- Cholesterol: 16mg
- Sodium: 331mg
- Total Carbohydrate: 25g
- Protein: 3g
- Fiber: 1g

101. Corn Meal Supper Biscuits

"These quick and easy corn meal biscuits with buttermilk bake up moist and tender, perfect with just about any hearty meal."

Serving: 14 | Prep: 20 m | Cook: 11 m | Ready in: 35 m

Ingredients

- Crisco® No-Stick Cooking Spray
- 1 1/2 cups Martha White® Self-Rising Flour
- 1/2 cup Martha White® Self-Rising Enriched White Corn Meal Mix
- 1 teaspoon sugar
- 1/3 cup Crisco® All-Vegetable Shortening*
- 3/4 cup buttermilk, plus
- 2 tablespoons buttermilk

Direction

- Heat oven to 450 degrees F. Lightly spray a cookie sheet with no-stick cooking spray. Combine flour, corn meal mix and sugar in medium bowl; mix well. With pastry blender or fork, cut in shortening until mixture resembles coarse crumbs.

- Add buttermilk; stir with fork until a soft dough forms and mixture pulls away from sides of bowl.
- Knead dough on lightly floured surface with floured hands just until smooth. Roll out dough to 1/2-inch thickness. Cut with floured 2-inch round cutter; place biscuits on prepared cookie sheet
- Bake 10 to 12 minutes or until golden brown. Serve warm.

Nutrition Information

- Calories: 75 calories
- Total Fat: 4.9 g
- Cholesterol: < 1 mg
- Sodium: 267 mg
- Total Carbohydrate: 15.1 g
- Protein: 2.2 g

102. Cornmeal Biscuits

This is an old Southern biscuit that has been in the family for years. The texture is slightly different but is still great. - -Maxine Reese, Candler, North Carolina

Serving: 13 biscuits. | Prep: 15 m | Cook: 10 m | Ready in: 25 m

Ingredients

- 1-1/2 cups all-purpose flour
- 1/2 cup cornmeal
- 1 tablespoon sugar
- 2 teaspoons baking powder
- 1/2 teaspoon baking soda
- 1/2 teaspoon salt
- 1/4 cup shortening
- 3/4 cup sour cream
- 1 egg
- 4 teaspoons butter, melted

Direction

- In a large bowl, combine the first six ingredients. Cut in shortening until mixture resembles coarse crumbs. In a small bowl, combine sour cream and egg; add to dry ingredients just until moistened. Turn onto a lightly floured surface; knead 8-10 times.
- Pat or roll out to 1/2-in. thickness; cut with a floured 2-1/2-in. biscuit cutter. Place 2 in. apart on a greased baking sheet. Brush with butter. Bake at 425 degrees for 8-12 minutes or until golden brown. Serve warm.

Nutrition Information

- Calories: 153 calories
- Total Fat: 8g
- Cholesterol: 29mg
- Sodium: 219mg
- Total Carbohydrate: 17g
- Protein: 3g
- Fiber: 1g

103. Cornmeal Cheddar Biscuits

Unlike traditional biscuits, this cheesy version lets you drop them from a spoon...so there's no mess and no fuss...and no precious time wasted! Serve them fresh-from-the-oven with chili or your favorite soup or stew.

Serving: 1 dozen. | Prep: 10 m | Cook: 15 m | Ready in: 25 m

Ingredients

- 1-1/2 cups all-purpose flour
- 1/2 cup yellow cornmeal
- 3 teaspoons baking powder
- 2 teaspoons sugar
- 1/4 to 1/2 teaspoon salt
- 1/2 cup cold butter
- 1/2 cup shredded cheddar cheese
- 1 cup milk

Direction

- In a large bowl, combine the flour, cornmeal, baking powder, sugar and salt. Cut in butter until mixture crumbly. Stir in cheese and milk just until moistened.
- Drop by 1/4 cupfuls 2 in. apart onto an ungreased baking sheet. Bake at 450 degrees for 12-15 minutes or until light golden brown. Serve warm.

Nutrition Information

- Calories: 177 calories
- Total Fat: 10g
- Cholesterol: 28mg
- Sodium: 265mg
- Total Carbohydrate: 18g
- Protein: 4g
- Fiber: 1g

104. Cornmeal Drop Biscuits

It's so easy to stir up a batch of these biscuits. The light golden biscuits are flecked with cheese and taste delicious spread with butter.--Rhonda McKee, Greensburg, Kansas

Serving: 10 servings. | Prep: 10 m | Cook: 30 m | Ready in: 40 m

Ingredients

- 1-1/3 cups all-purpose flour
- 1/2 cup cornmeal
- 2-1/2 teaspoons baking powder
- 1/2 teaspoon salt
- 1/2 teaspoon ground mustard
- 1/2 cup shortening
- 1/2 cup shredded cheddar cheese
- 1 cup 2% milk

Direction

- In a large bowl, combine the flour, cornmeal, baking powder, salt and mustard; cut in shortening until crumbly. Stir in cheese and milk just until moistened.
- Drop by 1/4 cupfuls 2 in. apart onto a greased baking sheet. Bake at 375 degrees for 26-28 minutes or until golden brown. Serve warm.

Nutrition Information

- Calories: 210 calories
- Total Fat: 12g
- Cholesterol: 9mg
- Sodium: 265mg
- Total Carbohydrate: 19g
- Protein: 4g
- Fiber: 1g

105. CornmealChive Drop Biscuits

"Cornmeal gives these biscuits a nice crunch," writes Angela Buchanan from Longmont, Colorado. "Use this recipe to make drop dumplings for soups or stews, too. Just drop the dough on top, cover and simmer for 10 minutes."

Serving: 6 biscuits. | Prep: 15 m | Cook: 15 m | Ready in: 30 m

Ingredients

- 1 cup all-purpose flour
- 1/4 cup cornmeal
- 1 teaspoon baking soda
- 1/4 teaspoon salt
- 1/4 cup cold butter
- 2/3 cup buttermilk
- 1 tablespoon minced chives

Direction

- In a small bowl, mix the flour, cornmeal, baking soda and salt. Cut in butter until mixture resembles coarse crumbs. Add buttermilk and chives; stir just until moistened.
- Drop by 1/4 cupfuls 2 in. apart onto a greased baking sheet. Bake at 375 degrees for 12-16 minutes or until golden brown. Serve warm.

Nutrition Information

- Calories: 175 calories
- Total Fat: 8g
- Cholesterol: 21mg
- Sodium: 391mg
- Total Carbohydrate: 22g
- Protein: 4g
- Fiber: 1g

106. Cracked Black Pepper PullApart Biscuits

These super-light and airy biscuits, with their peppery bite, are as good alongside a hearty dinner as they are for a savory morning treat with jam.

Serving: Makes 16 biscuits | Prep: 25 m | Cook: 1 h

Ingredients

- 4 tablespoons (1/2 stick) unsalted butter, melted, divided, plus 1/2 pound (2 sticks), cut into pieces, softened
- 4 cups all-purpose flour
- 2 cups cake flour
- 2 tablespoons baking powder
- 1 tablespoon freshly ground black pepper
- 2 teaspoons kosher salt
- 1 teaspoon baking soda
- 1/2 cup vegetable shortening
- 2 1/2 cups buttermilk
- 1 teaspoon flaky sea salt
- Two (8") cake pans or one (9x13") baking dish

Direction

- Preheat oven to 425°F. Grease cake pans or baking dish with 1 Tbsp. melted butter.
- Combine all-purpose flour, cake flour, baking powder, pepper, kosher salt, and baking soda in a large bowl. Add shortening and 1/2 pound softened butter. Using your hands or a fork, mix just until mixture is coarse and mealy. Stir in buttermilk just until a shaggy dough forms.

- Divide dough into 16 heaping 1/3-cup portions. Place 7 around the perimeter and 1 in the center of each cake pan (or nestle all 16 into baking dish). Brush biscuits with remaining 3 Tbsp. melted butter, sprinkle with sea salt, and bake until puffed and golden brown, 35–40 minutes. Let cool in pan 10 minutes. Invert onto a wire rack, then reinvert. Serve warm or at room temperature.

Nutrition Information

- Calories: 356
- Total Fat: 14 g (21%)
- Saturated Fat: 5 g (27%)
- Cholesterol: 18 mg (6%)
- Sodium: 349 mg (15%)
- Total Carbohydrate: 51 g (17%)
- Protein: 7 g (14%)
- Fiber: 2 g (7%)

107. Cranberry Biscuits

I like the texture and nutrition of potato rolls and the taste of orange-cranberry bread, so I combined them in these yummy breakfast biscuits. Dotted with dried cranberries and drizzled with a sweet glaze, these tender treats are a family favorite. -Debra Fulenwider, Colfax, California

Serving: about 1-1/2 dozen. | Prep: 40 m | Cook: 10 m | Ready in: 50 m

Ingredients

- 1-2/3 cups warm whole milk (70 deg to 80 degrees)
- 2 large eggs
- 3 tablespoons butter, softened
- 3/4 cup mashed potato flakes
- 1/4 cup sugar
- 2 teaspoons salt
- 1-1/4 teaspoons ground cinnamon
- 1 teaspoon grated orange zest
- 4 cups bread flour
- 1 tablespoon active dry yeast
- 1 cup dried cranberries

- ORANGE GLAZE:
- 1 cup confectioners' sugar
- 2 to 3 tablespoons orange juice
- 3 tablespoons chopped dried cranberries, optional

Direction

- In bread machine pan, place the first 10 ingredients in order suggested by manufacturer. Select dough setting (check dough after 5 minutes of mixing; add 1 to 2 tablespoons of water or flour if needed). Just before final kneading (your machine may audibly signal this), add cranberries.
- When cycle is completed, turn dough onto a lightly floured surface. Cover and let rest for 15 minutes. Roll or pat to 1/2-in. thickness. Cut with a 2-1/2-in. biscuit cutter. Place in a greased 15x10x1-in. baking pan. Cover and let rise in a warm place until almost doubled, about 40 minutes.
- Bake at 375 degrees for 10-15 minutes or until golden brown. For glaze, combine confectioners' sugar and enough orange juice to achieve a glaze consistency. Drizzle over warm biscuits. Sprinkle with chopped cranberries if desired.

Nutrition Information

- Calories: 198 calories
- Total Fat: 3g
- Cholesterol: 32mg
- Sodium: 306mg
- Total Carbohydrate: 39g
- Protein: 6g
- Fiber: 1g

108. Cranberry Apple Biscuits

Tangy cranberries and sweet apples blend beautifully with tender biscuits on this pretty holiday dessert. Serve the fruity treats alone or with vanilla ice cream.

Serving: 8 servings. | Prep: 15 m | Cook: 15 m | Ready in: 30 m

Ingredients

- 2 tablespoons butter, melted
- 2 tablespoons sugar
- 1/4 teaspoon ground cinnamon
- 1/4 teaspoon ground ginger
- 1 tube (16.3 ounces) large refrigerated flaky biscuits
- SAUCE:
- 3/4 cup sugar
- 1/2 teaspoon ground cinnamon
- 1/2 teaspoon ground ginger
- 3 cups diced peeled tart apples
- 1 cup fresh or frozen cranberries
- 1/2 cup water, divided
- 1 tablespoon lemon juice
- 2 tablespoons cornstarch

Direction

- Place butter in a shallow bowl. In another shallow bowl, combine the sugar, cinnamon and ginger. Dip the top of each biscuit in butter, then in sugar mixture. Place sugar side up 2 in. apart on an ungreased baking sheet. Bake at 350 degrees for 15-17 minutes or until golden brown. Remove to a wire rack.
- For sauce, in a saucepan, combine the sugar, cinnamon and ginger. Add the apples, cranberries, 1/4 cup water and lemon juice. Bring to a boil. Reduce heat; cover and simmer for 3-4 minutes, stirring occasionally. Combine cornstarch and remaining water until smooth. Stir into fruit mixture. Bring to a boil; cook and stir for 2 minutes or until thickened. Pour about 1/3 cup sauce over each biscuit.

Nutrition Information

- Calories: 349 calories
- Total Fat: 12g

- Cholesterol: 8mg
- Sodium: 612mg
- Total Carbohydrate: 57g
- Protein: 4g
- Fiber: 2g

109. CranberryWhite Chocolate Cornmeal Tea Biscuits

Little biscuits are flavored with dried cranberries and white chocolate for a sweet bite that's just right with coffee or as a snack.

Serving: 36 | Prep: 25 m | Ready in: 35 m

Ingredients

- Nonstick cooking spray
- ½ cup dried cranberries, coarsely chopped
- 1½ cups all-purpose flour
- ½ cup yellow cornmeal
- ¼ cup packed brown sugar or brown sugar substitute equivalent to ¼ cup brown sugar (see Tip)
- 1½ teaspoons baking powder
- ¼ teaspoon baking soda
- ¼ teaspoon salt
- ¼ cup butter
- 4 ounces white baking chocolate (with cocoa butter), chopped
- 1 egg white, lightly beaten
- 1 (8 ounce) carton light dairy sour cream
- 3 tablespoons fat-free milk

Direction

- Preheat oven to 375°F. Coat baking sheets with nonstick spray or line with parchment paper; set aside. Place cranberries in a small bowl; add enough boiling water to cover. Let stand for 5 minutes; drain well. Meanwhile, in a large bowl, combine flour, cornmeal, brown sugar, baking powder, baking soda, and salt. Using a pastry blender, cut in butter until mixture resembles coarse crumbs. Stir in drained cranberries and white chocolate. Make a well in the center of the flour mixture.
- In a small bowl, combine egg white, sour cream, and milk. Add egg white mixture all at once to flour mixture. Using a fork, stir until combined.
- Drop dough by well-rounded teaspoonfuls 2 inches apart onto prepared cookie sheets.
- Bake for 9 to 11 minutes or until edges are lightly browned and tops are set. Transfer biscuits to wire racks; cool completely.

Nutrition Information

- Calories: 75 calories
- Total Fat: 3 g
- Saturated Fat: 2 g
- Cholesterol: 6 mg
- Sodium: 55 mg
- Total Carbohydrate: 10 g
- Protein: 1 g
- Fiber: 0 g
- Sugar: 4 g

110. Creamed Corn Biscuits

Nothing is easier than these delicious muffins. They have the yummy corn taste in a quick biscuit.--Teri Lindquist, Gurnee, Illinois

Serving: about 1-1/2 dozen. | Prep: 15 m | Cook: 15 m | Ready in: 30 m

Ingredients

- 1-1/2 cups biscuit/baking mix
- 1 can (8-1/4 ounces) cream-style corn
- 1/4 cup butter, melted

Direction

- In a bowl, stir the biscuit mix and corn just until moistened. Drop by tablespoonfuls onto a greased baking sheet. Brush with butter. Bake at 375 degrees for 15-20 minutes or until golden brown. Serve warm.

Nutrition Information

- Calories: 146 calories
- Total Fat: 8g
- Cholesterol: 14mg
- Sodium: 382mg
- Total Carbohydrate: 17g
- Protein: 2g
- Fiber: 1g

111. Creamy PumpkinFilled Biscuits

Convenient refrigerator biscuits create these delicious pie-inspired treats. The warm and creamy pumpkin filling invites you to take bite after bite! -- Michelle Kester, Cleveland, Ohio

Serving: 8 servings. | Prep: 20 m | Cook: 10 m | Ready in: 30 m

Ingredients

- 1 package (8 ounces) cream cheese, softened
- 1 cup canned pumpkin
- 1/2 cup cold milk
- 1/2 cup whipped topping
- 1 package (3.4 ounces) instant vanilla pudding mix
- 1/2 teaspoon pumpkin pie spice
- 1 tube (16.3 ounces) large refrigerated flaky biscuits
- Oil for deep-fat frying
- Confectioners' sugar, optional

Direction

- In a small bowl, beat the first six ingredients until smooth; set aside. On a lightly floured surface, roll out each biscuit into a 6-in. circle. Spread 1/3 cup cream cheese mixture on half of each biscuit. Bring dough from opposite side over filling just until edges meet; pinch seams to seal.
- In a deep-fat fryer, heat oil to 375 degrees. Fry biscuits, a few at a time, for 1-2 minutes on each side or until golden brown. Drain on paper towels. Dust with confectioners' sugar while warm if desired. Serve immediately.

Nutrition Information

- Calories: 507 calories
- Total Fat: 36g
- Cholesterol: 33mg
- Sodium: 843mg
- Total Carbohydrate: 40g
- Protein: 7g
- Fiber: 2g

112. Crissis Sweet Potato Biscuits

"Yummy sweet potato biscuits that rival Steamer's biscuits in Chincoteague, Virginia. You'll taste no better than this! My family hates sweet potatoes, but they snatch these up every time I make them! You could also substitute pumpkin for the sweet potato and cardamom for the nutmeg."

Serving: 6 | Prep: 20 m | Cook: 20 m | Ready in: 40 m

Ingredients

- 1 cup sifted all-purpose flour
- 1/4 cup toasted wheat germ
- 2 tablespoons baking powder
- 1/2 teaspoon salt
- 1/3 cup butter, melted
- 1/4 cup evaporated milk, heated
- 1 cup mashed sweet potatoes
- 2 tablespoons milk
- 1 pinch ground nutmeg

Direction

- Preheat oven to 400 degrees F (200 degrees C). Grease a baking sheet.
- Into a large bowl, sift together the flour, wheat germ, baking powder, and salt. Mix in butter, evaporated milk, sweet potatoes, milk, and nutmeg, stirring by hand until dough is smooth.
- On a lightly floured board, roll out the dough until it is about 1/2-inch thick. With a sharp knife, cut into 3-inch squares or diamonds. Place squares on greased baking sheet, and bake for 15 to 20 minutes. Serve warm.

Nutrition Information

- Calories: 230 calories
- Total Fat: 11.9 g
- Cholesterol: 31 mg
- Sodium: 618 mg
- Total Carbohydrate: 26.7 g
- Protein: 4.9 g

113.Crunchy Biscuits

For a quick complement to the effortless main dish, Traci bakes Crunchy Biscuits. Convenient refrigerated biscuits get a tasty treatment when topped with crushed corn chips. "They couldn't be easier," she promises.

Serving: 8 biscuits. | Prep: 15 m | Cook: 15 m | Ready in: 30 m

Ingredients

- 1 tube (16.3 ounces) refrigerated home-style biscuits, separated into 8 biscuits
- 1 tablespoon butter, melted
- 1/3 cup crushed corn chips

Direction

- Arrange biscuits in greased 8-in. round baking pan. Brush with butter. Sprinkle with corn chips and gently press into the dough. Bake at 400 degrees for 14-16 minutes or until golden brown.

Nutrition Information

- Calories:
- Total Fat: g
- Cholesterol: mg
- Sodium: mg
- Total Carbohydrate: g
- Protein: g
- Fiber: g

114. Crusty Dinner Biscuits

These biscuits bake up with golden crusty outsides and moist and tender vegetables dish we both enjoy.--Sharon McClatchey, Muskogee, Oklahoma

Serving: 6 biscuits. | Prep: 10 m | Cook: 15 m | Ready in: 25 m

Ingredients

- 1 cup all-purpose flour
- 1 teaspoon baking powder
- 1/2 teaspoon salt
- 1/2 cup milk
- 1 tablespoon vegetable oil
- Half-and-half cream or milk, optional
- Butter and/or honey

Direction

- In a bowl, combine the flour, baking powder and salt. Combine milk and oil; pour over dry ingredients and stir just until moistened.
- Turn onto a floured surface; knead 5-6 times. Roll out to 1/2-in. thickness; cut with a floured 2-in. biscuit cutter. Place on a greased baking sheet.
- Brush tops with cream if desired. Bake at 425 degrees for 13-15 minutes or until golden brown. Serve warm with butter and/or honey.

Nutrition Information

- Calories: 108 calories
- Total Fat: 3g
- Cholesterol: 3mg
- Sodium: 274mg
- Total Carbohydrate: 17g
- Protein: 3g
- Fiber: 1g

115. Curry Tofu Scramble with Biscuits and Gravy

"Curry-flavored tofu sauteed with veggies, served over whole wheat biscuits and smothered in gravy."

Serving: 4 | Prep: 30 m | Cook: 36 m | Ready in: 1 h 6 m

Ingredients

- 2 1/4 cups whole wheat pastry flour
- 1/4 cup margarine
- 2 teaspoons baking powder
- 1/2 teaspoon salt
- 1 cup buttermilk, or as needed
- 1 tablespoon olive oil
- 1 cup chopped onion
- 1 clove garlic, minced
- 1 (16 ounce) package curry-flavored tofu
- 1 zucchini, diced
- 1 green bell pepper, diced
- salt and ground black pepper to taste
- 3 tablespoons margarine
- 3 tablespoons all-purpose flour
- 2 1/2 cups chicken stock, or to taste

Direction

- Preheat oven to 425 degrees F (220 degrees C). Grease a baking pan.
- Combine pastry flour, baking powder, and 1/2 teaspoon salt in a bowl. Mix well. Cut in 1/4 cup margarine with a pastry cutter or 2 knives until mixture resembles coarse oatmeal. Mix in buttermilk, 2 tablespoons at a time, until a soft dough is formed and no dry spots remain. Roll dough out into a 1/2- to 3/4-inch layer; cut out into circles using a biscuit cutter or aluminum can. Place dough circles on the prepared pan.
- Bake in the preheated oven until golden brown, 10 to 12 minutes.
- Heat a large nonstick skillet over medium-high heat. Add olive oil and onion; sauté until softened and translucent, about 5 minutes. Add garlic; sauté until fragrant, about 1 minute. Add tofu; cook and stir until slightly browned, about 6 minutes. Toss in zucchini and green bell pepper; cook until tender, about 5 minutes. Season with salt and pepper.
- Melt 3 tablespoons margarine in a saucepan over low heat. Add all-purpose flour; cook and stir until paste-like, about 2 minutes. Increase heat to medium; cook for 2 minutes. Whisk in stock slowly; bring to a boil. Cook until thickened to your desired consistency, about 5 minutes. Remove from heat.
- Tear biscuits in half; scoop tofu mixture over biscuit pieces and pour gravy on top.

Nutrition Information

- Calories: 559 calories
- Total Fat: 30 g
- Cholesterol: 3 mg
- Sodium: 1306 mg
- Total Carbohydrate: 57.3 g
- Protein: 20.6 g

116. CutOut Biscuits

After a couple of tries at doctoring the recipe, these biscuits came out so light and fluffy, I think of them as cloud puffs. A plate of these can be served hot or cold for breakfast, tea, luncheons, dinners or snack time.

Serving: 3 biscuits. | Prep: 15 m | Cook: 10 m | Ready in: 25 m

Ingredients

- 1 cup self-rising flour
- 4-1/2 teaspoons cold butter
- 1/4 cup ginger ale
- 1 tablespoon sour cream
- 1 tablespoon mayonnaise
- TOPPING:
- 2 teaspoons butter, melted
- 1/2 teaspoon sugar

Direction

- Place flour in a small bowl. Cut in butter until mixture resembles coarse crumbs. In another bowl, combine the ginger ale, sour cream and mayonnaise; stir into flour mixture just until moistened. Turn onto a lightly floured surface; knead 8-10 times.

- Pat out to 3/4-in. thickness; cut with a floured 2-1/2-in. biscuit cutter. Place 2 in. apart on an ungreased baking sheet. Brush with butter; sprinkle with sugar. Bake at 400 degrees for 9-11 minutes or until lightly browned. Serve warm.

Nutrition Information

- Calories: 259 calories
- Total Fat: 13g
- Cholesterol: 27mg
- Sodium: 566mg
- Total Carbohydrate: 32g
- Protein: 4g
- Fiber: 1g

117. Daddys Savory Tomato Biscuits

"My father was a man that could take an unstocked kitchen and make a gourmet meal. I watched him make these biscuits when we were out of milk. Just amazing!"

Serving: 18 | Prep: 15 m | Cook: 10 m | Ready in: 25 m

Ingredients

- 3 cups self-rising flour
- 1/8 teaspoon baking soda
- 1/8 teaspoon salt
- 1 teaspoon white sugar
- 1/2 cup shortening
- 1 cup tomato-vegetable juice cocktail

Direction

- Preheat oven to 400 degrees F (200 degrees C). Grease a baking sheet.
- Stir the flour, baking soda, salt, and sugar together in a bowl, and cut in the shortening with a pastry cutter until the mixture looks like crumbs. Mix in the vegetable juice cocktail just until moist, and turn out onto a well-

floured work surface. Gently knead several times just until dough holds together, roll out to 1/2-inch thick, and cut into rounds with a biscuit cutter. Place the biscuits onto the prepared baking sheet.

- Bake in the preheated oven until risen and lightly browned, 8 to 10 minutes.

Nutrition Information

- Calories: 128 calories
- Total Fat: 5.9 g
- Cholesterol: 0 mg
- Sodium: 324 mg
- Total Carbohydrate: 16.2 g
- Protein: 2.2 g

118. Dads Orangutan Bread

"This is a completely different twist on dad's monkey bread recipe. You will absolutely drool over it!"

Serving: 15 | Prep: 15 m | Cook: 30 m | Ready in: 45 m

Ingredients

- 2 tablespoons butter
- 1 cup white sugar
- 3/4 cup butter
- 1/4 cup orange juice
- 2 tablespoons grated orange zest
- 3 (10 ounce) cans refrigerated biscuits (10 biscuits per can)

Direction

- Preheat oven to 350 degrees F (175 degrees C). Grease a 9-inch fluted tube pan (such as Bundt(R)) with 2 tablespoons butter.
- Combine sugar, 3/4 cup butter, orange juice, and orange zest in a saucepan; warm over low heat until sugar is dissolved and butter is melted, about 5 minutes.
- Separate biscuits; cut in half. Layer half in the bottom of the prepared tube pan. Pour half of the orange juice mixture over the biscuits. Repeat both steps.

- Bake in the preheated oven until golden brown, about 25 minutes.

Nutrition Information

- Calories: 330 calories
- Total Fat: 18.4 g
- Cholesterol: 29 mg
- Sodium: 636 mg
- Total Carbohydrate: 38.2 g
- Protein: 3.9 g

119. Daisy Tea Biscuits

For a unique biscuit to serve at your next get-together, try this recipe. The petals of the flowers added an extra special touch.--Jeanne Nakjavani, Alfred, New York

Serving: 12 to 14 biscuits. | Prep: 25 m | Cook: 10 m | Ready in: 35 m

Ingredients

- 2-1/2 cups all-purpose flour
- 3 teaspoons baking powder
- 1/4 teaspoon baking soda
- 1/2 teaspoon salt
- 1/2 cup plus 2 tablespoons butter
- 3/4 to 1 cup half-and-half cream, room temperature
- 1/2 cup fresh daisy petals

Direction

- Preheat oven to 450 degrees. Sift flour; measure and sift again with baking powder, soda and salt. Cut in butter until mixture resembles coarse cornmeal. Add cream and daisy petals, mixing just enough to moisten. Turn out onto a lightly floured surface; knead quickly 8 to 10 times. Pat or roll out to desired thickness. Cut with biscuit cutter. Bake on greased baking sheet 10 to 15 minutes.

Nutrition Information

- Calories: 170 calories
- Total Fat: 10g
- Cholesterol: 28mg

- Sodium: 282mg
- Total Carbohydrate: 18g
- Protein: 3g
- Fiber: 1g

120. Dill Biscuits

These biscuits are quick way prepare and easy on your pocketbook

Serving: 6 servings. | Prep: 5 m | Cook: 10 m | Ready in: 15 m

Ingredients

- 1/4 cup butter, melted
- 1 tablespoon finely chopped onion
- 1 teaspoon dill weed
- 1 tube (10 ounces) refrigerated buttermilk biscuits

Direction

- In a shallow bowl, combine the butter, onion and dill. Cut biscuits in half lengthwise; toss in butter mixture. Arrange in a single layer in an ungreased 9-in. square baking pan.
- Bake at 450 degrees for 8-10 minutes or until lightly browned. Serve warm.

Nutrition Information

- Calories: 182 calories
- Total Fat: 9g
- Cholesterol: 20mg
- Sodium: 481mg
- Total Carbohydrate: 23g
- Protein: 4g
- Fiber: 0 g

121. Drop Biscuits and Gravy

"We enjoy these flaky biscuits covered with creamy gravy not only for breakfast, but sometimes for dinner," reports Darlene Brenden of Salem, Oregon. Priced at only 27 cents per serving, "It's hard to find a more stick-to-the-ribs meal and at such a low cost," she Note:s.

Serving: 4 servings. | Prep: 10 m | Cook: 10 m | Ready in: 20 m

Ingredients

- 1 cup all-purpose flour
- 1-1/2 teaspoons baking powder
- 1/8 teaspoon salt
- 1/2 cup 2% milk
- 2 tablespoons butter, melted
- GRAVY:
- 1/2 pound Jones No Sugar Pork Sausage Roll
- 1 tablespoon butter
- 3 tablespoons all-purpose flour
- 1-3/4 cups 2% milk
- 1/8 teaspoon salt
- 1/2 teaspoon pepper

Direction

- Preheat oven to 450 degrees. Whisk together flour, baking powder and salt. In another bowl, whisk together milk and butter; stir into dry ingredients just until blended. Drop four biscuits onto a parchment-paper lined baking sheet; bake until golden brown, 10-12 minutes.
- In a small saucepan, cook and crumble sausage over medium heat until no longer pink, 4-5 minutes. Stir in butter until melted; sprinkle with flour. Gradually stir in milk, salt and pepper. Bring to a boil, stirring constantly; cook and stir 2 minutes. Serve over biscuits.

Nutrition Information

- Calories: 454 calories
- Total Fat: 27g
- Cholesterol: 72mg
- Sodium: 864mg
- Total Carbohydrate: 36g
- Protein: 16g
- Fiber: 1g

122. Easy 7Up Biscuits

"These biscuits are delicious and not as fattening as the recipe might lead you to believe. That stick of butter is allotted through the whole recipe and the biscuits are so tasty that you won't need any toppings!"

Serving: 12 | Prep: 20 m | Cook: 10 m | Ready in: 40 m

Ingredients

- 1/2 cup butter
- 4 1/2 cups baking mix (such as Bisquick ®)
- 1 cup lemon-lime soda (such as 7-Up®)
- 1 cup sour cream

Direction

- Preheat oven to 425 degrees F (220 degrees C). Put butter in a 9x13-inch baking dish and place dish in the preheating oven until butter is melted.
- Mix baking mix, lemon-lime soda, and sour cream together in a bowl until dough holds together and is sticky. Turn dough onto a floured work surface and roll into 1-inch thick circle. Cut circles out of dough using a cookie cutter or the rim of a wine glass and place in the melted butter.
- Bake in the preheated oven until biscuits are golden brown, 10 to 12 minutes. Remove dish from oven and let stand until biscuits have absorbed all the butter.

Nutrition Information

- Calories: 301 calories
- Total Fat: 18.5 g
- Cholesterol: 29 mg
- Sodium: 634 mg
- Total Carbohydrate: 30.8 g
- Protein: 3.9 g

123. Easy Baking Powder Drop Biscuits

"These are the best breakfast biscuits, easy and perfect for sausage gravy!"

Serving: 12 | Prep: 15 m | Cook: 15 m | Ready in: 30 m

Ingredients

- 2 cups all-purpose flour
- 2 1/2 teaspoons baking powder
- 1/2 teaspoon salt
- 1 tablespoon white sugar
- 1/2 cup chilled butter, diced
- 1 1/4 cups whole milk

Direction

- Preheat an oven to 450 degrees F (230 degrees C).
- Mix flour, baking powder, salt, and sugar in a bowl. Cut in the cold butter with a knife or pastry blender until the mixture resembles coarse crumbs. Add milk a little at a time, stirring lightly between additions.
- Drop the batter by spoonfuls onto a cookie sheet, and bake for 12 to 15 minutes, until the tops are golden.

Nutrition Information

- Calories: 163 calories
- Total Fat: 8.7 g
- Cholesterol: 23 mg
- Sodium: 264 mg
- Total Carbohydrate: 18.4 g
- Protein: 3.1 g

124. Easy Biscuit Mixture

"Use as you would a baking mix. The possibilities are endless!"

Serving: 24

Ingredients

- 10 cups all-purpose flour
- 1/2 cup baking powder
- 1/4 cup white sugar
- 2 teaspoons salt
- 2 cups shortening

Direction

- In a large bowl mix together the flour, baking powder, sugar, and salt. Cut in shortening until mixture resembles coarse crumbs.
- Store in an airtight container for up to 6 weeks.

Nutrition Information

- Calories: 351 calories
- Total Fat: 17.6 g
- Cholesterol: 0 mg
- Sodium: 682 mg
- Total Carbohydrate: 43.1 g
- Protein: 5.4 g

125. Easy Biscuits

"This three-ingredient recipe gets biscuits on your table in a quick and easy manner for when you need biscuits now!"

Serving: 12 | Prep: 10 m | Cook: 25 m | Ready in: 35 m

Ingredients

- 2 1/4 cups self-rising flour
- 3/4 cup shortening
- 1 cup milk

Direction

- Combine and mix ingredients together. Pour out on floured waxed paper. Pat the dough out with your hands until dough is not sticky

(add a little flour if necessary). Fold double. Cut biscuits with a biscuit cutter.
- Bake on a cookie sheet at 425 degrees F (220 degrees C) for 20-25 minutes.

Nutrition Information

- Calories: 206 calories
- Total Fat: 13.4 g
- Cholesterol: 2 mg
- Sodium: 306 mg
- Total Carbohydrate: 18.3 g
- Protein: 3 g

126. Easy Cheddar Biscuits with Fresh Herbs

"These are great with a hearty meal like stew. Substitute parsley or basil for rosemary, if you like."

Serving: 16 | Prep: 15 m | Cook: 15 m | Ready in: 30 m

Ingredients

- 2 1/4 cups all-purpose baking mix
- 1/2 cup shredded Cheddar cheese
- 2 tablespoons fresh rosemary, chopped
- 1/4 cup sour cream
- 2 tablespoons Dijon mustard
- 1/3 cup milk
- 1 egg, lightly beaten

Direction

- Preheat oven to 425 degrees F (220 degrees C).
- In a medium bowl, stir together baking mix, cheese, and rosemary.
- In a separate bowl, stir together sour cream, mustard, and milk. Stir wet mixture into dry mixture until well combined. Drop dough in 2-inch rounds onto a baking sheet. Brush tops with beaten egg.
- Bake in preheated oven 12 to 15 minutes. Serve warm.

Nutrition Information

- Calories: 103 calories
- Total Fat: 5.2 g
- Cholesterol: 18 mg
- Sodium: 295 mg
- Total Carbohydrate: 11.3 g
- Protein: 2.9 g

127. Easy Cheese Drop Biscuits

It's hard to believe that these buttery bites call for only a few items. "I keep the ingredients for these biscuits on hand because my sons just love them," writes Marla Miller from Englewood, Tennessee.

Serving: 2 dozen. | Prep: 10 m | Cook: 20 m | Ready in: 30 m

Ingredients

- 2 cups self-rising flour
- 1 cup butter, melted
- 1 cup (8 ounces) sour cream
- 1 cup shredded cheddar cheese

Direction

- In a large bowl, combine all the ingredients until blended. Drop by rounded tablespoonfuls 2 in. apart onto lightly greased baking sheets.
- Bake at 350 degrees for 20-25 minutes or until golden brown. Cool for 5 minutes before removing from pans to wire racks. Serve warm.

Nutrition Information

- Calories: 274 calories
- Total Fat: 21g
- Cholesterol: 64mg
- Sodium: 461mg
- Total Carbohydrate: 16g
- Protein: 5g
- Fiber: 0 g

128. Easy Cheesy Biscuits

I'm a big fan of homemade biscuits but not the rolling and cutting that goes with them. The drop biscuit method solves everything. --Christina Addison, Blanchester, Ohio

Serving: 1 dozen. | Prep: 10 m | Cook: 20 m | Ready in: 30 m

Ingredients

- 3 cups all-purpose flour
- 3 teaspoons baking powder
- 1 tablespoon sugar
- 1 teaspoon salt
- 3/4 teaspoon cream of tartar
- 1/2 cup cold butter
- 1 cup shredded sharp cheddar cheese
- 1 garlic clove, minced
- 1/4 to 1/2 teaspoon crushed red pepper flakes
- 1-1/4 cups 2% milk

Direction

- Preheat oven to 450 degrees. In a large bowl, whisk flour, baking powder, sugar, salt and cream of tartar. Cut in butter until mixture resembles coarse crumbs. Stir in cheese, garlic and pepper flakes. Add milk; stir just until moistened.
- Drop dough by heaping 1/4 cupfuls 2 in. apart onto a greased baking sheet. Bake 18-20 minutes or until golden brown. Serve warm.

Nutrition Information

- Calories: 237 calories
- Total Fat: 12g
- Cholesterol: 32mg
- Sodium: 429mg
- Total Carbohydrate: 26g
- Protein: 7g
- Fiber: 1g

129. Easy German Biscuits

My mother-in-law, who was of German descent, gave me this delicious recipe for easy yeast biscuits. It's so special because it goes back in her family for generations.

Serving: 15 biscuits. | Prep: 20 m | Cook: 15 m | Ready in: 35 m

Ingredients

- 1 package (1/4 ounce) active dry yeast
- 1/2 cup warm water (110 degrees to 115 degrees)
- 2-1/2 cups all-purpose flour
- 1/3 cup sugar
- 2 teaspoons baking powder
- 1 teaspoon salt
- 1/4 teaspoon baking soda
- 1 cup buttermilk
- 1/4 cup vegetable oil

Direction

- Dissolve yeast in warm water. In a large bowl, combine flour, sugar, baking powder, salt and baking soda. Add yeast mixture, buttermilk and oil; stir well. Cover and refrigerate at least 12 hours. Punch down. Turn onto a floured surface and roll out to 1-in. thickness. Cut with a 2-in. biscuit cutter and place 2-in. apart on a greased baking sheet. Bake at 400 degrees for 12 minutes.

Nutrition Information

- Calories: 133 calories
- Total Fat: 4g
- Cholesterol: 1mg
- Sodium: 249mg
- Total Carbohydrate: 21g
- Protein: 3g
- Fiber: 1g

130. Easy Maple Bacon Monkey Bread

"Maple bacon monkey bread is extra gooey and cinnamon-sugar sweet with salty pieces of candied bacon throughout. Easy and delicious!"

Serving: 16 | Prep: 15 m | Cook: 58 m | Ready in: 1 h 23 m

Ingredients

- cooking spray
- 3/4 cup white sugar
- 2 tablespoons caramel instant pudding mix, uncooked
- 2 teaspoons ground cinnamon
- 2 (16.3 ounce) cans refrigerated biscuit dough, separated and cut into quarters
- 12 slices bacon strips, cooked and crumbled
- 1/2 cup butter
- 3/4 cup packed dark brown sugar
- 1/2 cup maple syrup
- 1 pinch salt

Direction

- Preheat the oven to 350 degrees F (175 degrees C). Coat the inside of a 9-inch fluted tube pan with cooking spray.
- Mix white sugar, pudding mix, and cinnamon together in a 1-gallon resealable plastic bag. Add the quartered biscuits and shake until well coated. Toss in the bacon and shake well to distribute. Transfer biscuits to the prepared tube pan. Save the sugar-cinnamon mixture left in the bottom of the bag.
- Melt butter in a small saucepan over medium heat. Stir in dark brown sugar, maple syrup, and salt. Bring mixture to a boil and carefully stir until it begins to foam, about 1 minute. Pour the saved sugar-cinnamon mixture into the saucepan and stir until dissolved, 2 to 3 minutes. Pour the melted sugar mixture over the biscuits in the tube pan.
- Bake in the preheated oven until the biscuits are puffed up and cooked through, 50 to 55 minutes. Cool in the pan for 10 minutes before inverting onto a serving plate.

Nutrition Information

- Calories: 363 calories
- Total Fat: 15.5 g
- Cholesterol: 21 mg
- Sodium: 733 mg
- Total Carbohydrate: 51.5 g
- Protein: 5.6 g

131. Easy Mayonnaise Biscuits

"This recipe is amazing."

Serving: 6 | Prep: 15 m | Cook: 30 m | Ready in: 45 m

Ingredients

- 1 cup self-rising flour
- 1/2 cup milk
- 1/4 cup mayonnaise

Direction

- Preheat oven to 375 degrees F (190 degrees C). Grease 6 large muffin cups.
- Stir flour, milk, and mayonnaise together in a bowl until smooth. Pour flour mixture into prepared muffin cups.
- Bake until golden brown, about 30 minutes.

Nutrition Information

- Calories: 150 calories
- Total Fat: 7.9 g
- Cholesterol: 5 mg
- Sodium: 325 mg
- Total Carbohydrate: 16.7 g
- Protein: 2.8 g

132. Easy Parmesan Biscuits

THIS recipe is simple but so good and a delicious addition to any meal. The children love to dip the ready-made biscuits in butter and coat it with the cheese. Warm from the oven, one biscuit per person usually isn't enough.

Serving: 5 biscuits. | Prep: 5 m | Cook: 10 m | Ready in: 15 m

Ingredients

- 1 tube (6 ounces) refrigerated buttermilk biscuits, separated into 5 biscuits
- 3 tablespoons butter, melted
- 1/2 cup grated Parmesan cheese

Direction

- Preheat oven to 400 degrees. Dip both sides of biscuits into melted butter, then into cheese. Place 1 in. apart in a well-greased 9-in. round pan. Bake until golden brown, 8-11 minutes. Serve warm.

Nutrition Information

- Calories: 177 calories
- Total Fat: 10g
- Cholesterol: 25mg
- Sodium: 462mg
- Total Carbohydrate: 16g
- Protein: 6g
- Fiber: 0 g

133. Easy Sour Cream Biscuits

"These light fluffy biscuits are some of the best you'll ever eat," assures LaDonna Reed of Ponca City, Oklahoma. She serves them with a sweet citrus butter that's also great on pancakes.

Serving: 1-1/2 dozen. | Prep: 20 m | Cook: 15 m | Ready in: 35 m

Ingredients

- 4 cups biscuit/baking mix
- 1 cup sour cream
- 1 cup lemon-lime soda
- ORANGE HONEY BUTTER:
- 1/2 cup butter, softened
- 1/3 cup honey
- 2 teaspoons grated orange zest

Direction

- Place the biscuit mix in a large bowl. Combine the sour cream and lemon-lime soda; stir into biscuit mix just until combined.
- Turn onto a floured surface; knead 4-5 times. Roll to 1/2-in. thickness; cut with a 2-1/2-in. biscuit cutter. Place on greased baking sheets. Bake at 400 degrees for 15-20 minutes or until golden brown.
- In a small bowl, beat the butter, honey and orange peel until fluffy. Serve with biscuits.

Nutrition Information

- Calories: 203 calories
- Total Fat: 11g
- Cholesterol: 22mg
- Sodium: 395mg
- Total Carbohydrate: 23g
- Protein: 2g
- Fiber: 1g

134. Easy Southern Biscuits

"These are the easiest biscuits to make in the world. Sweet and fluffy."

Serving: 10 | Prep: 10 m | Cook: 25 m | Ready in: 35 m

Ingredients

- 2 cups self-rising flour
- 2 tablespoons white sugar
- 1 cup milk
- 1/3 cup mayonnaise

Direction

- Preheat oven to 350 degrees F (175 degrees C). Line 10 muffin cups with paper muffin liners.
- In a large bowl, combine self-rising flour and sugar. Stir in milk and mayonnaise until a

smooth dough is formed. Spoon batter into prepared muffin cups.

- Bake in preheated oven for 25 to 30 minutes, until golden brown and doubled in size.

Nutrition Information

- Calories: 163 calories
- Total Fat: 6.5 g
- Cholesterol: 5 mg
- Sodium: 369 mg
- Total Carbohydrate: 22.4 g
- Protein: 3.3 g

135. Egg Bake with Sausage Biscuits

When I want to treat my family to a delicious down-home breakfast, this is the recipe I rely on. Sausage biscuits are a perfect partner for the egg and cheese casserole.

Serving: 12 servings. | Prep: 40 m | Cook: 25 m | Ready in: 01 h 05 m

Ingredients

- 6 tablespoons butter, divided
- 1/4 cup all-purpose flour
- 1-1/2 cups milk
- 1 cup heavy whipping cream
- 1/4 cup minced fresh parsley
- 1/4 teaspoon each dried basil, marjoram and thyme
- 3 cups shredded cheddar cheese
- 12 hard-boiled large eggs, thinly sliced
- 1 pound bacon strips, cooked and crumbled
- 1/2 cup dry bread crumbs
- SAUSAGE BISCUITS:
- 2 cups biscuit/baking mix
- 2/3 cup whole milk
- 3/4 pound Jones No Sugar Pork Sausage Roll, cooked and crumbled

Direction

- In a large saucepan, melt 4 tablespoons butter. Stir in flour until smooth; gradually whisk in milk and cream. Add the parsley, basil, marjoram and thyme. Bring to a boil; cook and stir for 1-2 minutes or until thickened. Remove from the heat; add cheese, stirring until melted.
- In a greased shallow 2-1/2-qt. baking dish, layer a third of the egg slices, a third of the bacon and about 1 cup cheese sauce. Repeat layers twice. Melt remaining butter; toss with bread crumbs. Sprinkle over the top. Bake, uncovered, at 400 degrees for 25-30 minutes or until bubbly and golden brown.
- In a bowl, combine biscuit mix and milk. Stir in sausage. Shape into 1-1/2-in. balls. Place 2-in. apart on an ungreased baking sheet. Bake at 400 deg. for 13-15 minutes or until lightly browned. Serve with casserole.

Nutrition Information

- Calories: 708 calories
- Total Fat: 55g
- Cholesterol: 333mg
- Sodium: 1330mg
- Total Carbohydrate: 22g
- Protein: 30g
- Fiber: 1g

136. Eggless Whole Wheat Biscuits

"This is such a fluffy, delicate biscuit recipe. It goes good with any soup or even just alone!!!"

Serving: 8 | Prep: 15 m | Cook: 10 m | Ready in: 25 m

Ingredients

- 1 cup all-purpose flour
- 1 cup whole wheat flour
- 4 teaspoons baking powder
- 1 tablespoon white sugar
- 3/4 teaspoon salt
- 1/4 cup butter
- 1 cup milk

Direction

- Preheat oven to 450 degrees F (230 degrees C).
- Whisk all-purpose flour, whole wheat flour, baking powder, sugar, and salt in a bowl. Cut butter into flour mixture using whisk until mixture resembles coarse crumbs. Add milk and stir until mixture is moistened.
- Turn the dough out onto a lightly floured surface and knead briefly, about 15 turns. Pat or roll the dough out into a 3/4-inch thick round. Cut circles with a 2-inch biscuit cutter or cup and arrange on a baking sheet.
- Bake in preheated oven until brown, 10 to 12 minutes. Serve warm.

Nutrition Information

- Calories: 181 calories
- Total Fat: 6.8 g
- Cholesterol: 18 mg
- Sodium: 516 mg
- Total Carbohydrate: 26.4 g
- Protein: 4.7 g

137. Eggnog Biscuits

"I was making biscuits during the holidays one year and substituted eggnog for milk," relates Angie Jones from West Point, Utah. "These yummy biscuits were the outcome." Whether you bake some for Christmas dinner or a weekday meal, the clever creations are sure to become a seasonal favorite.

Serving: 6-8 biscuits. | Prep: 20 m | Cook: 0 m | Ready in: 20 m

Ingredients

- 1 cup plus 1 tablespoon biscuit/baking mix
- 1/3 cup eggnog
- 1/4 to 1/2 teaspoon ground nutmeg

Direction

- In a small bowl, combine biscuit mix and eggnog just until moistened. Turn on a lightly floured surface; knead 8-10 times. Pat or roll

out to 1/2-in. thickness; cut with a floured 2-1/2-in. biscuit cutter.
- Place 2 in. apart on a greased baking sheet. Sprinkle with nutmeg. Bake at 450 degrees for 8-10 minutes or until lightly browned. Serve warm.

Nutrition Information

- Calories: 80 calories
- Total Fat: 3g
- Cholesterol: 6mg
- Sodium: 206mg
- Total Carbohydrate: 11g
- Protein: 2g
- Fiber: 0 g

138. EZ Cream Biscuits

"Just two ingredients! This is foolproof and good every time!! If you've ever enjoyed a famous chicken restaurant's biscuits, you've got to try these!"

Serving: 10 | Prep: 5 m | Cook: 15 m | Ready in: 20 m

Ingredients

- 2 cups self-rising flour
- 1 1/2 cups heavy cream

Direction

- Preheat the oven to 375 degrees F (190 degrees C).
- In a medium bowl, stir together the flour and cream just until blended. You should have a sticky dough. Use a large spoon to scrape the dough out onto a floured surface. Knead the dough once or twice, then pat or roll out to 1/2 inch thickness. Cut into circles using a biscuit cutter. Place on a baking sheet, spacing 1/2 inch apart. If you like drop biscuits, you can skip this part and just drop spoonfuls of the dough onto a baking sheet.
- Bake in the preheated oven until the bottoms and tops are golden brown, about 15 minutes.

Nutrition Information

- Calories: 212 calories
- Total Fat: 13.5 g
- Cholesterol: 49 mg
- Sodium: 331 mg
- Total Carbohydrate: 19.6 g
- Protein: 3.2 g

139. EZ Drop Biscuits

"These are a favorite of my boys. For an extra treat I drop a handful of shredded cheese in."

Serving: 12 | Prep: 15 m | Cook: 15 m | Ready in: 30 m

Ingredients

- 2 cups all-purpose flour
- 1 tablespoon baking powder
- 2 teaspoons white sugar
- 1/2 teaspoon cream of tartar
- 1/4 teaspoon salt
- 1/2 cup melted butter
- 1 cup milk

Direction

- Preheat oven to 450 degrees F (230 degrees C).
- In a large bowl, combine flour, baking powder, sugar, cream of tartar and salt. Stir in butter and milk just until moistened. Drop batter on a lightly greased cookie sheet by the tablespoon.
- Bake in preheated oven until golden on the edges, about 8 to 12 minutes. Serve warm.

Nutrition Information

- Calories: 157 calories
- Total Fat: 8.3 g
- Cholesterol: 22 mg
- Sodium: 196 mg
- Total Carbohydrate: 17.8 g
- Protein: 2.9 g

140. Fair Scones

"A hallmark of the Puyallup and Evergreen State Fairs in Washington State. Now you can make them at home any time of year. Just like at the fair, they are best served hot, with butter and raspberry jam."

Serving: 8 | Prep: 15 m | Cook: 15 m | Ready in: 30 m

Ingredients

- 2 1/2 cups all-purpose flour
- 2 tablespoons white sugar
- 2 teaspoons baking powder
- 1/2 teaspoon salt
- 6 tablespoons shortening
- 1/2 cup milk

Direction

- Preheat an oven to 450 degrees F (230 degrees C).
- Whisk flour, sugar, baking powder, and salt together in a large bowl. Cut shortening into flour mixture with a fork or pastry knife until crumbly texture. Add milk; mix until just combined.
- Turn dough onto a floured surface; knead until completely mixed, about 1 minute. Divide into 2 equal pieces. Roll or pat each piece into a 3/4-inch round. Cut each round into 4 pieces. Arrange pieces on a baking sheet.
- Bake in the preheated oven until golden brown, about 15 minutes.

Nutrition Information

- Calories: 247 calories
- Total Fat: 10.3 g
- Cholesterol: 1 mg
- Sodium: 274 mg
- Total Carbohydrate: 34 g
- Protein: 4.5 g

141. Fast Food Biscuits

"These easy biscuits are perfect for those times when you crave fast food but don't want to leave the house!"

Serving: 6 | Prep: 10 m | Cook: 20 m | Ready in: 30 m

Ingredients

- 1/4 cup lemon-lime flavored carbonated beverage
- 1/3 cup buttermilk
- 2 cups baking mix
- 2 tablespoons butter, melted

Direction

- Preheat oven to 450 degrees F (230 degrees C). Lightly grease a baking sheet.
- Pour soda and buttermilk into a large bowl. Stir in baking mixing until dough pulls together. Knead dough in bowl until smooth.
- Flatten dough and cut into 6 rounds. Place biscuits on pan and brush with melted butter.
- Bake in preheated oven until golden brown, about 18 to 20 minutes. Let cool 10 minutes before serving.

Nutrition Information

- Calories: 207 calories
- Total Fat: 10 g
- Cholesterol: 11 mg
- Sodium: 547 mg
- Total Carbohydrate: 26.4 g
- Protein: 3.3 g

142. FeatherLight Biscuits

I usually used a glass or baking powder can lid as a cutter so the biscuits would be bigger than average size...and I always baked some extras to send home with the kids. They liked to split them and fill them with cheese or peanut butter and strawberry jam. --Eleanore Hill, Fresno, California

Serving: about 2 dozen. | Prep: 20 m | Cook: 10 m | Ready in: 30 m

Ingredients

- 6 cups buttermilk baking mix
- 1/4 cup sugar
- 1 package (1/4 ounce) active dry yeast
- 1/3 cup shortening
- 1 to 1-1/4 cups warm water (120 degrees to 130 degrees)
- 1/4 cup butter, melted

Direction

- In a large bowl, combine the baking mix, sugar and yeast. Cut in shortening until mixture resembles coarse crumbs. Stir in enough warm water to form a soft and slightly sticky dough. Turn onto a floured surface; knead gently 3-4 times.
- Roll dough to 3/4-in. thickness; cut with a 2-1/2-in. round biscuit cutter. Place on ungreased baking sheets. Brush tops with melted butter. Bake at 400 degrees for 10-12 minutes or until lightly browned.

Nutrition Information

- Calories: 173 calories
- Total Fat: 9g
- Cholesterol: 5mg
- Sodium: 397mg
- Total Carbohydrate: 21g
- Protein: 2g
- Fiber: 1g

143. Flaky Biscuits

"Biscuits with extra flakiness. They're light and airy, not hard, even after a few days."

Serving: 12 | Prep: 10 m | Cook: 10 m | Ready in: 20 m

Ingredients

- 2 1/2 cups buttermilk baking mix
- 1 teaspoon baking powder
- 1 pinch salt
- 2/3 cup milk
- 1/2 tablespoon malt vinegar

Direction

- Preheat oven to 450 degrees F (230 degrees C). Lightly grease two baking sheets.
- In a large bowl, stir together baking mix, baking powder and salt. Mix in milk and vinegar until a loose dough forms. Turn out onto a lightly floured surface and knead briefly; about 10 times. Break dough apart into 12 equal pieces and place on prepared baking sheets.
- Bake in preheated oven for 8 to 10 minutes, or until light brown.

Nutrition Information

- Calories: 114 calories
- Total Fat: 4.1 g
- Cholesterol: 2 mg
- Sodium: 365 mg
- Total Carbohydrate: 16.6 g
- Protein: 2.4 g

144. Flaky Biscuits with Herb Butter

Nothing says "spring" like fresh herbs...and these flaky, flavorful biscuits are the ideal way to showcase tarragon and chives. They can be on the table in 30 minutes, which makes them an ideal choice for last-minute entertaining. — Theresa Stanek, Evans City, Pennsylvania

Serving: 1 dozen. | Prep: 20 m | Cook: 10 m | Ready in: 30 m

Ingredients

- 2 cups all-purpose flour
- 3 teaspoons baking powder
- 1 tablespoon sugar
- 1-1/2 teaspoons minced fresh chives
- 1-1/2 teaspoons minced fresh tarragon
- 1 teaspoon salt
- 1/2 teaspoon garlic powder
- 1/2 cup shortening
- 3/4 cup 2% milk
- HERB BUTTER:
- 1/2 cup butter, softened
- 1-1/2 teaspoons minced fresh chives
- 1-1/2 teaspoons minced fresh tarragon
- 1/2 teaspoon garlic powder

Direction

- In a small bowl, combine the first seven ingredients. Cut in shortening until mixture resembles coarse crumbs. Stir in milk just until moistened. Turn onto a lightly floured surface; knead 8-10 times.
- Pat or roll out to 1/2-in. thickness; cut with a floured 2-1/2-in. biscuit cutter. Place 2 in. apart on an ungreased baking sheet.
- Bake at 425 degrees for 8-12 minutes or until golden brown.
- Meanwhile, in a small bowl, beat the butter ingredients until blended; serve with warm biscuits.

Nutrition Information

- Calories: 229 calories
- Total Fat: 16g
- Cholesterol: 21mg

- Sodium: 359mg
- Total Carbohydrate: 18g
- Protein: 3g
- Fiber: 1g

145. Flaky Dill Biscuits

The dill weed in these lovely golden biscuits really comes through. My friends like them because they're fluffy, tender and delicious. I like them because they don't take as much time to make as yeast rolls. -Audrey Lockau, Kitchener, Ontario

Serving: 9 servings. | Prep: 15 m | Cook: 10 m | Ready in: 25 m

Ingredients

- 2 cups all-purpose flour
- 3 teaspoons baking powder
- 2 to 3 teaspoons dill weed
- 3/4 teaspoon salt
- 1/4 teaspoon pepper
- 1/2 cup cold butter
- 2 eggs, lightly beaten
- 1/2 cup plus 1 tablespoon half-and-half cream, divided

Direction

- In a large bowl, combine the flour, baking powder, dill, salt and pepper. Cut in butter until the mixture resembles coarse crumbs. With a fork, stir in eggs and 1/2 cup cream just until moistened.
- Drop by 1/4 cupfuls 2 in. apart onto an ungreased baking sheet. Brush tops with remaining cream. Bake at 450 degrees for 10-12 minutes or until golden brown. Serve warm.

Nutrition Information

- Calories: 228 calories
- Total Fat: 13g
- Cholesterol: 82mg
- Sodium: 455mg
- Total Carbohydrate: 22g
- Protein: 5g
- Fiber: 1g

146. Flaky Italian Biscuits

Keeping the biscuit mix on hand makes it easy to stir up a batch of these tender Italian biscuits. Spread them with butter hellip;or omit the Italian seasoning and serve them with honey. --Tami Christman, Soda Springs, Idaho

Serving: 8 biscuits. | Prep: 15 m | Cook: 15 m | Ready in: 30 m

Ingredients

- 2 cups Biscuit Baking Mix
- 1 teaspoon Italian seasoning
- 1/2 cup half-and-half cream

Direction

- In a small bowl, mix biscuit baking mix and Italian seasoning; stir in cream just until moistened. Turn onto a lightly floured surface; knead gently 10 times. Pat or roll out to 1/2-in. thickness; cut with a 2-1/2-in. biscuit cutter.
- Place 2 in. apart on an ungreased baking sheet. Bake at 425 degrees for 13-16 minutes or until golden brown. Serve warm.

Nutrition Information

- Calories:
- Total Fat: g
- Cholesterol: mg
- Sodium: mg
- Total Carbohydrate: g
- Protein: g
- Fiber: g

147. Flaky Sweet Potato Biscuits

Flaky and bursting with flavor from honey and sweet potatoes, these biscuits are wonderful any time, but they're best right from the oven. – DeLynne Rutledge, Lovelady, Texas

Serving: 17 biscuits. | Prep: 15 m | Cook: 15 m | Ready in: 30 m

Ingredients

- 2 cups all-purpose flour
- 1/3 cup yellow cornmeal
- 2-1/2 teaspoons baking powder
- 1/2 teaspoon salt
- 1/3 cup cold butter, cubed
- 1 cup mashed sweet potato
- 1/2 cup fat-free milk
- 2 tablespoons honey

Direction

- In a large bowl, combine the flour, cornmeal, baking powder and salt. Cut in butter until mixture resembles coarse crumbs. Stir in the sweet potato, milk and honey just until moistened. Turn onto a lightly floured surface; knead 5-8 times. Pat out to 1/2-in. thickness; cut with a floured 2-in. biscuit cutter.
- Place 2 in. apart on an ungreased baking sheet. Bake at 400 degrees for 14-18 minutes or until lightly browned. Serve warm.

Nutrition Information

- Calories: 120 calories
- Total Fat: 4g
- Cholesterol: 10mg
- Sodium: 162mg
- Total Carbohydrate: 19g
- Protein: 2g
- Fiber: 1g

148. Flaky Whole Wheat Biscuits

Whole wheat flour gives these biscuits a nutty, homey flavor. Ever since I started making these, white flour biscuits just don't taste as good! Pair them with soup or slather them with whipped cream and sweetened berries for a dessert treat. – Trisha Kruse, Eagle, Idaho

Serving: 10 biscuits. | Prep: 15 m | Cook: 10 m | Ready in: 25 m

Ingredients

- 1 cup all-purpose flour
- 1 cup whole wheat flour
- 3 teaspoons baking powder
- 1 tablespoon brown sugar
- 1 teaspoon baking soda
- 1/2 teaspoon salt
- 1/4 cup cold butter
- 1 cup 2% milk

Direction

- In a large bowl, combine the first six ingredients. Cut in butter until mixture resembles coarse crumbs. Stir in milk just until moistened. Turn onto a lightly floured surface; knead 8-10 times.
- Pat or roll out to 1/2-in. thickness; cut with a floured 2-1/2-in. biscuit cutter. Place 2 in. apart on an ungreased baking sheet.
- Bake at 425 degrees for 8-10 minutes or until golden brown.

Nutrition Information

- Calories: 144 calories
- Total Fat: 6g
- Cholesterol: 14mg
- Sodium: 417mg
- Total Carbohydrate: 21g
- Protein: 4g
- Fiber: 2g

149. Fluffy Biscuits

If you're looking for a fluffy biscuit recipe, this one is the best. These golden-brown rolls bake up tall, light and tender. Their mild flavor tastes even better when the warm biscuits are spread with butter or jam. --Nancy Horsburgh, Everett, Ontario

Serving: about 1 dozen. | Prep: 20 m | Cook: 10 m | Ready in: 30 m

Ingredients

- 2 cups all-purpose flour
- 4 teaspoons baking powder
- 1 tablespoon sugar
- 1/2 teaspoon salt
- 1/2 cup shortening
- 1 large egg
- 2/3 cup 2% milk

Direction

- Preheat oven to 450 degrees. In a bowl, whisk together first four ingredients. Cut in shortening until the mixture resembles coarse crumbs. Whisk together egg and milk. Add to dry ingredients; stir just until moistened.
- On a well-floured surface, knead dough gently 8-10 times. Roll to 3/4-in. thickness; cut with a floured 2-1/2-in. biscuit cutter. Place on a lightly greased baking sheet.
- Bake until golden brown, 8-10 minutes. Serve warm.

Nutrition Information

- Calories: 166 calories
- Total Fat: 9g
- Cholesterol: 17mg
- Sodium: 271mg
- Total Carbohydrate: 18g
- Protein: 3g
- Fiber: 1g

150. Fluffy Cathead Biscuits with Honey Butter

Cathead biscuits are a Southern staple whose name refers to their large size (about as big as a cat's head). The dough for this hand-rolled biscuit recipe is made by incorporating flour into the wet ingredients, instead of the reverse. The result is a fluffy (rather than flaky) biscuit, ready to be split and spread with flavorful honey butter.

Serving: Makes 12 biscuits | Prep: 20 m | Cook: 45 m

Ingredients

- 1/2 cup buttermilk powder
- 3 tablespoons baking powder
- 1 1/2 teaspoons kosher salt
- Pinch of sugar
- 6 tablespoons lard or bacon fat, cut into pieces and slightly softened
- 6 tablespoons unsalted butter, cut into pieces and slightly softened, plus more, melted, if desired
- 3 1/2–4 cups all-purpose flour, divided, plus more
- 1/2 cup flavorful honey (such as buckwheat)
- 1/4 cup unsalted butter, slightly softened
- 1/2 teaspoon sea salt or kosher salt

Direction

- For the biscuits: Arrange rack in middle of oven; preheat to 400°F. Whisk buttermilk powder, baking powder, salt, and sugar in a large bowl until evenly distributed and no lumps remain. Add 2 cups water and whisk to combine. Add lard and butter.
- Add 2 cups flour and mix with a fork until mixture resembles porridge. Using fork, press fats against side of bowl to cut into smaller, irregular, flattened pieces.
- Fold in remaining 1 1/2–2 cups flour by the half cup with fork until a wet dough forms. Turn out dough onto a well-floured surface. Dust top of dough with more flour. Gently fold dough into itself until it feels like a pillow and is no longer sticky. Using a floured bench scraper or butter knife, divide dough into 12 equal pieces.

- Working with 1 piece at a time, dip cut sides in flour and gently roll into a ball with your hands. Nestle each ball side by side in a large cast-iron skillet or on a rimmed baking sheet. Bake biscuits until lightly browned, 25–30 minutes. Brush with melted butter, if desired. Serve with honey butter.
- For the honey butter: Combine honey, butter, and salt in a medium bowl. Mash with fork until just combined but not emulsified.
- Cooks' Note: If you can't find buttermilk powder, substitute 2 cups store-bought buttermilk (omit water). White Lily self-rising flour can be substituted for all-purpose flour (omit baking powder and salt).

Nutrition Information

- Calories: 334
- Total Fat: 16 g (25%)
- Saturated Fat: 9 g (44%)
- Cholesterol: 32 mg (11%)
- Sodium: 304 mg (13%)
- Total Carbohydrate: 43 g (14%)
- Protein: 5 g (9%)
- Fiber: 1 g (4%)

151.Fluffy Herb Drop Biscuits

I grow many herbs, so I can just go out to the garden and pick them. These biscuits contain my favorite ones. -- Melissa McCabe, Long Beach, California

Serving: 1 dozen. | Prep: 10 m | Cook: 10 m | Ready in: 20 m

Ingredients

- 2 cups all-purpose flour
- 2 teaspoons baking powder
- 1/2 teaspoon salt
- 1/4 teaspoon baking soda
- 3/4 cup buttermilk
- 1/3 cup canola oil
- 2 tablespoons minced fresh basil

- 2 teaspoons minced fresh rosemary

Direction

- Preheat oven to 450 degrees. In a large bowl, whisk flour, baking powder, salt and baking soda. In another bowl, whisk buttermilk, oil, basil and rosemary; stir into dry ingredients just until moistened.
- Drop by rounded tablespoonfuls 2 in. apart onto an ungreased baking sheet. Bake 10-12 minutes or until light brown. Serve warm.

Nutrition Information

- Calories: 137 calories
- Total Fat: 7g
- Cholesterol: 1mg
- Sodium: 208mg
- Total Carbohydrate: 17g
- Protein: 3g
- Fiber: 1g

152. Fluffy Sour Cream Biscuits

"Fluffy and delicious."

Serving: 6 | Prep: 15 m | Cook: 10 m | Ready in: 25 m

Ingredients

- 1 1/4 cups all-purpose flour
- 2 teaspoons baking powder
- 3/4 teaspoon salt
- 1/8 teaspoon baking soda
- 3 tablespoons shortening
- 1/3 cup milk
- 1/3 cup sour cream

Direction

- Preheat oven to 425 degrees F (220 degrees C).
- Combine flour, baking powder, salt, and baking soda in a bowl; cut in shortening until mixture is crumbly. Add milk and sour cream until dough comes together.

- Turn dough onto a floured work surface; knead 10 times. Roll out dough and cut into biscuits. Place biscuits on a baking sheet.
- Bake in the preheated oven until biscuits are lightly browned, about 10 minutes.

Nutrition Information

- Calories: 186 calories
- Total Fat: 9.6 g
- Cholesterol: 7 mg
- Sodium: 492 mg
- Total Carbohydrate: 21.5 g
- Protein: 3.5 g

153. Fluffy Whole Wheat Biscuits

"These light and fluffy biscuits, made with all-purpose and whole wheat flour, are perfect for breakfast or dinner."

Serving: 12 | Prep: 15 m | Cook: 10 m | Ready in: 25 m

Ingredients

- 1 cup all-purpose flour
- 1 cup whole wheat flour
- 4 teaspoons baking powder
- 1 tablespoon white sugar
- 3/4 teaspoon salt
- 1/4 cup butter
- 1 cup buttermilk

Direction

- Preheat oven to 450 degrees F (230 degrees C).
- Combine all-purpose flour, whole wheat flour, baking powder, sugar, and salt in bowl. Cut in butter with a knife or pastry blender until mixture resembles coarse crumbs; stir in buttermilk until just moistened.
- Turn dough out on a lightly floured surface; knead gently 8 to 10 times. Roll to about 3/4-inch thickness; cut with a 2 1/2-inch biscuit cutter. Place biscuits on an ungreased baking sheet.
- Bake in preheated oven until biscuits are lightly browned, 10 to 12 minutes.

Nutrition Information

- Calories: 119 calories
- Total Fat: 4.3 g
- Cholesterol: 11 mg
- Sodium: 357 mg
- Total Carbohydrate: 17.7 g
- Protein: 3.2 g

154. French Onion Drop Biscuits

These simple drop biscuits have a golden color and mild onion flavor. As Galelah Dowell of Fairland, Oklahoma Note:s, "They're fast to fix and fabulous!"

Serving: 1 dozen. | Prep: 10 m | Cook: 10 m | Ready in: 20 m

Ingredients

- 2 cups biscuit/baking mix
- 1 carton (8 ounces) French onion dip
- 1/4 cup 2% milk

Direction

- In a large bowl, combine baking mix and onion dip. Stir in milk just until moistened. Drop by rounded tablespoonfuls 2 in. apart onto a baking sheet coated with cooking spray.
- Bake at 450 degrees for 10-14 minutes or until golden brown. Serve warm.

Nutrition Information

- Calories: 121 calories
- Total Fat: 6g
- Cholesterol: 0 mg
- Sodium: 382mg
- Total Carbohydrate: 14g
- Protein: 2g
- Fiber: 0 g

155. Fresh Alberta Biscuits

"Pioneer biscuits, the same ones Grammy used to make. You can use either lard or shortening."

Serving: 24 | Prep: 20 m | Cook: 20 m | Ready in: 40 m

Ingredients

- 6 cups all-purpose flour
- 1/2 cup nonfat dry milk powder
- 1/4 cup white sugar
- 1/4 cup baking powder
- 2 teaspoons cream of tartar
- 2 teaspoons salt
- 2 cups shortening
- 1 1/2 cups water, or as needed

Direction

- Preheat oven to 400 degrees F (200 degrees C).
- Whisk together flour, dry milk powder, sugar, baking powder, cream of tartar, and salt in a large bowl. Cut shortening into flour mixture with a knife or pastry blender until mixture resembles coarse crumbs. Stir water into mixture until uniformly moistened and a soft dough forms.
- Turn dough out onto a lightly floured surface and, with floured hands, knead until smooth, about 8 to 10 turns. Roll dough out to 3/4-inch thickness with a floured rolling pin. Cut biscuits with a 2 1/2-inch round cookie cutter; place onto a baking sheet. Press dough trimmings together, roll out again, and cut remaining dough into rounds.
- Bake biscuits in the preheated oven until golden, about 20 minutes. Serve warm.

Nutrition Information

- Calories: 283 calories
- Total Fat: 17.4 g
- Cholesterol: < 1 mg
- Sodium: 387 mg
- Total Carbohydrate: 27.8 g
- Protein: 4.1 g

156. Frosted CinnamonRaisin Biscuits

I created this recipe several years ago after sampling something similar at a popular chain restaurant. These easy drop biscuits are a great accompaniment to a country-style breakfast.

Serving: 1 dozen. | Prep: 15 m | Cook: 15 m | Ready in: 30 m

Ingredients

- 2 cups all-purpose flour
- 1/4 cup sugar
- 2 teaspoons baking powder
- 1 teaspoon salt
- 1/4 teaspoon baking soda
- 1/3 cup shortening
- 2/3 cup buttermilk
- 1/3 cup raisins
- 1-1/2 teaspoons ground cinnamon
- FROSTING:
- 1-1/2 cups confectioners' sugar
- 2 tablespoons butter, softened
- 1-1/2 teaspoons vanilla extract
- 3 to 5 teaspoons warm water

Direction

- In a large bowl, combine the first five ingredients; cut in shortening until mixture resembles coarse crumbs. Stir in buttermilk just until moistened. Turn onto a floured surface; sprinkle with raisins and cinnamon. Knead 8-10 times (cinnamon will have a marbled appearance).
- Drop batter into 12 mounds 2 in. apart on a greased baking sheet. Bake at 425 degrees for 12-16 minutes or until golden brown.
- For frosting, combine the sugar, butter, vanilla and enough water to achieve desired consistency. Frost warm biscuits. Serve immediately.

Nutrition Information

- Calories: 235 calories

- Total Fat: 8g
- Cholesterol: 6mg
- Sodium: 324mg
- Total Carbohydrate: 39g
- Protein: 3g
- Fiber: 1g

157. Fruity PullApart Bread

Who doesn't love to start the day with monkey bread? This skillet version is packed with bright berries and dolloped with irresistibly rich cream cheese. A sprinkle of fresh basil brings it all together. --Darla Andrews, Schertz, Texas

Serving: 8 servings. | Prep: 15 m | Cook: 35 m | Ready in: 50 m

Ingredients

- 1 tube (16.3 ounces) large refrigerated flaky honey butter biscuits
- 1/2 cup packed dark brown sugar
- 1/2 cup granulated sugar
- 1/3 cup butter, melted
- 1 cup fresh blueberries
- 1 cup chopped fresh strawberries
- 4 ounces cream cheese, softened
- 1 tablespoon minced fresh basil

Direction

- Preheat oven to 350 degrees. Separate dough into eight biscuits; cut biscuits into fourths.
- In a shallow bowl, combine sugars. Dip biscuits in melted butter, then in sugar mixture. Place biscuits in a greased 10-1/4-in. cast-iron skillet. Top with fresh berries; dollop with cream cheese. Bake until biscuits are golden brown and cooked through, 35-40 minutes. Sprinkle with basil.

Nutrition Information

- Calories: 383 calories
- Total Fat: 20g
- Cholesterol: 30mg
- Sodium: 641mg
- Total Carbohydrate: 49g

- Protein: 5g
- Fiber: 2g

158. Garden Biscuits

"These flaky yeast biscuits – speckled with carrot, parsley and green onion – smell wonderful while baking. So it's hard to resist eating one right from the oven," Note:s Kerry Dority of Camdenton, Missouri.

Serving: 15 biscuits. | Prep: 20 m | Cook: 10 m | Ready in: 30 m

Ingredients

- 2-1/2 cups all-purpose flour
- 1 tablespoon sugar
- 1 package (1/4 ounce) active dry yeast
- 1-1/2 teaspoons baking powder
- 1/2 teaspoon baking soda
- 1/4 teaspoon salt
- 1/2 cup shortening
- 1 cup buttermilk
- 2 tablespoons water
- 1/4 cup finely shredded carrot
- 2 tablespoons minced fresh parsley
- 2 tablespoons finely chopped green onion

Direction

- In a large bowl, combine the flour, sugar, yeast, baking powder, baking soda and salt. Cut in shortening until mixture resembles coarse crumbs.
- In a small saucepan, heat buttermilk and water to 120 degrees -130 degrees. Add buttermilk mixture, carrot, parsley and onion to yeast mixture; stir just until moistened.
- Turn onto a lightly floured surface; knead until a soft dough forms, about 6-8 minutes. Pat or roll out to 1/2-in. thickness; cut with a floured 2-1/2-in. biscuit cutter. Place 1 in. apart on ungreased baking sheets.
- Bake at 450 degrees for 8-10 minutes or until golden brown. Serve warm.

Nutrition Information

- Calories: 147 calories
- Total Fat: 7g
- Cholesterol: 1mg
- Sodium: 140mg
- Total Carbohydrate: 18g
- Protein: 3g
- Fiber: 1g

159. Garden Herb Drop Biscuits

Since we live in military housing, we usually doesn't have much yard space for a garden. We decided to purchase our own 5th-wheel travel trailer that stays in a park, so now I have herbs and vegetables growing anywhere I can put them! I like using my my veggies and herbs in new dishes, and this one was especially great.--Dreama Crump, Hephzibah, Georgia

Serving: 1 dozen. | Prep: 20 m | Cook: 15 m | Ready in: 35 m

Ingredients

- 2-1/4 cups biscuit/baking mix
- 1 cup shredded cheddar cheese
- 2 green onions, finely chopped
- 1 tablespoon minced fresh parsley or 1 teaspoon dried parsley flakes
- 1 tablespoon minced fresh basil or 1 teaspoon dried basil
- 2 teaspoons minced fresh oregano or 1/2 teaspoon dried oregano
- 1/2 teaspoon sugar
- 1/4 teaspoon garlic powder
- 2/3 cup plus 1 tablespoon 2% milk, divided
- 1/3 cup sour cream
- 2 teaspoons spicy brown mustard
- 1 large egg

Direction

- Preheat oven to 425 degrees. In a large bowl, mix the first eight ingredients. In a small bowl, whisk 2/3 cup milk, sour cream and mustard

until blended. Add to baking mix mixture; stir just until moistened.
- Drop by 1/4 cupfuls 2 in. apart onto a greased baking sheet. In a small bowl, whisk egg with remaining milk; brush over tops. Bake 12-14 minutes or until golden brown. Serve warm.

Nutrition Information

- Calories:
- Total Fat: g
- Cholesterol: mg
- Sodium: mg
- Total Carbohydrate: g
- Protein: g
- Fiber: g

160. Garlic Blue Cheese and Bacon Biscuits

"Amazing garlic, blue cheese, and bacon biscuits! Soft and moist. Great as a side with any meal."

Serving: 12 | Prep: 15 m | Cook: 15 m | Ready in: 30 m

Ingredients

- 2 cups all-purpose flour
- 1 teaspoon baking powder
- 1/2 teaspoon salt
- 1/2 teaspoon ground black pepper
- 6 tablespoons butter, frozen and grated
- 1 1/4 cups crumbled blue cheese
- 4 slices cooked bacon, crumbled
- 2 cloves garlic, minced
- 1 cup buttermilk
- 1/4 cup butter, melted
- 1 clove garlic, minced

Direction

- Preheat oven to 450 degrees F (230 degrees C). Line a baking sheet with parchment paper.
- Whisk flour, baking powder, salt, and pepper together into a large bowl. Mash grated butter into the flour mixture until the result resembles coarse crumbs. Mix blue cheese,

bacon, and 2 cloves minced garlic into the flour mixture.

- Make a well in the center of the flour mixture. Pour buttermilk into the well and mix with your hands until the dry ingredients are just moistened. Drop mixture by heaping spoonfuls onto prepared baking sheet.
- Bake in preheated oven until lightly browned, 12 to 15 minutes. Switch oven to preheat the broiler.
- Stir melted butter and 1 clove minced garlic together in a small bowl; brush over the top of the biscuits.
- Heat biscuits under the broiler just until the tops are browned, about 2 minutes.

Nutrition Information

- Calories: 231 calories
- Total Fat: 14.9 g
- Cholesterol: 39 mg
- Sodium: 470 mg
- Total Carbohydrate: 17.7 g
- Protein: 6.7 g

161. Garlic Cheddar Biscuits

Make these quick and savory drop biscuits to serve alongside a big bowl of chili or as the base for an incredible breakfast sandwich.

| Prep: 15 m | Cook: 27 m

Ingredients

- 2 3/4 cups all-purpose flour
- 1 tbsp Davis or Clabber Girl Baking Powder
- 1/2 tsp garlic powder, plus an extra 1/4 tsp (optional)
- 1/2 tsp salt
- 1 cup shortening
- 1 cup buttermilk
- 1 cup shredded cheddar cheese
- 2 tbsp butter, melted

Direction

- Preheat oven to 425°F. Combine flour, baking powder, 1/2 teaspoon garlic powder and salt. Using a pastry blender or 2 forks cut in shortening until mixture is crumbly. With a fork, add buttermilk and cheese and stir until mixture forms a soft dough. Drop dough by 1/4 cupfuls onto greased cookie sheet. Combine butter and remaining 1/4 teaspoon garlic powder (if using); brush on biscuit tops. Bake 10-12 minutes or until golden brown.
- This recipe is made available as a courtesy by Davis, a trademark of the Clabber Girl Corporation.

Nutrition Information

- Calories: 319
- Total Fat: 23 g (35%)
- Saturated Fat: 7 g (37%)
- Cholesterol: 16 mg (5%)
- Sodium: 192 mg (8%)
- Total Carbohydrate: 23 g (8%)
- Protein: 6 g (12%)
- Fiber: 1 g (3%)

162. Garlic Cheese Biscuits

"Light, tasty biscuits - just as good as the ones served at a popular seafood restaurant chain."

Serving: 10 | Prep: 10 m | Cook: 10 m | Ready in: 20 m

Ingredients

- 2 cups buttermilk baking mix
- 2/3 cup milk
- 1/2 cup shredded Cheddar cheese
- 1/4 cup butter, melted
- 1/2 teaspoon garlic powder

Direction

- Preheat oven to 450 degrees F (230 degrees C).

- Combine baking mix, milk and cheddar cheese in mixing bowl. Beat with wooden spoon till soft dough forms.
- Drop dough by spoonfuls onto ungreased cookie sheet. Bake 8-10 minutes until golden brown.
- Mix butter and garlic powder and brush over warm biscuits before removing from cookie sheet.

Nutrition Information

- Calories: 152 calories
- Total Fat: 7.1 g
- Cholesterol: 19 mg
- Sodium: 536 mg
- Total Carbohydrate: 18.3 g
- Protein: 4.1 g

---

163. Garlic Onion Cheese Biscuits

Laced with garlicky goodness, melted cheese and a lick of onion, these quick, buttery muffins are easy enough for weekday suppers but special enough for any company dinner.

Serving: 1 dozen. | Prep: 20 m | Cook: 10 m | Ready in: 30 m

Ingredients

- 2 cups all-purpose flour
- 1 tablespoon sugar
- 2 teaspoons baking powder
- 1 teaspoon onion powder
- 1 teaspoon garlic powder
- 1/4 teaspoon salt
- 1/4 teaspoon baking soda
- 1/4 cup cold butter, cubed
- 2 cups shredded cheddar-Monterey Jack cheese, divided
- 1/2 cup grated Parmesan cheese
- 1 cup buttermilk

Direction

- In a large bowl, combine the flour, sugar, baking powder, onion powder, garlic powder, salt and baking soda. Cut in butter until mixture resembles coarse crumbs. Stir in 1-1/4 cups cheddar-Monterey Jack cheese and Parmesan cheese. Stir in buttermilk just until moistened.
- Turn onto a lightly floured surface; knead 6-8 times. Pat or roll out to 1/2-in. thickness; cut with a floured 2-1/2-in. biscuit cutter. Place 2 in. apart on a greased baking sheet. Sprinkle with remaining cheddar-Monterey Jack cheese. Bake at 400 degrees for 10-15 minutes or until golden brown. Serve warm.

Nutrition Information

- Calories: 204 calories
- Total Fat: 10g
- Cholesterol: 30mg
- Sodium: 355mg
- Total Carbohydrate: 19g
- Protein: 8g
- Fiber: 1g

---

164. Garlic Potato Biscuits

We grow our own potatoes and garlic, so these delectable biscuits are on our table often. I make biscuits a lot because they're quicker and easier than rolls.

Serving: 15 biscuits. | Prep: 25 m | Cook: 10 m | Ready in: 35 m

Ingredients

- 1 large potato (1/2 pound), peeled and diced
- 3 to 4 garlic cloves, peeled
- 1/3 cup butter, softened
- 1 teaspoon salt
- 1/4 teaspoon pepper
- 2 cups all-purpose flour
- 3 teaspoons baking powder
- 1/3 cup milk

Direction

- Place potato and garlic in a saucepan; cover with water. Bring to a boil. Reduce heat; cover and simmer until tender. Drain. Add butter, salt and pepper to potato and garlic; mash. In a large bowl, combine flour and baking powder; stir in potato mixture until mixture resembles coarse crumbs. Add milk and stir well.
- Turn dough onto a lightly floured surface. Roll out to 1/2-in. thickness. Cut with a floured 2-in. biscuit cutter. Place 1 in. apart on an ungreased baking sheet. Bake at 450 degrees for 10-12 minutes or until golden brown. Serve warm.

Nutrition Information

- Calories: 120 calories
- Total Fat: 4g
- Cholesterol: 12mg
- Sodium: 283mg
- Total Carbohydrate: 18g
- Protein: 2g
- Fiber: 1g

165. GarlicHerb Butter Drop Biscuits

"Excellent drop biscuits made with lots of real butter, garlic, and herbs!"

Serving: 12 | Prep: 15 m | Cook: 15 m | Ready in: 30 m

Ingredients

- 2 cups all-purpose flour
- 1 tablespoon baking powder
- 2 teaspoons white sugar
- 1/2 teaspoon cream of tartar
- 1/3 teaspoon garlic powder
- 1/4 teaspoon salt
- 1/2 cup chilled unsalted butter, cut into cubes
- 1 cup shredded mild Cheddar cheese
- 1 teaspoon dried Italian seasoning
- 1 cup cold whole milk
- 2 tablespoons salted butter, melted

- 1/2 teaspoon dried parsley flakes
- 1/2 teaspoon garlic powder

Direction

- Preheat oven to 400 degrees F (200 degrees C). Grease a baking sheet.
- Sift flour, baking powder, white sugar, cream of tartar, 1/3 teaspoon garlic powder, and salt together in a large bowl. Mash unsalted butter cubes into the flour mixture with a pastry cutter or large fork until coarsely blended. Mix Cheddar cheese and Italian seasoning into the flour mixture.
- Pour milk over the flour mixture while stirring until you get a tough and sticky dough. Drop dough by the tablespoon onto the prepared baking sheet.
- Bake in preheated oven until lightly browned, about 15 minutes.
- Stir melted salted butter, parsley flakes, and 1/2 teaspoon garlic powder together in a bowl; brush over biscuits immediately upon removing from the oven.

Nutrition Information

- Calories: 215 calories
- Total Fat: 13.6 g
- Cholesterol: 37 mg
- Sodium: 214 mg
- Total Carbohydrate: 18.2 g
- Protein: 5.3 g

166. Ginger Buttermilk Biscuits

After we had cinnamon-topped biscuits at a restaurant, I came up with my own version at home. I keep crystallized ginger on hand so I can whip up a batch at a moment's notice!--Rebecca Littlejohn, Vista, California

Serving: 20 biscuits. | Prep: 15 m | Cook: 10 m | Ready in: 25 m

Ingredients

- 2 cups all-purpose flour

- 2 tablespoons brown sugar
- 2 teaspoons baking powder
- 1 teaspoon ground ginger
- 1/2 teaspoon salt
- 1/2 teaspoon baking soda
- 1/2 teaspoon ground cinnamon
- 1/3 cup shortening
- 1/2 cup finely chopped crystallized ginger
- 3/4 cup buttermilk
- 2 tablespoons butter, melted
- Coarse sugar, optional

Direction

- Preheat oven to 425 degrees. In a large bowl, whisk the first seven ingredients. Cut in shortening until mixture resembles coarse crumbs. Stir in crystallized ginger. Add buttermilk; stir just until moistened.
- Turn onto a lightly floured surface; knead gently 8-10 times. Pat or roll dough to 1/2-in. thickness; cut with a floured 2-in. biscuit cutter. Place 1 in. apart on a parchment paper-lined baking sheet. Brush tops with butter. If desired, sprinkle with coarse sugar. Bake 7-8 minutes or until bottoms are golden brown. Serve warm.

Nutrition Information

- Calories: 114 calories
- Total Fat: 5g
- Cholesterol: 3mg
- Sodium: 161mg
- Total Carbohydrate: 16g
- Protein: 2g
- Fiber: 0 g

167. Glazed Cinnamon Biscuits

"I often make this easy, delicious variation of glazed cinnamon rolls for our family as a breakfast treat on weekends," reports Sue Gronholz of Beaver Dam, Wisconsin.

Serving: 1 dozen. | Prep: 20 m | Cook: 20 m | Ready in: 40 m

Ingredients

- 2 cups all-purpose flour
- 4 teaspoons baking powder
- 1/2 teaspoon salt
- 6 tablespoons butter, divided
- 3/4 cup whole milk
- 1/4 cup sugar
- 1 teaspoon ground cinnamon
- GLAZE:
- 1 cup confectioners' sugar
- 1 tablespoon butter, melted
- 5 to 6 teaspoons whole milk
- 1/8 teaspoon vanilla extract

Direction

- In a large bowl, combine dry ingredients. Cut in 4 tablespoons of the butter until mixture resembles coarse crumbs. Stir in milk just until moistened. Turn onto a lightly floured surface; knead gently 8-10 times. Roll into an 11x8-in. rectangle about 1/2 in. thick. Melt remaining butter; brush 1 tablespoon over dough. Combine sugar and cinnamon; sprinkle over butter. Roll up jelly-roll style, starting with long edge. Cut into 12 equal slices. Place with cut side down in a greased 8-in. square baking pan. Brush with remaining butter. Bake at 450 degrees for 18 to 20 minutes or until golden brown. Cool for 5 minutes. Combine glaze ingredients; spread over warm biscuits. Serve immediately.

Nutrition Information

- Calories: 201 calories
- Total Fat: 7g
- Cholesterol: 20mg
- Sodium: 308mg

- Total Carbohydrate: 31g
- Protein: 3g
- Fiber: 1g

168. Glazed Cranberry Biscuits

My family likes biscuits for breakfast. One Sunday, I decided to make those golden goodies extra special by adding white chips, dried cranberries and a simple orange glaze. --Lori Daniels, Beverly, West Virginia

Serving: about 1 dozen. | Prep: 30 m | Cook: 15 m | Ready in: 45 m

Ingredients

- 2 cups all-purpose flour
- 2 teaspoons baking powder
- 1/2 teaspoon salt
- 1/2 teaspoon grated orange zest
- 1/2 teaspoon ground cinnamon
- 1/4 cup shortening
- 1/4 cup cold butter
- 3/4 cup 2% milk
- 1/4 cup orange juice
- 1 cup dried cranberries
- 1/2 cup white baking chips
- DRIZZLE:
- 1-1/2 cups confectioners' sugar
- 2 tablespoons orange juice
- 1/4 teaspoon orange extract

Direction

- In a large bowl, combine the first five ingredients. Cut in shortening and butter until mixture resembles coarse crumbs. Stir in milk and orange juice just until moistened. Stir in cranberries and baking chips.
- Turn onto a lightly floured surface; knead gently 8-10 times. Pat or roll out to 3/4-in. thickness; cut with a floured 2-1/2-in. biscuit cutter.
- Place 2 in. apart on a greased baking sheet. Bake at 400 degrees for 12-16 minutes or until lightly browned. In a small bowl, combine the confectioners' sugar, orange juice and extract; drizzle over biscuits. Serve warm.

Nutrition Information

- Calories: 285 calories
- Total Fat: 11g
- Cholesterol: 12mg
- Sodium: 206mg
- Total Carbohydrate: 45g
- Protein: 3g
- Fiber: 1g

169. GlutenFree Biscuits

"You would never know these are gluten-free!"

Serving: 15 | Prep: 25 m | Cook: 15 m | Ready in: 40 m

Ingredients

- 1 1/2 cups sorghum flour
- 1 cup millet flour
- 1/2 cup tapioca starch
- 4 teaspoons baking powder
- 2 teaspoons xanthan gum
- 1 1/2 teaspoons baking soda
- 1 1/2 teaspoons salt
- 1/2 cup cold butter
- 1 cup milk
- 1 egg, beaten
- 1 tablespoon cider vinegar
- 2 tablespoons rice flour, or as needed

Direction

- Preheat oven to 350 degrees F (175 degrees C). Grease 1 baking sheet.
- Whisk sorghum flour, millet flour, tapioca starch, baking powder, xanthan gum, baking soda, and salt together in a large bowl. Cut in butter with a pastry blender or 2 knives until there are no large pieces left.
- Mix milk, egg, and vinegar together in a small bowl. Pour over flour and butter mixture; stir until dough comes together.
- Dust a flat work surface with rice flour. Roll dough out to 1/2-inch thickness; cut into 15

biscuits with a biscuit cutter. Arrange biscuits on the baking sheet.

- Bake in the preheated oven until the tops are golden brown, 15 to 20 minutes.

Nutrition Information

- Calories: 174 calories
- Total Fat: 7.2 g
- Cholesterol: 30 mg
- Sodium: 559 mg
- Total Carbohydrate: 23.7 g
- Protein: 3.8 g

170. Golden Biscuits

All you need is milk and Quick Baking Mix to make these flaky biscuits. They're wonderful served warm with butter and honey...or use as a base for creamed dishes.

Serving: 9 biscuits. | Prep: 10 m | Cook: 15 m | Ready in: 25 m

Ingredients

- 3 cups Quick Baking Mix
- 2/3 cup milk

Direction

- Place mix in a bowl. Add milk; stir just until combined. Turn onto a lightly floured surface; knead 10-15 times. Pat or roll out to 1/2-in. thickness; cut with a 2-1/2-in. biscuit cutter.
- Place 2 in. apart on ungreased baking sheets. Bake at 425 degrees for 12-14 minutes or until golden brown. Serve warm.

Nutrition Information

- Calories:
- Total Fat: g
- Cholesterol: mg
- Sodium: mg
- Total Carbohydrate: g
- Protein: g
- Fiber: g

171. Golden Butter Biscuits

"This is one of our favorite recipes," writes Pat Howard of Georgetown, Texas. "I keep the dough in the refrigerator and take it out just before the meal to bake. We love 'em hot from the oven."

Serving: 4 biscuits. | Prep: 15 m | Cook: 10 m | Ready in: 25 m

Ingredients

- 3/4 teaspoon active dry yeast
- 1 tablespoon warm water (110 degrees to 115 degrees)
- 1-1/4 cups all-purpose flour
- 1 tablespoon sugar
- 1 teaspoon baking powder
- 1/4 teaspoon salt
- 1/8 teaspoon baking soda
- 1/2 cup buttermilk
- 1 tablespoon canola oil
- 1 tablespoon butter, melted

Direction

- In a small bowl, dissolve yeast in warm water. In a large bowl, combine the flour, sugar, baking powder, salt and baking soda. Add the yeast mixture, buttermilk and oil; toss with a fork until dough forms a ball.
- Turn onto a lightly floured surface; knead 10-12 times. Roll out to 3/4-in. thickness; cut with a floured 2-1/2-in. biscuit cutter. Place 2 in. apart on a baking sheet coated with cooking spray. Brush with butter. Cover and let rise until doubled, about 30 minutes.
- Bake at 400 degrees for 10-15 minutes or until golden brown. Serve warm.

Nutrition Information

- Calories: 212 calories
- Total Fat: 6g
- Cholesterol: 5mg
- Sodium: 344mg
- Total Carbohydrate: 35g

- Protein: 5g
- Fiber: 1g

- Protein: g
- Fiber: g

172. Golden Sourdough Biscuits

I obtained this recipe from a friend when we were exchanging sourdough recipes a few years ago. These soft biscuits are best enjoyed straight from the oven. -- Stephanie Church, Delaware, Ohio

Serving: 1 dozen. | Prep: 15 m | Cook: 15 m | Ready in: 30 m

Ingredients

- 2 cups all-purpose flour
- 1 teaspoon baking powder
- 1 teaspoon salt
- 1/2 teaspoon baking soda
- 1/2 cup cold butter
- 1 cup Sourdough Starter
- 1/2 cup buttermilk
- Additional butter, melted

Direction

- In a large bowl, combine the flour, baking powder, salt and baking soda; cut in butter until mixture resembles coarse crumbs. Combine Sourdough Starter and buttermilk; stir into crumb mixture with a fork until dough forms a ball.
- Turn onto a well-floured surface; knead 10-12 times. Roll to 1/2-in. thickness. Cut with a floured 2-1/2-in. biscuit cutter. Place 2 in. apart on a greased baking sheet.
- Bake at 425 degrees for 12-15 minutes or until golden brown. Brush with melted butter. Remove from pan to a wire rack to cool.

Nutrition Information

- Calories:
- Total Fat: g
- Cholesterol: mg
- Sodium: mg
- Total Carbohydrate: g

173. Grandmas Baking Powder Biscuits

"This is my grandmother's biscuit recipe. It is my all-time favorite and has a really good flavor to it. Be sure not to roll out too thin, you want high biscuits! I usually just pat out the dough to the desired thickness, usually 1/2 inch."

Serving: 12 | Prep: 15 m | Cook: 10 m | Ready in: 25 m

Ingredients

- 2 cups all-purpose flour
- 2 tablespoons white sugar
- 4 teaspoons baking powder
- 1/2 teaspoon cream of tartar
- 1/2 teaspoon salt
- 1/2 cup vegetable shortening
- 1 egg
- 2/3 cup milk

Direction

- Preheat an oven to 450 degrees F (230 degrees C).
- Sift flour, sugar, baking powder, cream of tartar, and salt into a bowl. Use a pastry cutter to chop vegetable shortening into the flour mixture until it resembles coarse crumbs. Whisk egg and milk together in a separate bowl and slowly add milk mixture to flour mixture, stirring as you pour, until dough is moistened and well-mixed. Drop dough by spoonfuls onto an ungreased baking sheet.
- Bake in the preheated oven until biscuits have risen and are golden brown, 10 to 12 minutes.

Nutrition Information

- Calories: 173 calories
- Total Fat: 9.4 g
- Cholesterol: 17 mg
- Sodium: 271 mg
- Total Carbohydrate: 19.1 g
- Protein: 3.1 g

174. Grandmas Biscuits

Homemade biscuits add a warm and comforting touch to any meal. My grandmother makes these tender biscuits to go with her seafood chowder. --Melissa Obernesser, Utica, New York

Serving: 10 biscuits. | Prep: 15 m | Cook: 10 m | Ready in: 25 m

Ingredients

- 2 cups all-purpose flour
- 3 teaspoons baking powder
- 1 teaspoon salt
- 1/3 cup shortening
- 2/3 cup 2% milk
- 1 large egg, lightly beaten

Direction

- Preheat oven to 450 degrees. In a large bowl, whisk flour, baking powder and salt. Cut in shortening until mixture resembles coarse crumbs. Add milk; stir just until moistened.
- Turn onto a lightly floured surface; knead gently 8-10 times. Pat dough into a 10x4-in. rectangle. Cut rectangle lengthwise in half; cut crosswise to make 10 squares.
- Place 1 in. apart on an ungreased baking sheet; brush tops with egg. Bake 8-10 minutes or until golden brown. Serve warm.

Nutrition Information

- Calories: 165 calories
- Total Fat: 7g
- Cholesterol: 20mg
- Sodium: 371mg
- Total Carbohydrate: 20g
- Protein: 4g
- Fiber: 1g

175. Grandmas Sweet Potato Biscuits

The recipe for these mild-tasting biscuits was my grandmother's. They're a family favorite that we always serve at holidays. --Nancy Daugherty, Cortland, Ohio

Serving: 1-1/2 dozen. | Prep: 20 m | Cook: 10 m | Ready in: 30 m

Ingredients

- 2-1/2 cups all-purpose flour
- 1 tablespoon baking powder
- 1 teaspoon salt
- 1/3 cup shortening
- 1 can (15-3/4 ounces) sweet potatoes
- 3/4 cup whole milk

Direction

- In a large bowl, combine the flour, baking powder and salt. Cut in shortening until mixture resembles coarse crumbs. In another bowl, mash the sweet potatoes and milk. Add to the crumb mixture just until combined.
- Turn onto a floured surface; knead 8-10 times. Roll to 1/2-in. thickness; cut with a 2-1/2-in. biscuit cutter. Place on ungreased baking sheets.
- Bake at 425 degrees for 8-10 minutes or until golden brown. Remove to wire racks. Serve warm.

Nutrition Information

- Calories: 124 calories
- Total Fat: 4g
- Cholesterol: 1mg
- Sodium: 214mg
- Total Carbohydrate: 19g
- Protein: 2g
- Fiber: 1g

176. Greek Yogurt Biscuits

"No milk, no eggs, no problem. These biscuits utilize Greek yogurt for creaminess, and carbonated water or seltzer water for an added light flakiness! The result is a biscuit that melts in your mouth! Yum!"

Serving: 12 | Prep: 20 m | Cook: 10 m | Ready in: 35 m

Ingredients

- 2 cups all-purpose flour
- 2 tablespoons white sugar
- 2 teaspoons baking powder
- 1/2 teaspoon salt
- 1/4 teaspoon baking soda
- 1/2 cup cold butter, cut into small cubes
- 1/2 cup cold nonfat Greek yogurt
- 1/4 cup cold seltzer, or more as needed

Direction

- Preheat oven to 425 degrees F (220 degrees C). Line a baking sheet with parchment paper.
- Whisk flour, sugar, baking powder, salt, and baking soda together in a bowl. Cut in butter with a knife until mixture resembles coarse crumbs.
- Place the bowl in the freezer for 5 minutes.
- Stir in Greek yogurt until dough is combined. Add 1/4 cup seltzer; mix until dough is smooth. Add more seltzer if dough appears dry.
- Place dough on a floured piece of parchment paper and pat into a flat rectangle. Fold the rectangle in thirds. Rotate dough 90 degrees, gather any crumbs, and flatten into a rectangle again. Repeat folding, turning, and flattening twice more.
- Flatten dough to 1/2-inch thickness. Cut into twelve 2 1/2-inch rounds. Transfer rounds to a baking sheet.
- Bake in the preheated oven until golden brown, 10 to 15 minutes.

Nutrition Information

- Calories: 157 calories
- Total Fat: 7.9 g
- Cholesterol: 20 mg
- Sodium: 263 mg
- Total Carbohydrate: 18.6 g
- Protein: 3.1 g

177. Green Onion Biscuits

The savory flavor of green onions comes through in these easy drop biscuits that are best right out of the oven. They have a crusty exterior and soft interior. -Test Kitchen

Serving: 16 biscuits. | Prep: 10 m | Cook: 15 m | Ready in: 25 m

Ingredients

- 2 cups all-purpose flour
- 1 teaspoon baking powder
- 1/2 teaspoon salt
- 1/4 teaspoon baking soda
- 1/4 teaspoon onion powder
- 1 cup buttermilk
- 1/2 cup finely chopped green onions
- 3 tablespoons canola oil
- Refrigerated butter-flavored spray

Direction

- In a large bowl, combine the first five ingredients. Combine the buttermilk, onions and oil; stir into dry ingredients just until moistened.
- Drop by heaping teaspoonfuls 2 in. apart onto baking sheets coated with cooking spray. Spritz tops with butter-flavored spray. Bake at 400 degrees for 14-18 minutes or until golden brown. Serve warm.

Nutrition Information

- Calories: 85 calories
- Total Fat: 3g
- Cholesterol: 1mg
- Sodium: 124mg
- Total Carbohydrate: 12g
- Protein: 2g
- Fiber: 1g

178. Green Onion Drop Biscuits

These golden gems, developed by our Test Kitchen, are beyond scrumptious-crunchy on the outside and moist and tender inside. You'll want to save a few biscuits for mini ham sandwiches on Easter Monday. Feel free to substitute chives for green onions.

Serving: 10 servings. | Prep: 15 m | Cook: 15 m | Ready in: 30 m

Ingredients

- 2 cups all-purpose flour
- 1/2 cup thinly sliced green onions
- 2 teaspoons sugar
- 2 teaspoons baking powder
- 1/2 teaspoon salt
- 1/4 teaspoon baking soda
- 6 tablespoons cold butter, cubed
- 1 egg
- 3/4 cup buttermilk

Direction

- In a small bowl, combine the flour, onions, sugar, baking powder, salt and baking soda. Cut in butter until mixture resembles coarse crumbs. Combine egg and buttermilk; stir into crumb mixture just until moistened.
- Drop by 1/4 cupfuls 2 in. apart onto a greased baking sheet. Bake at 400 degrees for 12-15 minutes or until golden brown. Serve warm.

Nutrition Information

- Calories: 171 calories
- Total Fat: 8g
- Cholesterol: 40mg
- Sodium: 326mg
- Total Carbohydrate: 21g
- Protein: 4g
- Fiber: 1g

179. Ground Beef Pinwheels with Mushroom Sauce

"A favorite family recipe."

Serving: 5 | Prep: 20 m | Cook: 25 m | Ready in: 45 m

Ingredients

- Meat:
- 1 pound ground beef
- 1/2 onion, chopped
- 1 clove garlic, minced
- 1/4 teaspoon ground black pepper
- Pastry:
- 2 cups all-purpose flour
- 4 teaspoons baking powder
- 1 teaspoon salt
- 1/2 cup shortening
- 3/4 cup milk
- Mushroom Sauce:
- 2 (10.75 ounce) cans cream of mushroom soup
- 1 (10.75 ounce) can milk

Direction

- Preheat oven to 400 degrees F (200 degrees C).
- Heat a large skillet over medium-high heat. Cook and stir beef in the hot skillet until a bit of the fat renders, 2 to 3 minutes; add onion, garlic, and black pepper. Continue to cook and stir the beef mixture until the beef is browned completely, 3 to 5 minutes more.
- Combine flour, baking powder, and salt in a large bowl. Cut shortening into the flour mixture with a pastry cutter or fork. Slowly pour 3/4 cup milk into the mixture while stirring with a fork to form a soft dough; knead 8 to 10 times and roll out into a 12x8-inch rectangle.
- Spread the beef mixture in an even layer onto the pastry rectangle to cover, leaving one of the longer edges clear. Begin with longer end not left clear and roll pastry and filling tightly into a cylinder, pinching the edge left clear to seal.
- Use a thread to cut cylinder into ten 1 1/2-inch slices; arrange pinwheels onto a baking sheet.

- Bake in preheated oven until pastry is no longer doughy, 15 to 20 minutes.
- Stir cream of mushroom soup and 1 can of milk together in a saucepan; bring to a simmer and cook until hot, 2 to 3 minutes. Spoon over the baked pinwheels.

Nutrition Information

- Calories: 692 calories
- Total Fat: 41 g
- Cholesterol: 65 mg
- Sodium: 1736 mg
- Total Carbohydrate: 54.3 g
- Protein: 25.9 g

180. Ham Green Onion Biscuits

I started with my grandmother's biscuits and added a bit of my personality. When I make them with my kids, it feels like she's with us. --Amy Chase, Vanderhoof, British Columbia

Serving: about 1 dozen. | Prep: 20 m | Cook: 10 m | Ready in: 30 m

Ingredients

- 2 cups all-purpose flour
- 3 teaspoons baking powder
- 1 teaspoon sugar
- 1/4 teaspoon garlic salt
- Dash pepper
- 6 tablespoons cold butter, cubed
- 1 cup finely chopped fully cooked ham
- 2 green onions, chopped
- 3/4 cup 2% milk

Direction

- Preheat oven to 450 degrees. In a large bowl, whisk the first five ingredients. Cut in butter until mixture resembles coarse crumbs. Stir in ham and green onions. Add milk; stir just until moistened.
- Turn dough onto a lightly floured surface; knead gently 8-10 times. Pat or roll dough to

1/2-in. thickness; cut with a floured 2-1/2-in. biscuit cutter. Place 2 in. apart on an ungreased baking sheet. Bake 10-12 minutes or until golden brown. Serve warm.

Nutrition Information

- Calories: 151 calories
- Total Fat: 7g
- Cholesterol: 23mg
- Sodium: 315mg
- Total Carbohydrate: 17g
- Protein: 5g
- Fiber: 1g

181. Ham and Cheese Biscuits

These specially stuffed biscuits are a must throughout the year. I get asked to make them for school parties, bridal luncheons and holiday get-togethers.

Serving: 6-8 servings. | Prep: 15 m | Cook: 10 m | Ready in: 25 m

Ingredients

- 2 packages heat and serve pull-apart rolls (24 rolls)
- 1-1/2 pounds shaved fully cooked ham
- 6 slices (6 to 8 ounces) Swiss cheese, quartered
- 1/4 cup butter, melted
- 1 tablespoon prepared mustard
- 1/2 teaspoon Worcestershire sauce
- 1 tablespoon poppy seeds

Direction

- Separate rolls. Divide ham and cheese into 24 portions and place in the center of each roll. Place in a greased 13-in. x 9-in. baking pan.
- In a small bowl, combine the butter, mustard and Worcestershire sauce. Pour over rolls. Sprinkle with poppy seeds. Bake at 350 degrees for 10-15 minutes.

Nutrition Information

- Calories: 364 calories
- Total Fat: 18g
- Cholesterol: 48mg
- Sodium: 881mg
- Total Carbohydrate: 28g
- Protein: 17g
- Fiber: 2g

182. Ham and Swiss Biscuits

"These can be made ahead and frozen. To heat them up, place on an ungreased baking sheet in a 375° oven for 6 to 10 minutes or until heated through. They go great with the soup and salad." – Trisha Kruse, Eagle, Idaho

Serving: 10 biscuits. | Prep: 10 m | Cook: 10 m | Ready in: 20 m

Ingredients

- 2 cups biscuit/baking mix
- 1/4 pound fully cooked ham, finely chopped
- 1/2 cup shredded Swiss cheese
- 2/3 cup 2% milk
- 1 large egg, beaten
- 1 tablespoon honey mustard
- 2 teaspoons dried minced onion

Direction

- In a small bowl, combine the biscuit mix, ham and cheese. Combine the milk, egg, mustard and onion. Stir into biscuit mixture just until moistened. Drop by 1/4 cupfuls 2 in. apart onto a greased baking sheet.
- Bake at 425 degrees for 10-12 minutes or until golden brown. Serve warm. Refrigerate leftovers.

Nutrition Information

- Calories: 300 calories
- Total Fat: 13g
- Cholesterol: 63mg
- Sodium: 883mg
- Total Carbohydrate: 34g
- Protein: 13g

- Fiber: 1g

183. Ham Biscuits

Our home economists make ordinary biscuits them even heartier by stirring in ground ham. These handheld goodies are great fresh from the oven.

Serving: 10 biscuits. | Prep: 30 m | Cook: 15 m | Ready in: 45 m

Ingredients

- 1 cup cubed fully cooked ham
- 1 cup all-purpose flour
- 1 teaspoon baking powder
- 1/4 teaspoon baking soda
- 1/4 teaspoon each onion powder, garlic powder and ground mustard
- 3 tablespoons shortening
- 1 teaspoon minced chives
- 6 tablespoons buttermilk
- 1 tablespoon butter, melted

Direction

- In a food processor, process ham until ground; set aside. In a large bowl, combine the flour, baking powder, baking soda, onion powder, garlic powder and mustard. Cut in shortening until mixture is crumbly. Fold in ham and chives. Add buttermilk; stir just until the dough clings together.
- Turn onto a lightly floured surface; knead gently 10-12 times. Roll dough to 1/2-in. thickness. Cut with a floured 2-1/2-in. biscuit cutter. Place 1 in. apart on a greased baking sheet. Bake at 450 degrees for 13-15 minutes or until golden brown. Brush with butter. Serve warm.

Nutrition Information

- Calories: 116 calories
- Total Fat: 6g
- Cholesterol: 11mg
- Sodium: 272mg

- Total Carbohydrate: 10g
- Protein: 4g
- Fiber: 0 g

184. Ham Cheddar Biscuits

From Broken Arrow, Oklahoma, Sarah Marshall writes, "My husband often skipped breakfast until I created these savory biscuits that have become his favorite. I keep a batch in the freezer, and he reheats a few in the microwave on busy mornings.

Serving: 20 biscuits. | Prep: 10 m | Cook: 10 m | Ready in: 20 m

Ingredients

- 2-1/4 cups biscuit/baking mix
- 3/4 cup milk
- 3/4 cup shredded cheddar cheese
- 1/2 cup chopped fully cooked ham

Direction

- In a bowl, combine the biscuit mix and milk just until moistened. Stir in the cheese and ham. Drop by rounded tablespoonfuls onto greased baking sheets.
- Bake at 450 degrees for 8-10 minutes or until golden brown. Serve warm.

Nutrition Information

- Calories: 81 calories
- Total Fat: 4g
- Cholesterol: 8mg
- Sodium: 245mg
- Total Carbohydrate: 9g
- Protein: 3g
- Fiber: 0 g

185. Ham on Biscuits

I enjoy entertaining friends at luncheons. They always compliment me on these special little ham sandwiches made on cheesy homemade biscuits. Usually, I use Smithfield ham, but if salty ham is not your preference, any thin-sliced ham works well. --Betsy Hedeman, Timonium, Maryland

Serving: 8 sandwiches. | Prep: 20 m | Cook: 10 m | Ready in: 30 m

Ingredients

- 1 cup all-purpose flour
- 2 teaspoons sugar
- 1-1/8 teaspoons baking powder
- 1/4 teaspoon baking soda
- 1/8 teaspoon salt
- 2 tablespoons cold butter
- 1/2 cup 4% cottage cheese
- 1 egg
- 3 tablespoons milk
- 8 teaspoons butter, softened
- 1/2 pound sliced deli ham

Direction

- Preheat oven to 450 degrees. In a small bowl, combine flour, sugar, baking powder, baking soda and salt; cut in cold butter until mixture resembles coarse crumbs. In a small bowl, beat cottage cheese 2 minutes. Beat in egg and milk until blended. Stir into crumb mixture just until moistened.
- Turn onto a lightly floured surface; knead 8-10 times. Pat or roll out to 1/2-in. thickness; cut out eight biscuits with a floured 2-1/2-in. biscuit cutter.
- Place 1 in. apart on an ungreased baking sheet. Bake 8-12 minutes or until golden brown. Split biscuits in half; spread with softened butter. Place ham on biscuit bottoms; replace tops.

Nutrition Information

- Calories: 350 calories
- Total Fat: 18g
- Cholesterol: 121mg
- Sodium: 1021mg

- Total Carbohydrate: 29g
- Protein: 18g
- Fiber: 1g

186. Handy Sausage Biscuits

These are similar to old-fashioned biscuits made from scratch, but they're even better thanks to the tasty sausage throughout. It's almost impossible to stop eating them. I like to serve these biscuits with an egg dish or soup. -- Nancy Parker, Seguin, Texas

Serving: 2-3 dozen. | Prep: 25 m | Cook: 10 m | Ready in: 35 m

Ingredients

- 3/4 pound Jones No Sugar Pork Sausage Roll sausage
- 2-2/3 cups all-purpose flour
- 2 tablespoons sugar
- 1-1/2 teaspoons baking powder
- 1/2 teaspoon baking soda
- 1/2 teaspoon salt
- 1/2 cup shortening
- 1 package (1/4 ounce) active dry yeast
- 1/4 cup warm water (110 degrees to 115 degrees)
- 1 cup buttermilk
- Melted butter

Direction

- In a skillet, cook sausage over medium heat until no longer pink; drain well and set aside. In a bowl, combine flour, sugar, baking powder, baking soda and salt; cut in shortening until crumbly. Stir in the sausage.
- In another bowl, dissolve yeast in water; let stand for 5 minutes. Add buttermilk. Stir into dry ingredients just until moistened.
- On a lightly floured surface, gently knead dough 6-8 times. Roll out to 1/2-in. thickness; cut with a 2 in. biscuit cutter. Place on lightly greased baking sheets.

- Brush tops with butter. Bake at 450 degrees for 10-12 minutes or until golden brown. Serve warm.

Nutrition Information

- Calories: 83 calories
- Total Fat: 5g
- Cholesterol: 4mg
- Sodium: 113mg
- Total Carbohydrate: 8g
- Protein: 2g
- Fiber: 0 g

187. Heart Biscuits

"Mom always made heart-shaped biscuits for Valentine's Day," says Tina Christensen of Addison, Illinois. "When I realized how easy they were, I continued the tradition! They're great anytime of year served warm with a honey or cinnamon spread."

Serving: about 1 dozen. | Prep: 20 m | Cook: 12 m | Ready in: 32 m

Ingredients

- 2 cups all-purpose flour
- 1 tablespoon baking powder
- 1 teaspoon salt
- 1/2 cup cold butter
- 3/4 cup milk
- HONEY SPREAD:
- 1/2 cup butter, softened
- 1/4 cup honey
- CINNAMON SPREAD:
- 1/2 cup butter, softened
- 3/4 cup sugar
- 3 teaspoons ground cinnamon

Direction

- In a bowl, combine dry ingredients. Cut in butter until mixture resembles coarse crumbs. With a fork, stir in milk until the mixture forms a ball.

- Turn onto a lightly floured surface; knead five to six times. Roll to 1/2-in. thickness; cut with a 2-in. heart-shaped cookie or biscuit cutter. Place on an ungreased baking sheet. Bake at 450 degrees for 10-12 minutes or until golden brown.
- For honey spread, combine butter and honey in a bowl; beat until smooth. For cinnamon spread, combine butter, sugar and cinnamon in a bowl; beat until smooth. Serve with the warm biscuits.

Nutrition Information

- Calories: 357 calories
- Total Fat: 23g
- Cholesterol: 63mg
- Sodium: 536mg
- Total Carbohydrate: 35g
- Protein: 3g
- Fiber: 1g

188. Herb Biscuits

"This is a great recipe for showers, luncheons, or other parties. It can be easily doubled or tripled."

Serving: 8 | Prep: 10 m | Cook: 12 m | Ready in: 22 m

Ingredients

- 1 (12 ounce) package refrigerated buttermilk biscuit dough
- 1/2 cup melted butter
- 1 1/2 teaspoons dried parsley
- 1 1/2 teaspoons dried dill weed
- 1/4 teaspoon dried minced onion

Direction

- In a medium bowl, blend melted butter with the dried parsley, dill weed, and onion flakes.
- Cut buttermilk biscuits into quarters. Roll each biscuit quarter in herb butter. Place in 8 inch cake pan, with pieces touching. Pour remaining butter over biscuits.
- Bake in a 425 degree F (220 degrees C) oven for 12 minutes. Serve warm.

Nutrition Information

- Calories: 238 calories
- Total Fat: 17.2 g
- Cholesterol: 31 mg
- Sodium: 502 mg
- Total Carbohydrate: 18.4 g
- Protein: 3 g

189. Herb Buttermilk Biscuits

"Light and fluffy, melt-in-your-mouth goodness!"

Serving: 12 | Prep: 20 m | Cook: 8 m | Ready in: 28 m

Ingredients

- 2 cups sifted all-purpose flour
- 1 tablespoon baking powder
- 1 pinch salt
- 1 1/2 teaspoons white sugar
- 1 1/2 teaspoons dried thyme
- 1 1/2 teaspoons dried savory
- 1 teaspoon kelp powder
- 1 tablespoon dried parsley
- 1 tablespoon dried basil
- 1/3 cup unsalted butter, softened
- 3/4 cup buttermilk

Direction

- Preheat oven to 450 degrees F (230 degrees C). Whisk together the flour, baking powder, salt, sugar, thyme, savory, kelp, parsley, and basil in a large bowl.
- Cut in the butter with a knife or pastry blender until the mixture resembles coarse crumbs. Drizzle the buttermilk slowly over the flour mixture while tossing lightly with a fork, just until the flour mixture is moistened. Turn the dough out onto a floured board, and knead 4 to 5 times. Pat the dough into a circle, 3/4 inch thick, and cut biscuits with a 2 inch cookie cutter. Place biscuits 2 inches apart on a baking sheet.

- Bake in the preheated oven until golden brown, about 8 minutes. Serve warm.

Nutrition Information

- Calories: 133 calories
- Total Fat: 5.5 g
- Cholesterol: 14 mg
- Sodium: 147 mg
- Total Carbohydrate: 18 g
- Protein: 2.9 g

---

minutes or until lightly browned. Serve warm. Refrigerate any leftovers.

Nutrition Information

- Calories: 104 calories
- Total Fat: 5g
- Cholesterol: 22mg
- Sodium: 276mg
- Total Carbohydrate: 11g
- Protein: 3g
- Fiber: 0 g

---

190. Herb Sausage Biscuits

Flavored with sausage and cheese, these savory drop biscuits from Marion Lowery make a nice accompaniment to almost any meal. "The leftovers are great for breakfast- warm in the microwave in the morning when everyone is on the run," suggests the Medford, Oregon baker.

Serving: 14 biscuits. | Prep: 20 m | Cook: 10 m | Ready in: 30 m

Ingredients

- 1/4 pound Johnsonville TM ; Ground Mild Italian sausage
- 2 cups biscuit/baking mix
- 1/4 cup shredded cheddar cheese
- 2 teaspoons minced fresh oregano or 3/4 teaspoon dried oregano
- 2 teaspoons dried minced onion
- 1/2 teaspoon minced fresh cilantro
- 1 egg, lightly beaten
- 2/3 cup milk

Direction

- In a small skillet, cook sausage over medium heat until no longer pink; drain. In a large bowl, combine the biscuit mix, cheese, oregano, onion and cilantro. Whisk egg and milk; stir into dry ingredients just until moistened. Stir in sausage.
- Drop by heaping tablespoonfuls onto greased baking sheets. Bake at 425 degrees for 8-10

---

191. Herbed Biscuits

These savory biscuits bake up golden and tender. The blend of herb seasonings is irresistible. Keep the convenient seasoning mix on hand for a variety of uses.--Jane Everett, Pinehurst, North Carolina

Serving: 6 biscuits (1/2 cup seasoning mix). | Prep: 20 m | Cook: 10 m | Ready in: 30 m

Ingredients

- SEASONING MIX:
- 2 tablespoon each dried oregano, marjoram and basil
- 4 teaspoons dried savory
- 2 teaspoons dried rosemary, crushed
- 2 teaspoons rubbed sage
- BISCUITS:
- 1/4 cup chopped onion
- 2 tablespoons butter, divided
- 1-1/2 cups all-purpose flour
- 2 teaspoons baking powder
- 1/2 teaspoon salt
- 1/4 cup shortening
- 1 egg
- 1/3 cup milk
- 2 tablespoons grated Parmesan or Romano cheese

Direction

- Combine seasoning mix ingredients. Store in an airtight container in a cool, dry place.

- For biscuits, sauté 1 tablespoon mix and onion in 1 tablespoon butter in a skillet until onion is tender; set aside.
- In a bowl, combine flour, baking powder and salt. Cut in shortening until crumbly. Combine egg, milk and onion mixture; stir into dry ingredients just until moistened. Turn onto a floured surface; knead 10-15 times. Roll to 3/4-in. thickness; cut with a 2-1/2-in. biscuit cutter. Place on an ungreased baking sheet. Melt remaining butter; brush over biscuits. Sprinkle with cheese. Bake at 450 degrees for 10-14 minutes or until golden brown.

Nutrition Information

- Calories: 265 calories
- Total Fat: 14g
- Cholesterol: 49mg
- Sodium: 419mg
- Total Carbohydrate: 28g
- Protein: 6g
- Fiber: 3g

192. Herbed Sausage Gravy Over Cheese Biscuits

The gang at my house loves anything with biscuits, and this oregano flavored sausage gravy is the best we've ever tasted! It's a real favorite with my husband and two toddlers. --Lynn Crosby, Homerville, Ohio

Serving: 4 servings. | Prep: 20 m | Cook: 15 m | Ready in: 35 m

Ingredients

- 2-1/4 cups all-purpose flour
- 3 teaspoons baking powder
- 1/2 teaspoon salt
- 1/2 cup 2% milk
- 1/4 cup canola oil
- 1/2 teaspoon dried oregano
- 1 ounce part-skim mozzarella cheese, cut into 8 cubes (about 1/2-in.)
- GRAVY:
- 1/2 pound Jones No Sugar Pork Sausage Roll sausage
- 3/4 cup 2% milk
- 1 teaspoon dried oregano
- 1/4 cup all-purpose flour
- 1 cup cold water

Direction

- Preheat oven to 450 degrees. Whisk flour, baking powder and salt. Stir in milk and oil just until moistened. Turn onto a lightly floured surface; knead gently 8-10 times. Roll to 1/2-in. thickness; cut with a floured 2-1/2-in. biscuit cutter. Place a pinch of oregano in the center of each biscuit; top with a cheese cube.
- Moisten edge of dough with water and pull up over cheese, forming a pouch; pinch tightly to seal. Place seam side down on a lightly greased baking sheet, pressing lightly with hand. Bake until golden brown, 12-15 minutes.
- Meanwhile, in a large skillet, cook sausage over medium heat until no longer pink; drain. Stir in milk and oregano. Mix flour and water until smooth; add to sausage mixture. Bring to a boil; cook and stir until thickened, about 2 minutes. For each serving, spoon about 1/3 cup gravy over two biscuits.

Nutrition Information

- Calories: 626 calories
- Total Fat: 31g
- Cholesterol: 46mg
- Sodium: 1132mg
- Total Carbohydrate: 65g
- Protein: 20g
- Fiber: 2g

193. Herbed Sour Cream Biscuits

"Being a student can make cooking impossible," writes Audrey Hurd of Fountain Hills, Arizona. "So I took an easy biscuit recipe and added an herb mixture of my own...and voila! These tender rolls make my quick home meals a real treat."

Serving: 6 biscuits. | Prep: 15 m | Cook: 10 m | Ready in: 25 m

Ingredients

- 1 cup biscuit/baking mix
- 1/2 teaspoon sugar
- 1 garlic clove, minced
- Dash dried rosemary, crushed
- 1/4 teaspoon dried basil
- 1/4 cup club soda
- 2 tablespoons sour cream

Direction

- In a small bowl, combine the biscuit mix, sugar, garlic, rosemary and basil. Combine club soda and sour cream; stir into dry ingredients just until moistened.
- Drop by heaping tablespoonfuls 2 in. apart onto a baking sheet coated with cooking spray. Bake at 400 degrees for 10-12 minutes or until golden brown. Serve warm.

Nutrition Information

- Calories: 94 calories
- Total Fat: 4g
- Cholesterol: 3mg
- Sodium: 257mg
- Total Carbohydrate: 13g
- Protein: 2g
- Fiber: 0 g

194. Herman Biscuits

"This is a great biscuit recipe for using Herman sourdough starter."

Serving: 12 | Prep: 15 m | Cook: 30 m | Ready in: 2 h

Ingredients

- 1 cup Herman Sourdough Starter
- 1 cup all-purpose flour
- 1/4 teaspoon baking soda
- 2 teaspoons baking powder
- 1/4 teaspoon salt
- 1/4 cup vegetable oil

Direction

- Bring Herman Starter to room temperature.
- Stir together flour, baking soda, baking powder and salt.
- Stir flour mixture and oil into Herman Starter. It will form a soft dough.
- On a lightly floured surface knead dough until smooth. Pinch off small pieces of dough and shape into balls OR roll dough out and cut with a biscuit cutter. Place biscuits onto a greased baking sheet, cover and let rise in a warm place for 1 hour.
- Preheat oven to 350 degrees F (175 degrees C).
- Bake in biscuits in the preheat oven for about 30 minutes or until golden. Serve warm.

Nutrition Information

- Calories: 79 calories
- Total Fat: 4.7 g
- Cholesterol: 0 mg
- Sodium: 156 mg
- Total Carbohydrate: 8.2 g
- Protein: 1.1 g

195. HighRise Buttermilk Biscuits

"This recipe comes from chats with friends and many weekend mornings of making biscuits. Pay close attention to technique -- it is certainly as important as the ingredients -- and you'll surely make a moist, airy, tasty biscuit with good rise. Important: Use fresh, aluminum-free baking powder; this is less salty than regular baking powder and allows you to add more without affecting taste."

Serving: 9 | Prep: 30 m | Cook: 14 m | Ready in: 54 m

Ingredients

- 4 cups cake flour
- 2 1/2 tablespoons aluminum-free baking powder
- 2 teaspoons salt
- 1/2 cup cold unsalted butter, cut into small chunks
- 1 1/3 cups buttermilk, or more as needed
- 1 tablespoon salted butter, melted

Direction

- Preheat oven to 500 degrees F (260 degrees C).
- Mix flour, baking powder, and salt together in the bowl of a stand mixer with a paddle attachment. Add unsalted butter and mix at medium speed until well incorporated and the mixture resembles wet sand, about 4 minutes.
- Remove the bowl from the mixer and fold in buttermilk until dough sticks together.
- Dump dough onto a flour work surface; pat into a rectangle. Pat remaining dry crumbs into the mixture by hand.
- Cut dough in half with a floured bench knife; stack cut halves on top of each other. Press layers together to about 1 1/2-inch thickness, shaping a long rectangle as you go. Repeat 3 to 5 times.
- Cut dough into 8 even squares with the bench knife. Cut off uneven edges and put these scraps to the side; clean cuts on all sides will encourage rise. Pat scraps together to make 1 odd-shaped ninth biscuit.
- Place biscuits close together in a 9-inch square pan and brush with melted salted butter. Place pan on top of the warm stove for 10 to 15 minutes to rise.
- Bake biscuits in the preheated oven, checking halfway through bake time, until tops are golden brown and a toothpick inserted into the center comes out clean, 14 to 18 minutes.

Nutrition Information

- Calories: 349 calories
- Total Fat: 12.4 g
- Cholesterol: 32 mg
- Sodium: 973 mg
- Total Carbohydrate: 52.5 g
- Protein: 6.5 g

196. Holiday Breakfast Sandwiches

"These have become a Christmas morning tradition that I have shared with many people. Taste like apple pie for breakfast!"

Serving: 8 | Prep: 15 m | Cook: 15 m | Ready in: 30 m

Ingredients

- 1/3 cup firmly packed brown sugar
- 2 tablespoons all-purpose flour
- 1/2 teaspoon ground cinnamon
- 1 (10 ounce) can refrigerated biscuit dough
- 1 cup shredded sharp Cheddar cheese
- 2 large Granny Smith apples - peeled, cored, and cut into rings
- 1 tablespoon margarine, melted

Direction

- Preheat oven to 350 degrees F (175 degrees C). Lightly grease a baking sheet.
- Whisk brown sugar, flour, and cinnamon together in a bowl.
- Remove biscuit dough from the can and separate into biscuits. Press into 3-inch circles on the prepared baking sheet. Sprinkle Cheddar cheese over each circle; top with

apple rings. Sprinkle brown sugar mixture evenly over apple rings. Drizzle margarine on top.

- Bake in the preheated oven until biscuits are lightly browned, about 15 minutes.

Nutrition Information

- Calories: 260 calories
- Total Fat: 11.8 g
- Cholesterol: 18 mg
- Sodium: 475 mg
- Total Carbohydrate: 32.5 g
- Protein: 7 g

197. Homemade Biscuit Mix

"Add a few simple ingredients, bake, and viola! You'll have hot, tasty homemade biscuits fast!"

Serving: 48 | Prep: 15 m | Ready in: 15 m

Ingredients

- 10 cups all-purpose flour
- 1/2 cup baking powder
- 2 tablespoons white sugar
- 2 teaspoons salt
- 1 1/4 cups vegetable oil

Direction

- Combine flour, baking powder, sugar and salt in a mixing bowl. Add oil and mix with a fork or pastry blender; you should have small lumps throughout the mixture.
- Store in an airtight container in a cool, dry place for up to three months.

Nutrition Information

- Calories: 148 calories
- Total Fat: 5.9 g
- Cholesterol: 0 mg
- Sodium: 341 mg
- Total Carbohydrate: 21 g
- Protein: 2.7 g

198. Homemade Buttermilk Biscuits

These old-fashioned biscuits from Bonita Coleman of Camarillo, California are simple to make and rich in homemade taste.

Serving: 4 biscuits. | Prep: 10 m | Cook: 10 m | Ready in: 20 m

Ingredients

- 3/4 cup all-purpose flour
- 1 teaspoon baking powder
- 1/8 teaspoon salt
- 2 tablespoons butter-flavored shortening
- 1/4 cup buttermilk

Direction

- In a small bowl, combine the flour, baking powder and salt. Cut in shortening until mixture resembles coarse crumbs. Stir in buttermilk just until moistened.
- Turn onto a lightly floured surface; knead 5-7 times. Pat or roll out to 1/2-in. thickness; cut with a 2-1/2-in. biscuit cutter.
- Place on a baking sheet coated with cooking spray. Bake at 450 degrees for 10-12 minutes or until golden brown. Serve warm.

Nutrition Information

- Calories: 146 calories
- Total Fat: 6g
- Cholesterol: 1mg
- Sodium: 190mg
- Total Carbohydrate: 19g
- Protein: 3g
- Fiber: 1g

199. Homemade Cheese Biscuits

These savory biscuits from Lynn Tice of Osage City, Kansas couldn't be simpler to make! With from-scratch flavor and a golden-brown cheese topping, they're sure to be a hit.

Serving: 10 biscuits. | Prep: 15 m | Cook: 10 m | Ready in: 25 m

Ingredients

- 1 tube (12 ounces) refrigerated buttermilk biscuits
- 1/4 cup prepared Italian salad dressing
- 1/3 cup grated Parmesan cheese
- 1/2 cup shredded part-skim mozzarella cheese

Direction

- Separate biscuits; dip the top of each in salad dressing, then in Parmesan cheese. Place cheese side up on an ungreased baking sheet; sprinkle with mozzarella cheese.
- Bake at 400 degrees for 9-11 minutes or until golden brown. Serve warm.

Nutrition Information

- Calories: 130 calories
- Total Fat: 5g
- Cholesterol: 6mg
- Sodium: 459mg
- Total Carbohydrate: 17g
- Protein: 5g
- Fiber: 0 g

200. Honey Biscuits

These lightly sweet biscuits are a great complement to all sorts of stews, soups, and chilies. Monterey Jack cheese adds an extra layer of flavor in these flaky bites.

Serving: about 1 dozen. | Prep: 20 m | Cook: 10 m | Ready in: 30 m

Ingredients

- 2 cups all-purpose flour
- 3 teaspoons baking powder
- 1 teaspoon salt
- 1/2 cup plus 1 tablespoon cold butter, divided
- 3/4 cup milk
- 1/2 cup shredded Monterey Jack cheese
- 1 tablespoon honey

Direction

- In a bowl, combine the flour, baking powder and salt. Cut in 1/2 cup butter until mixture resembles coarse crumbs. Stir in milk and cheese until mixture forms a ball.
- Turn onto a lightly floured surface; knead 5-6 times. Roll out to 1/2-in. thickness; cut with a floured 2-in. biscuit cutter. Place on an ungreased baking sheet.
- In a small microwave-safe bowl, combine honey and remaining butter. Microwave on high until melted. Brush over biscuits. Bake at 450 degrees for 10-12 minutes or until golden brown. Serve warm.

Nutrition Information

- Calories: 314 calories
- Total Fat: 18g
- Cholesterol: 50mg
- Sodium: 714mg
- Total Carbohydrate: 31g
- Protein: 7g
- Fiber: 1g

201. Honey Butter Biscuits

"These biscuits are rolled up with honey butter to make them sweet and delicious."

Serving: 12 | Prep: 20 m | Cook: 12 m | Ready in: 32 m

Ingredients

- 2 cups all-purpose flour
- 2 teaspoons baking powder
- 1 teaspoon salt
- 1/3 cup vegetable shortening
- 3/4 cup milk

- 1/2 cup honey
- 1/2 cup butter

Direction

- Preheat oven to 350 degrees F (175 degrees C).
- Sift flour, baking powder, and salt together into a bowl. Combine shortening with flour mixture using fingers until the mixture is crumbly and resembles cornmeal. Stir milk in gradually until dough is well combined.
- Place dough on a floured surface; shape into a 1/2-inch thick rectangle about 12 inches wide.
- Put honey and butter into a microwave-safe bowl; microwave until melted, 15 to 20 seconds. Stir.
- Spread 1/2 the honey-butter mixture on the dough surface; roll up like a jellyroll and cut into 12 slices, about 1 inch thick. Arrange biscuits on a baking sheet 1/2-inch apart; spread remaining honey-butter on each.
- Bake in the preheated oven until golden, 12 to 15 minutes.

Nutrition Information

- Calories: 246 calories
- Total Fat: 13.9 g
- Cholesterol: 25 mg
- Sodium: 337 mg
- Total Carbohydrate: 28.5 g
- Protein: 2.8 g

202. Honey Sweet Potato Biscuits

I make at least one batch of these hearty biscuits each week. They pair perfectly with soups, stews and even breakfast entrees!--Mary Ellen Swanson, Rainsville, Alabama

Serving: 10 biscuits. | Prep: 20 m | Cook: 15 m | Ready in: 35 m

Ingredients

- 1 cup plus 3 tablespoons all-purpose flour
- 3/4 cup whole wheat flour
- 1/2 cup toasted wheat germ

- 2 teaspoons baking powder
- 1/2 teaspoon baking soda
- 1/2 teaspoon salt
- 1-1/4 cups buttermilk
- 2/3 cup mashed sweet potato
- 1/4 cup butter, melted
- 2 tablespoons honey

Direction

- In a large bowl, combine the first six ingredients. In another bowl, whisk the buttermilk, sweet potato, butter and honey; stir into dry ingredients just until moistened.
- Turn onto a lightly floured surface; knead 8-10 times. Pat or roll out to 3/4-in. thickness; cut with a floured 2-1/2-in. biscuit cutter.
- Place 2 in. apart on a greased baking sheet. Bake at 400 degrees for 15-20 minutes or until golden brown. Serve warm.

Nutrition Information

- Calories: 185 calories
- Total Fat: 6g
- Cholesterol: 13mg
- Sodium: 332mg
- Total Carbohydrate: 29g
- Protein: 6g
- Fiber: 3g

203. HoneyGlazed Drop Biscuits

A handful of ingredients are all you'll need for these moist biscuits brushed with a sweet glaze. "I make these easy biscuits for my church and by special request," says Diane Patton of Toledo, Ohio. "I made 350 the last time!" Diane adds, "I use a small ice cream scoop to drop the batter onto pans."

Serving: 16 biscuits. | Prep: 10 m | Cook: 10 m | Ready in: 20 m

Ingredients

- 3-1/4 cups self-rising flour
- 1 cup milk
- 1/2 cup mayonnaise
- 1/2 cup honey

- 1/2 cup butter, melted

Direction

- In a large bowl, combine the flour, milk and mayonnaise just until moistened. Turn onto a lightly floured surface; knead 8-10 times. Drop by tablespoonfuls 2 in. apart onto a greased baking sheet.
- Bake at 425 degrees for 10-14 minutes or until golden brown. Combine honey and butter; brush 1/2 cup over hot biscuits. Serve warm with remaining honey butter.

Nutrition Information

- Calories: 223 calories
- Total Fat: 12g
- Cholesterol: 20mg
- Sodium: 396mg
- Total Carbohydrate: 27g
- Protein: 3g
- Fiber: 0 g

204. How to Make Cream Biscuits

"Not only is this one of America's greatest biscuit recipes, it's also by far the easiest. If you can stir, you can make cream biscuits. They are so light, moist, flaky, and perfect, you're going to be shocked."

Serving: 10 | Prep: 15 m | Cook: 10 m | Ready in: 25 m

Ingredients

- 2 cups self-rising flour
- 1 tablespoon white sugar
- 1 1/2 cups heavy whipping cream
- 2 tablespoons butter, melted, or as needed

Direction

- Move an oven rack to the enter position of your oven; preheat oven to 500 degrees F (260 degrees C). Line a baking sheet with aluminum foil.
- Combine self-rising flour and sugar in a mixing bowl; stir in cream until almost all the flour has been incorporated and dough is wet and sticky.
- Turn dough onto a well-floured work surface and gently press it into a rectangle about 1/2-inch thick. Use a bench scraper to lift up ends of dough and fold dough into thirds. Press dough again into a thick rectangle.
- Roll dough out into a 6x10-inch rectangle about 1/2-inch thick. Cut rounds from the dough using a 3-inch biscuit cutter. Gently press dough scraps together into a thick disk, roll out 1/2-inch thick, and cut 3 more biscuits. If any dough remains, lightly press it flat and cut one more biscuit from the remaining dough.
- Arrange biscuits on prepared baking sheet. Brush tops of biscuits generously with melted butter.
- Bake in the preheated oven until biscuits are golden brown, 10 to 12 minutes. Brush hot biscuits with melted butter again and let stand 2 to 3 minutes to cool slightly before serving.

Nutrition Information

- Calories: 237 calories
- Total Fat: 15.8 g
- Cholesterol: 55 mg
- Sodium: 347 mg
- Total Carbohydrate: 20.8 g
- Protein: 3.2 g

205. HurryUp Biscuits

When I was young, my mom would make these biscuits with fresh cream she got from a local farmer. I don't go to those lengths, but the family recipe is still a real treat. -- Beverly Sprague, Baltimore, Maryland

Serving: 1 dozen. | Prep: 10 m | Cook: 20 m | Ready in: 30 m

Ingredients

- 3 cups all-purpose flour
- 4 teaspoons baking powder

- 4 teaspoons sugar
- 1 teaspoon salt
- 2 cups heavy whipping cream

Direction

- Preheat oven to 375 degrees. In a large bowl, whisk flour, baking powder, sugar and salt. Add cream; stir just until moistened.
- Drop by 1/4 cupfuls 1 in. apart onto greased baking sheets. Bake 17-20 minutes or until bottoms are golden brown. Serve warm.

Nutrition Information

- Calories: 256 calories
- Total Fat: 15g
- Cholesterol: 54mg
- Sodium: 346mg
- Total Carbohydrate: 26g
- Protein: 4g
- Fiber: 1g

206. Iced Cinnamon Biscuits

In Grand Valley, Ontario, Wendy Masters serves these biscuits oven-fresh for breakfast or brunch. "They are wonderfully light and have an appealing cinnamon flavor," she says. "The plump raisins and simple icing add the right touch of sweetness."

Serving: about 1 dozen. | Prep: 15 m | Cook: 15 m | Ready in: 30 m

Ingredients

- 2 cups all-purpose flour
- 1/4 cup sugar
- 1 tablespoon baking powder
- 1 teaspoon salt
- 1 teaspoon ground cinnamon
- 1/4 teaspoon baking soda
- 1/3 cup shortening
- 1/2 cup raisins
- 3/4 cup buttermilk
- ICING:
- 1/3 cup confectioners' sugar

- 1 to 2 teaspoons milk

Direction

- In a bowl, combine the first six ingredients; cut in shortening until mixture resembles coarse crumbs. Stir in raisins. Add buttermilk; stir just until moistened. Turn onto a lightly floured surface; knead 4-5 times. Roll to 1/2-in. thickness; cut with a 2-1/2-in. biscuit cutter. Place with sides barely touching on a greased baking sheet. Bake at 425 degrees for 12-17 minutes or until golden brown. Combine the icing ingredients; drizzle over biscuits. Serve warm.

Nutrition Information

- Calories: 179 calories
- Total Fat: 6g
- Cholesterol: 1mg
- Sodium: 340mg
- Total Carbohydrate: 29g
- Protein: 3g
- Fiber: 1g

207. Iced Cinnamon Raisin Biscuits

"A quick and easy breakfast item reminiscent of a famous fast-food version."

Serving: 12 | Prep: 15 m | Cook: 10 m | Ready in: 25 m

Ingredients

- Biscuits:
- 2 1/2 cups baking mix (such as Bisquick®)
- 2 tablespoons white sugar
- 1 teaspoon ground cinnamon
- 2/3 cup milk
- 1/2 cup raisins
- Glaze:
- 2/3 cup confectioners' sugar
- 1 teaspoon warm water
- 1/4 teaspoon vanilla extract

Direction

- Preheat oven to 450 degrees F (230 degrees C).
- Whisk baking mix, white sugar, and cinnamon together in a bowl; stir in milk until dough is just combined. Fold raisins into dough. Knead dough about 10 times and roll out to 1/2-inch thickness. Cut round biscuits using a biscuit cutter or cookie cutter; arrange on a baking sheet.
- Bake in the preheated oven until lightly browned, 8 to 10 minutes.
- Stir confectioners' sugar, water, and vanilla extract together until glaze is smooth; drizzle over warm biscuits.

Nutrition Information

- Calories: 165 calories
- Total Fat: 4.1 g
- Cholesterol: 1 mg
- Sodium: 321 mg
- Total Carbohydrate: 30.7 g
- Protein: 2.4 g

208. Iced Raisin Biscuits

Whip up a warm, mouthwatering breakfast treat in a snap! Sweet raisins and maple syrup bring out the best in this seasonally-inspired spice blend.

Serving: 10 biscuits. | Prep: 20 m | Cook: 15 m | Ready in: 35 m

Ingredients

- 2 cups all-purpose flour
- 1 tablespoon sugar
- 3 teaspoons baking powder
- 1 teaspoon ground cinnamon
- 1/2 teaspoon salt
- 1/8 teaspoon ground nutmeg
- 1/2 cup cold butter, cubed
- 1/3 cup raisins
- 1/2 cup 2% milk
- 3 tablespoons maple syrup

- ICING:
- 1/2 cup confectioners' sugar
- 1/8 teaspoon rum extract
- 2-1/4 teaspoons 2% milk

Direction

- In a large bowl, combine the first six ingredients. Cut in butter until mixture resembles coarse crumbs. Add raisins. In a small bowl, combine milk and syrup; stir into crumb mixture just until moistened.
- Turn onto a lightly floured surface; knead 8-10 times. Pat or roll out to 1/2-in. thickness; cut with a floured 2-1/2-in. biscuit cutter.
- Place 1 in. apart on an ungreased baking sheet. Bake at 450 degrees for 12-15 minutes or until golden brown.
- Meanwhile, combine the confectioners' sugar, extract and enough milk to achieve desired consistency. Drizzle over warm biscuits. Serve warm.

Nutrition Information

- Calories: 239 calories
- Total Fat: 10g
- Cholesterol: 25mg
- Sodium: 310mg
- Total Carbohydrate: 35g
- Protein: 3g
- Fiber: 1g

209. Individual Orange Cranberry Biscuits

Perfect for a holiday brunch or a breakfast treat for houseguests, these tender biscuits are bursting with tart cranberries, orange zest, and the gentle perfume of vanilla.

Serving: 12 biscuits | Prep: 15 m | Cook: 1 h 10 m

Ingredients

- 1 1/4 cups (150 g) whole wheat flour, preferably homemade

- 1 cup (125 g) unbleached all-purpose flour
- 2 1/4 teaspoons baking powder
- 1/2 teaspoon baking soda
- 1/4 teaspoon sea salt
- 1 1/4 cups (300 ml) plain 0% Greek yogurt, stirred
- 1/4 cup (60 ml) fresh orange juice
- 1/3 cup firmly packed (73 g) light brown sugar
- 1 tablespoon grated orange zest
- 1 teaspoon vanilla extract
- 1 cup (100 g) frozen cranberries, coarsely chopped
- 1/4 cup (60 ml) reduced-fat (2%) milk

Direction

- Preheat the oven to 400°F (200°C). Line a baking sheet with parchment paper or a silicone baking mat.
- Combine the flours, baking powder, baking soda, and salt in a medium bowl.
- Place the yogurt, orange juice, brown sugar, orange zest, and vanilla into the Vitamix container in the order listed and secure the lid. Select Variable 1. Turn the machine on and slowly increase the speed to Variable 10, then to High. Blend for 20 seconds.
- Pour the yogurt mixture into the flour mixture and fold in the cranberries.
- On a floured surface, pat the dough into a 9-inch (23-cm) round about 1/2 inch (1.3 cm) thick. Cut into 12 wedges.
- Place the wedges on the baking sheet and brush the tops with the milk. Bake for 30 to 35 minutes, until lightly browned.
- Remove from the baking sheet and cool on a wire rack.
- Amount per biscuit: calories 130, total fat 0.5 g, saturated fat 0 g, cholesterol 0 mg, sodium 210 mg, total carbohydrate 26 g, dietary fiber 2 g, sugars 8 g, protein 5 g

210. Irish Cheddar Spring Onion Biscuits

"By layering and folding the cheese into the dough, à la puff pastry, we get all the cheesy flavor without making the biscuit too dense."

Serving: 6 | Prep: 20 m | Cook: 20 m | Ready in: 40 m

Ingredients

- 2 cups self-rising flour, plus more for kneading
- 1/4 teaspoon baking soda
- 7 tablespoons very cold butter, cut into pieces
- 3/4 cup buttermilk, plus additional for brushing
- 1/2 cup shredded Irish Cheddar cheese, divided, plus more for topping
- 1/4 cup sliced green onions, divided

Direction

- Preheat oven to 400 degrees F (200 degrees C). Line a baking sheet with parchment paper.
- Whisk self-rising flour and baking soda together in a mixing bowl. Add cold butter and cut it into flour with a pastry blender until texture resembles coarse crumbs, 5 to 7 minutes. Make a well in the center of the flour mixture and pour in the buttermilk. Stir with a fork just until mixture starts to come together to form a shaggy dough.
- Transfer dough to a floured work surface. Press into a roughly shaped rectangle. Fold into thirds using a bench scraper. Press again into a rectangle. Flour surface if the dough seems sticky. Roll dough with a rolling pin to 1/2-inch thickness. Sprinkle with half of the shredded cheese and half of the green onions. Fold dough into thirds. Dust with flour, if necessary, and roll out again to about 1/2-inch thickness. Top with remaining cheese and green onions. Fold into thirds and roll out again to about 1/2 inch thickness. Cut biscuits with a 2- or 3-inch biscuit cutter.
- Transfer biscuits to prepared baking sheet. Brush lightly with buttermilk. Sprinkle tops with about a teaspoon of grated cheese.

- Bake in preheated oven until cooked through and golden brown, about 20 minutes. Transfer to a rack to cool.

Nutrition Information

- Calories: 318 calories
- Total Fat: 17.2 g
- Cholesterol: 47 mg
- Sodium: 768 mg
- Total Carbohydrate: 32.8 g
- Protein: 7.7 g

211. Italian Drop Biscuits

I'd been making garlic cheese biscuits for years before I tried spicing them up with some green chilies. These biscuits go well with soups as well as Mexican and Italian foods. -LaDonna Reed Ponca City, Oklahoma

Serving: 1-1/2 dozen. | Prep: 10 m | Cook: 10 m | Ready in: 20 m

Ingredients

- 2 cups biscuit/baking mix
- 1 cup shredded cheddar cheese
- 1/2 cup cold water
- 2 tablespoons chopped green chilies
- 1/4 cup butter, melted
- 1 teaspoon dried parsley flakes
- 1/2 teaspoon Italian seasoning
- 1/4 teaspoon garlic powder

Direction

- In a large bowl, combine the biscuit mix, cheese, water and chilies just until moistened. Drop by heaping tablespoonfuls onto a greased baking sheet.
- Bake at 450 degrees for 8-10 minutes or until golden brown. In a small bowl, combine the butter, parsley, Italian seasoning and garlic powder; brush over warm biscuits.

Nutrition Information

- Calories: 99 calories
- Total Fat: 6g
- Cholesterol: 13mg
- Sodium: 235mg
- Total Carbohydrate: 9g
- Protein: 2g
- Fiber: 0 g

212. ItalianStyle Drop Biscuits

My husband and I worked together to create this recipe by adding green chilies to our favorite garlic-cheese biscuits. They're even better this way!--LaDonna Reed, Ponca City, Oklahoma

Serving: 6 biscuits. | Prep: 10 m | Cook: 10 m | Ready in: 20 m

Ingredients

- 1 cup biscuit/baking mix
- 1/2 cup shredded cheddar cheese
- 2 tablespoons chopped green chilies
- 1/4 cup cold water
- 4 teaspoons butter, melted
- 1/2 teaspoon dried parsley flakes
- 1/4 teaspoon garlic powder
- 1/4 teaspoon Italian seasoning

Direction

- In a small bowl, combine the biscuit mix, cheese and chilies. Stir in water until a soft dough forms.
- Drop dough into six mounds 2 in. apart on a baking sheet coated with cooking spray. Bake at 450 degrees for 8-10 minutes or until golden brown.
- In a small bowl, combine the butter, parsley, garlic powder and Italian seasoning. Brush over biscuits. Serve warm.

Nutrition Information

- Calories: 115 calories

- Total Fat: 5g
- Cholesterol: 11mg
- Sodium: 320mg
- Total Carbohydrate: 15g
- Protein: 4g
- Fiber: 0 g

213. Jalapeno Cheddar Biscuits

These tender biscuits with a cheesy richness have a nice level of heat that will appeal to all ages. — Florence McNulty, Montebello, California

Serving: 15 biscuits. | Prep: 10 m | Cook: 15 m | Ready in: 25 m

Ingredients

- 2 cups all-purpose flour
- 3 teaspoons baking powder
- 1/2 teaspoon salt
- 1/2 teaspoon dried thyme
- 1/2 teaspoon paprika
- 5 tablespoons cold butter
- 3/4 cup 2% milk
- 1 cup shredded sharp cheddar cheese
- 3 tablespoons diced pickled jalapeno slices

Direction

- In a large bowl, combine the flour, baking powder, salt, thyme and paprika. Cut in butter until mixture resembles coarse crumbs. Stir in the milk, cheese and jalapeno.
- Turn onto a lightly floured surface; knead 8-10 times. Pat or roll out to 1/2-in. thickness; cut with a floured 2-1/2-in. biscuit cutter. Place 2 in. apart on an ungreased baking sheet.
- Bake at 450 degrees for 12-14 minutes or until golden brown. Serve warm.

Nutrition Information

- Calories: 129 calories
- Total Fat: 6g
- Cholesterol: 19mg
- Sodium: 276mg

- Total Carbohydrate: 14g
- Protein: 4g
- Fiber: 1g

214. Jam Biscuits

My teenage granddaughter, Holly, and I have enjoyed cooking together since she was 4 years old. We like to make these golden biscuits for holiday gatherings. Fill the centers with homemade jam, orange marmalade or cheese. --Mary Lindsay, Dunrango, Colorado

Serving: about 2-1/2 dozen. | Prep: 30 m | Cook: 20 m | Ready in: 50 m

Ingredients

- 4 teaspoons active dry yeast
- 5 tablespoons warm water (110 degrees to 115 degrees)
- 5 cups all-purpose flour
- 1/4 cup sugar
- 4 teaspoons baking powder
- 1 teaspoon salt
- 1/4 teaspoon baking soda
- 1 cup shortening
- 1-1/2 cups warm buttermilk (110 degrees to 115 degrees)
- Raspberry or plum jelly or jam

Direction

- In a small bowl, dissolve yeast in warm water; set aside. In a large bowl, combine the flour, sugar, baking powder, salt and baking soda; cut in shortening until mixture resembles coarse crumbs. Add yeast mixture to buttermilk; stir into dry ingredients until combined.
- Turn dough onto a lightly floured surface. Knead 5-6 times. Roll or pat to 1/2-in. thickness. Cut with a 2-1/2-in. biscuit cutter. Cut a 1-in. slit at an angle halfway through center of each biscuit. Separate dough at cut; fill with 1/4 to 1/2 teaspoon of jelly or jam. Place on ungreased baking sheets (do not let

rise). Bake at 400 degrees for 16-20 minutes or until golden brown.

Nutrition Information

- Calories: 147 calories
- Total Fat: 7g
- Cholesterol: 0 mg
- Sodium: 156mg
- Total Carbohydrate: 18g
- Protein: 3g
- Fiber: 1g

215. Jamaican Fried Dumplings

"Flat fried buttery dough usually served with cod fish in Jamaica, as a big weekend breakfast, slightly different from the American dumplings."

Serving: 6 | Prep: 10 m | Cook: 10 m | Ready in: 20 m

Ingredients

- 4 cups all-purpose flour
- 2 teaspoons baking powder
- 1 1/2 teaspoons salt
- 1/2 cup butter
- 1/2 cup cold water
- 1 cup vegetable oil for frying

Direction

- In a large bowl, stir together the flour, baking powder and salt. Rub in the butter until it is in pieces no larger than peas. Mix in water 1 tablespoon at a time just until the mixture is wet enough to form into a ball. The dough should be a firm consistency. Knead briefly.
- Heat the oil in a large heavy skillet over medium heat until hot. Break off pieces of the dough and shape into a patty - kind of like a flat biscuit. Place just enough of the dumplings in the pan so they are not crowded. Fry on each side until golden brown, about 3 minutes per side. Remove from the pan and drain on paper towels before serving.

Nutrition Information

- Calories: 472 calories
- Total Fat: 19.8 g
- Cholesterol: 41 mg
- Sodium: 855 mg
- Total Carbohydrate: 64 g
- Protein: 8.8 g

216. Jellied Biscuits

These biscuits are a pleasure to serve because that look so lovely with the colorful jelly.--Marsha Ransom, South Haven, Michigan

Serving: about 1 dozen. | Prep: 15 m | Cook: 10 m | Ready in: 25 m

Ingredients

- 2 cups all-purpose flour
- 4 teaspoons baking powder
- 2 teaspoon sugar
- 1/2 teaspoon salt
- 1/2 teaspoon cream of tartar
- 1/2 cup shortening
- 3/4 cup milk
- 1/3 cup jelly

Direction

- In a bowl, combine flour, baking powder, sugar, salt and cream of tartar. Cut in shortening until the mixture resembles coarse crumbs. Add milk, stir quickly with a fork just until mixed. Drop by rounded tablespoonfuls onto a greased baking sheet. Make a deep thumbprint in tops; fill each with 1 teaspoon of jelly. Bake at 450 degrees for 10-12 minutes or until biscuits are browned.

Nutrition Information

- Calories: 184 calories
- Total Fat: 9g
- Cholesterol: 2mg
- Sodium: 240mg

- Total Carbohydrate: 23g
- Protein: 3g
- Fiber: 1g

217. Johnnys Biscuits

"These are the most wonderful biscuits you'll ever put in your mouth. They are the biggest, best tasting, lightest, and fluffiest biscuits I've ever had. They're not very hard to make either."

Serving: 9 | Prep: 20 m | Cook: 20 m | Ready in: 40 m

Ingredients

- 2 cups self-rising flour
- 1/8 teaspoon baking soda
- 3/4 teaspoon salt
- 1 1/2 tablespoons white sugar
- 2 tablespoons shortening
- 2 tablespoons butter, softened
- 1 1/4 cups buttermilk
- 1 cup all-purpose flour
- 1 1/2 tablespoons butter, melted

Direction

- Preheat oven to 475 degrees F (245 degrees C). Spray a 10 1/2 inch cast iron skillet with nonstick cooking spray.
- In a medium bowl, combine flour, baking soda, salt and sugar. Cut in the shortening and softened butter with a fork until the lumps are pea size. Gently stir in the buttermilk until all of the flour is incorporated; do not over mix. The dough should be very wet. If not, add more buttermilk to achieve a sloppy consistency. Let stand for 2 to 3 minutes.
- Place all-purpose flour in a bowl. Spray an ice cream scoop or large spoon with vegetable spray and scoop out dough. Drop each biscuit one at a time into the flour. Using well-floured hands, pick up each piece and pass from hand to hand lightly to shake off excess flour and shape it into a soft round. Place the biscuits gently into cast iron skillet. They will be a tight

fit. Do not mash the biscuits down! Brush tops lightly with melted butter.
- Bake at 475 degrees F (245 degrees C) for 16 to 18 minutes. Cool before serving.

Nutrition Information

- Calories: 235 calories
- Total Fat: 8 g
- Cholesterol: 13 mg
- Sodium: 632 mg
- Total Carbohydrate: 34.9 g
- Protein: 5.4 g

218. JPs Big Daddy Biscuits

"This recipe will produce the biggest biscuits in the history of the world! Serve these gems with butter, preserves, honey, gravy or they can also be used as dinner rolls...you get the picture. The dough can also be prepared several hours, and up to a day ahead of time. If so, turn dough out onto aluminum foil that has been either floured, lightly buttered or lightly sprayed with cooking spray. Roll up foil until it is sealed, and refrigerate. Don't be surprised if your biscuits rise even higher because the baking powder has had more time to act in the dough. You may have to make a few batches before you get desired results: desired results equals huge mongo biscuits."

Serving: 6 | Prep: 30 m | Cook: 15 m | Ready in: 45 m

Ingredients

- 2 cups all-purpose flour
- 1 tablespoon baking powder
- 1 teaspoon salt
- 1 tablespoon white sugar
- 1/3 cup shortening
- 1 cup milk

Direction

- Preheat oven to 425 degrees F (220 degrees C).
- In a large bowl, whisk together the flour, baking powder, salt, and sugar. Cut in the shortening until the mixture resembles coarse meal. Gradually stir in milk until dough pulls away from the side of the bowl.

- Turn out onto a floured surface, and knead 15 to 20 times. Pat or roll dough out to 1 inch thick. Cut biscuits with a large cutter or juice glass dipped in flour. Repeat until all dough is used. Brush off the excess flour, and place biscuits onto an ungreased baking sheet.
- Bake for 13 to 15 minutes in the preheated oven, or until edges begin to brown.

Nutrition Information

- Calories: 282 calories
- Total Fat: 12.6 g
- Cholesterol: 3 mg
- Sodium: 649 mg
- Total Carbohydrate: 36.4 g
- Protein: 5.6 g

219. Kale and Onion Mini Biscuits

"A very light biscuit with tasty caraway seeds makes a good accompaniment for soups and stews at dinner time."

Serving: 50 | Prep: 25 m | Cook: 20 m | Ready in: 1 h 25 m

Ingredients

- 1 cup finely chopped kale
- 2 1/2 cups all-purpose flour
- 1 cup whole wheat pastry flour
- 1 tablespoon caraway seeds
- 2 teaspoons baking powder
- 1 teaspoon baking soda
- 1 teaspoon salt
- 1/2 cup butter, softened
- 2 tablespoons soft goat cheese
- 2 tablespoons white sugar
- 2 eggs
- 1/2 cup finely chopped onion

Direction

- Preheat oven to 300 degrees F (150 degrees C). Scatter kale over a large baking sheet.

- Place kale in the preheated oven until dried, about 10 minutes; remove to cool completely, about 10 minutes.
- Whisk all-purpose flour, whole wheat pastry flour, caraway seeds, baking powder, baking soda, and salt together in a bowl.
- Beat butter, goat cheese, and sugar together in a bowl until creamy; beat in eggs. Stir kale and onion into butter mixture; stir in flour mixture until a soft dough forms. Gather dough into a ball, wrap in plastic wrap, and chill in the refrigerator for 30 minutes.
- Preheat oven to 375 degrees F (190 degrees C). Line baking sheets with parchment paper.
- Roll dough out on a lightly-floured surface 1/2-inch thick; cut into rounds with a small cookie cutter. Place rounds on prepared baking sheets about 1 inch apart.
- Bake in the preheated oven until lightly browned, about 10 minutes.

Nutrition Information

- Calories: 53 calories
- Total Fat: 2.2 g
- Cholesterol: 13 mg
- Sodium: 109 mg
- Total Carbohydrate: 7.1 g
- Protein: 1.3 g

220. Kentucky Biscuits

"This is a great recipe, different than the usual biscuit. Serve piping hot with butter, jam, or honey."

Serving: 12 | Prep: 15 m | Cook: 15 m | Ready in: 30 m

Ingredients

- 2 cups all-purpose flour
- 2 1/2 teaspoons baking powder
- 1/2 teaspoon baking soda
- 1 dash salt
- 1 tablespoon white sugar
- 1/2 cup butter
- 3/4 cup buttermilk

Direction

- Preheat oven to 400 degrees F (200 degrees C).
- In a bowl, mix the flour, baking powder, baking soda, salt, and sugar. Cut in 1/2 cup butter until the mixture resembles coarse crumbs. Mix in the buttermilk. Turn out onto a lightly floured surface, and knead 2 minutes. Transfer to an ungreased baking sheet, roll into a 6x6 inch square, and cut into 12 even sections. Do not separate.
- Bake 15 minutes in the preheated oven, until a knife inserted in the center of the square comes out clean. Separate into biscuits, and serve hot.

Nutrition Information

- Calories: 154 calories
- Total Fat: 8 g
- Cholesterol: 21 mg
- Sodium: 231 mg
- Total Carbohydrate: 17.9 g
- Protein: 2.7 g

221. Kids Favorite Biscuits

Six-year-old Dustin Chasteen of Weaverville, North Carolina combines two kid-favorite flavors--peanut butter and jelly--in a new way. Refrigerated biscuits with a warm, gooey filling make a yummy lunch or snack.

Serving: 10 servings. | Prep: 5 m | Cook: 10 m | Ready in: 15 m

Ingredients

- 1 tube (12 ounces) refrigerated flaky buttermilk biscuits
- 1/2 cup peanut butter
- 1/2 cup jelly

Direction

- Separate biscuits; pat onto the bottom and up the sides of greased muffin cups. Bake at 450 degrees for 8-10 minutes or until golden brown.

- Remove to a wire rack.
- Place a scant tablespoonful of peanut butter in each warm biscuit cup; top with a scant tablespoonful of jelly. Serve immediately.

Nutrition Information

- Calories: 198 calories
- Total Fat: 7g
- Cholesterol: 0 mg
- Sodium: 351mg
- Total Carbohydrate: 29g
- Protein: 6g
- Fiber: 1g

222. Lemon Blueberry Biscuits

Lemon and blueberries make such a fresh and flavorful combination in all kinds of baked goods, especially these biscuits.

Serving: 1 dozen. | Prep: 30 m | Cook: 15 m | Ready in: 45 m

Ingredients

- 2 cups all-purpose flour
- 1/2 cup sugar
- 2 teaspoons baking powder
- 1/2 teaspoon baking soda
- 1/4 teaspoon salt
- 1 cup (8 ounces) lemon yogurt
- 1 large egg
- 1/4 cup butter, melted
- 1 teaspoon grated lemon zest
- 1 cup fresh or frozen blueberries
- GLAZE:
- 1/2 cup confectioners' sugar
- 1 tablespoon lemon juice
- 1/2 teaspoon grated lemon zest

Direction

- Preheat oven to 400 degrees. In a large bowl, whisk the first five ingredients. In another bowl, whisk yogurt, egg, melted butter and lemon zest until blended. Add to flour mixture; stir just until moistened. Fold in blueberries.

- Drop by 1/3 cupfuls 1 in. apart onto a greased baking sheet. Bake 15-18 minutes or until light brown.
- In a small bowl, combine glaze ingredients; stir until smooth. Drizzle over warm biscuits.

Nutrition Information

- Calories: 193 calories
- Total Fat: 5g
- Cholesterol: 29mg
- Sodium: 223mg
- Total Carbohydrate: 35g
- Protein: 4g
- Fiber: 1g

223. Lemon Tea Biscuits

With subtle lemon flavor, these flaky biscuits make a nice addition to a small buffet or light lunch. Try them the next time you host a holiday tea party for friends, family or co-workers. --Jane Rossen, Binghamton, New York

Serving: 16 biscuits (1/2 cup butter). | Prep: 25 m | Cook: 10 m | Ready in: 35 m

Ingredients

- 4 cups all-purpose flour
- 1/4 cup sugar
- 1-1/2 teaspoons baking soda
- 1 teaspoon salt
- 2/3 cup shortening
- 1 cup 2% milk
- 6 tablespoons lemon juice
- LEMON BUTTER:
- 1/2 cup butter, softened
- 4-1/2 teaspoons lemon juice
- 2 teaspoons grated lemon peel
- 1 tablespoon finely chopped onion, optional

Direction

- In a large bowl, combine the flour, sugar, baking soda and salt. Cut in shortening until

mixture resembles fine crumbs. Stir in milk and lemon juice just until moistened. Turn onto a lightly floured surface; knead 8-10 times.

- Roll out to 1/2-in. thickness; cut with a floured 2-1/2-in. biscuit cutter. Place 2 in. apart on ungreased baking sheets. Bake at 450 degrees for 8-10 minutes or until golden brown.
- Meanwhile, in a small bowl, combine lemon butter ingredients until blended. Serve with warm biscuits.

Nutrition Information

- Calories: 261 calories
- Total Fat: 14g
- Cholesterol: 17mg
- Sodium: 313mg
- Total Carbohydrate: 28g
- Protein: 4g
- Fiber: 1g

224. Lime Biscuits

"I whipped these up one night to go with our Mexican chicken stew, but they would be equally yummy for a fun twist on strawberry shortcake! The lime flavor is refreshing but not overpowering."

Serving: 12 | Prep: 20 m | Cook: 15 m | Ready in: 35 m

Ingredients

- 3/4 cup milk
- 1 tablespoon fresh lime juice
- 2 cups all-purpose flour
- 1 tablespoon baking powder
- 1 lime, zested
- 1 teaspoon salt
- 1/2 teaspoon baking soda
- 10 tablespoons unsalted butter, cut into pieces

Direction

- Preheat oven to 400 degrees F (200 degrees C).
- Mix milk and lime juice together in a bowl.

- Whisk flour, baking powder, lime zest, salt, and baking soda together in a separate bowl; mix butter into flour mixture using two knives or a pastry blender until crumbly. Stir milk mixture into flour mixture until just moistened.
- Transfer dough to a lightly floured work surface; knead a few times. Gently shape dough into a 3/4-inch thick disk; cut into 12 biscuits using a 2 1/2-inch floured cutter or the rim of a small juice glass. Reshape scraps as needed. Arrange biscuits on a baking sheet.
- Bake in the preheated oven until golden, 15 to 20 minutes.

Nutrition Information

- Calories: 169 calories
- Total Fat: 10.1 g
- Cholesterol: 27 mg
- Sodium: 376 mg
- Total Carbohydrate: 17.1 g
- Protein: 2.8 g

225. Lunch Biscuits

"Biscuits with various fillings - perfect for kids' lunch boxes! Once cooled, store biscuits in a sealed container or freeze."

Serving: 8 | Prep: 10 m | Cook: 20 m | Ready in: 40 m

Ingredients

- cooking spray
- 1 cup shredded Cheddar cheese
- 1/2 cup chopped ham
- 1 (10 ounce) can refrigerated buttermilk biscuit dough, each cut into small pieces
- 2 tablespoons pizza sauce

Direction

- Preheat oven to 375 degrees F (190 degrees C). Spray 8 muffin cups with cooking spray.
- Mix Cheddar cheese and ham together in a bowl; fold in biscuit dough pieces. Add pizza

sauce and lightly mix. Spoon mixture into the prepared muffin cups.
- Bake in the preheated oven until biscuits are puffed and browned, about 20 minutes. Cool for 10 minutes before removing from muffin cups.

Nutrition Information

- Calories: 184 calories
- Total Fat: 10.2 g
- Cholesterol: 19 mg
- Sodium: 552 mg
- Total Carbohydrate: 16 g
- Protein: 7.1 g

226. Makeover Cheddar Biscuits

Here's our crack at the never-ending biscuits from Red Lobster. Made from scratch with lighter ingredients, they're just as cheesy and buttery as the original.

Serving: 15 biscuits. | Prep: 20 m | Cook: 10 m | Ready in: 30 m

Ingredients

- 1 cup all-purpose flour
- 1 cup cake flour
- 1-1/2 teaspoons baking powder
- 3/4 teaspoon salt
- 1/2 teaspoon garlic powder, divided
- 1/4 teaspoon baking soda
- 4 tablespoons cold butter, divided
- 1/3 cup finely shredded cheddar cheese
- 1 cup buttermilk
- 1/2 teaspoon dried parsley flakes

Direction

- In a large bowl, combine the flours, baking powder, salt, 1/4 teaspoon garlic powder and baking soda. Cut in 3 tablespoons butter until mixture resembles coarse crumbs; add cheese. Stir in buttermilk just until moistened.
- Drop by two tablespoonfuls 2 in. apart onto baking sheets coated with cooking spray. Bake

at 425 degrees for 10-12 minutes or until golden brown. Melt remaining butter; stir in parsley and remaining garlic powder. Brush over biscuits. Serve warm.

Nutrition Information

- Calories: 106 calories
- Total Fat: 4g
- Cholesterol: 11mg
- Sodium: 233mg
- Total Carbohydrate: 14g
- Protein: 3g
- Fiber: 0 g

227. Maple Cinnamon Biscuits

Pass around a basket of these oven-fresh biscuits for a memorable breakfast or brunch. Full of maple and cinnamon flavors, they're enhanced by a scattering of nuts.
--Mary Relyea, Canastota, New York

Serving: 1 dozen. | Prep: 15 m | Cook: 15 m | Ready in: 30 m

Ingredients

- 2-1/2 cups all-purpose flour
- 3 tablespoons cinnamon-sugar, divided
- 3 teaspoons baking powder
- 1/2 teaspoon baking soda
- 1/2 teaspoon salt
- 1/2 cup cold butter, cubed
- 1/2 cup buttermilk
- 1/2 cup maple syrup
- 1/2 cup finely chopped pecans
- 2 tablespoons 2% milk

Direction

- In a large bowl, combine the flour, 2 tablespoons cinnamon-sugar, baking powder, baking soda and salt. Cut in butter until mixture resembles coarse crumbs. Stir in buttermilk and syrup just until moistened. Fold in pecans.

- Turn onto a floured surface; knead 8-10 times. Roll out to 1/2-in. thickness; cut with a floured 2-1/2-in. biscuit cutter.
- Place 2 in. apart on an ungreased baking sheet. Brush with milk; sprinkle with remaining cinnamon-sugar.
- Bake at 400 degrees for 12-15 minutes or until golden brown. Serve warm.

Nutrition Information

- Calories: 246 calories
- Total Fat: 11g
- Cholesterol: 21mg
- Sodium: 334mg
- Total Carbohydrate: 33g
- Protein: 4g
- Fiber: 1g

228. Maple Leaf Biscuits

These corn bread biscuits not only have a pretty maple leaf shape, but a mild maple flavor and glossy sheen from a syrup and butter mixture brushed on top.

Serving: about 1-1/2 dozen. | Prep: 20 m | Cook: 10 m | Ready in: 30 m

Ingredients

- 1-1/2 cups all-purpose flour
- 1/2 cup cornmeal
- 1 tablespoon baking powder
- 1 teaspoon sugar
- 1/2 teaspoon salt
- 1/2 teaspoon cream of tartar
- 1/3 cup shortening
- 2/3 cup milk
- 1 tablespoon butter, melted
- 1 tablespoon maple syrup

Direction

- In a bowl, combine flour, cornmeal, baking powder, sugar, salt and cream of tartar. Cut in shortening until mixture resembles coarse crumbs. Stir in milk just until moistened.

- Turn onto a floured surface; lightly knead 10-12 times. Roll or pat to 1/2-in. thickness. Cut with a 2-1/2-in. maple leaf cookie cutter or a biscuit cutter. Place on a lightly greased baking sheet. Combine butter and syrup; lightly brush over tops of biscuits.
- Bake at 425 degrees for 10-12 minutes or until golden brown. Brush with remaining syrup mixture.

Nutrition Information

- Calories: 100 calories
- Total Fat: 5g
- Cholesterol: 3mg
- Sodium: 144mg
- Total Carbohydrate: 12g
- Protein: 2g
- Fiber: 1g

229. Martha White Hot Rize Biscuits

"With self-rising flour, homemade biscuits are easy and ready in just 30 minutes."

Serving: 14 | Prep: 20 m | Cook: 11 m | Ready in: 31 m

Ingredients

- Crisco® Original No-Stick Cooking Spray
- 2 cups Martha White® Self-Rising Flour
- 1/4 stick Crisco® Baking Sticks All-Vegetable Shortening*
- 3/4 cup milk

Direction

- Heat oven to 450 degrees F. Spray a cookie sheet lightly with no-stick cooking spray. Place flour in large bowl. Cut in shortening with pastry blender or fork until mixture resembles coarse crumbs. Add milk; stir with fork until soft dough forms and mixture begins to pull away from sides of bowl.

- Knead dough on lightly floured surface just until smooth. Roll out dough to 1/2-inch thickness. Cut with floured 2-inch round cutter. Place biscuits with sides touching on prepared cookie sheet.
- Bake 10 to 12 minutes or until golden brown. Serve warm.

Nutrition Information

- Calories: 101 calories
- Total Fat: 3.9 g
- Cholesterol: 1 mg
- Sodium: 223 mg
- Total Carbohydrate: 13.8 g
- Protein: 2.1 g

230. Mayonnaise Biscuits

"This is a simple but tasty biscuit recipe. You don't taste the mayo, but it gives the biscuits a light and fluffy texture. For rolled and cut biscuits, use just enough milk to hold it together."

Serving: 12 | Prep: 10 m | Cook: 12 m | Ready in: 22 m

Ingredients

- 2 cups self-rising flour
- 1 cup milk
- 6 tablespoons mayonnaise

Direction

- Preheat oven to 400 degrees F (200 degrees C).
- In a large bowl, stir together flour, milk, and mayonnaise until just blended. Drop by spoonfuls onto lightly greased baking sheets.
- Bake for 12 minutes in the preheated oven, or until golden brown.

Nutrition Information

- Calories: 133 calories
- Total Fat: 6.1 g
- Cholesterol: 4 mg
- Sodium: 312 mg

- Total Carbohydrate: 16.6 g
- Protein: 2.8 g

- Fiber: 1g

231. Mexican Drop Biscuits

*"We love these golden biscuits with big bowls of soup,"
Teresa Spencer Note:s from Wauwatosa, Wisconsin. "The
green chilies and taco cheese add extra zip to everyday
meals."*

*Serving: 1 dozen. | Prep: 10 m | Cook: 10 m | Ready in:
20 m*

Ingredients

- 2 cups biscuit/baking mix
- 1 cup shredded Mexican cheese blend
- 1 can (4 ounces) chopped green chilies, undrained
- 1/2 cup water
- 3 tablespoons butter, melted
- 1 teaspoon dried parsley flakes
- 1/4 teaspoon garlic powder
- 1/4 teaspoon dried oregano
- 1/4 teaspoon dried thyme
- 1/8 teaspoon cayenne pepper

Direction

- In a small bowl, combine the biscuit mix, cheese and chilies. Stir in water just until moistened. Drop into 12 mounds 2 in. apart onto a greased baking sheet. Bake at 450 degrees for 10-15 minutes or until golden brown.
- In a small bowl, combine the butter, parsley, garlic powder, oregano, thyme and cayenne pepper; brush over biscuits. Serve warm.

Nutrition Information

- Calories: 140 calories
- Total Fat: 8g
- Cholesterol: 15mg
- Sodium: 379mg
- Total Carbohydrate: 13g
- Protein: 3g

232. Mini Butter Biscuits

*When my mom dropped her homemade rolls while on the
way to my house one Thanksgiving, I improvised and
whipped up a batch of these buttery bite-sized biscuits.
Since then they've been part of our traditional
Thanksgiving meal.*

*Serving: About 3-1/2 dozen. | Prep: 15 m | Cook: 15 m |
Ready in: 30 m*

Ingredients

- 2 cups self-rising flour
- 1 cup cold butter, cubed
- 1 cup (8 ounces) sour cream

Direction

- Place flour in a bowl; cut in butter until mixture resembles coarse crumbs. Stir in sour cream until just until moistened.
- Drop by rounded tablespoonfuls into ungreased miniature muffin cups. Bake at 450 degrees for 11-15 minutes or until lightly browned. Cool for 5 minutes before removing from pans to wire racks.

Nutrition Information

- Calories: 137 calories
- Total Fat: 11g
- Cholesterol: 31mg
- Sodium: 231mg
- Total Carbohydrate: 9g
- Protein: 2g
- Fiber: 0 g

233. Mini Cheese Biscuits

"To complete the meal, I pass a basket of Mini Cheese Biscuits," Chris Note:s. "We're garlic lovers, so we enjoy the flavor of these easy biscuits. If your taste buds prefer, omit the minced garlic altogether. "Friends and family tell me these treats are best warm from the oven," Chris adds. "But then, they never last long enough to cool off!"

Serving: about 1 dozen. | Prep: 15 m | Cook: 10 m | Ready in: 25 m

Ingredients

- 2 cups biscuit/baking mix
- 1/2 cup shredded cheddar cheese
- 2 garlic cloves, minced
- 2/3 cup milk
- 2 tablespoons butter, melted
- 1/4 teaspoon garlic powder

Direction

- In a bowl, combine biscuit mix, cheese and garlic. With a fork, stir in milk just until moistened. Drop by rounded tablespoonfuls onto a lightly greased baking sheet. Bake at 450 degrees for 9-11 minutes or until golden brown. Combine butter and garlic powder; brush over biscuits.

Nutrition Information

- Calories: 124 calories
- Total Fat: 7g
- Cholesterol: 12mg
- Sodium: 306mg
- Total Carbohydrate: 13g
- Protein: 3g
- Fiber: 0 g

234. Mini Italian Biscuits

I tasted biscuits like these at a seafood restaurant and really liked them. I experimented in my kitchen until I was able to get the same flavor in these fast little bites.--Elaine Whiting,Salt Lake City, Utah

Serving: about 3 dozen. | Prep: 10 m | Cook: 10 m | Ready in: 20 m

Ingredients

- 2 cups biscuit/baking mix
- 1/2 cup finely shredded cheddar cheese
- 1/2 teaspoon garlic powder
- 1/2 teaspoon dried oregano
- 1/2 teaspoon dried basil
- 2/3 cup milk

Direction

- In a large bowl, combine the biscuit mix, cheese, garlic powder, oregano and basil. Stir in milk just until moistened.
- Drop by rounded teaspoonfuls onto a lightly greased baking sheet. Bake at 450 degrees for 7-8 minutes or until golden brown. Serve warm.

Nutrition Information

- Calories: 36 calories
- Total Fat: 2g
- Cholesterol: 2mg
- Sodium: 96mg
- Total Carbohydrate: 4g
- Protein: 1g
- Fiber: 0 g

235. Mini Sour Cream Biscuits

These buttery mini muffins are flaky, tender and a snap to make because you start with convenient biscuit mix. Sara Dukes of Bartow, Georgia shared the recipe.

Serving: 1 dozen. | Prep: 10 m | Cook: 15 m | Ready in: 25 m

Ingredients

- 1 cup biscuit/baking mix
- 1/2 cup sour cream
- 1/4 cup butter, melted

Direction

- In a large bowl, combine all ingredients just until combined. Drop by rounded tablespoonfuls into greased miniature muffin pans.
- Bake at 425 degrees for 15-18 minutes or until golden brown.

Nutrition Information

- Calories: 94 calories
- Total Fat: 7g
- Cholesterol: 17mg
- Sodium: 170mg
- Total Carbohydrate: 6g
- Protein: 1g
- Fiber: 0 g

236. Moist Sweet Potato Biscuits

Moist and sweet, these biscuits are a delightful addition to any holiday meal-- even breakfast. They don't need butter...but they'll taste even better when you spread some on.

Serving: about 1-1/2 dozen. | Prep: 20 m | Cook: 15 m | Ready in: 35 m

Ingredients

- 3-1/2 cups all-purpose flour
- 4-1/2 teaspoons baking powder
- 1 teaspoon salt
- 1/2 teaspoon ground cinnamon
- 1-1/2 cups mashed cooked sweet potatoes (prepared without milk and butter)
- 1/2 cup butter, melted
- 1/2 cup sugar
- 2 tablespoons milk

Direction

- In a large bowl, combine the flour, baking powder, salt and cinnamon. In another bowl, combine sweet potatoes, butter, sugar and milk; add to flour mixture and mix well.
- Turn onto a floured surface; knead 8-10 times. Roll to 1/2-in. thickness. Cut with a 2-1/2-in. biscuit cutter; place on greased baking sheet. Bake at 400 degrees for 15-18 minutes or until golden brown.

Nutrition Information

- Calories: 184 calories
- Total Fat: 5g
- Cholesterol: 14mg
- Sodium: 287mg
- Total Carbohydrate: 31g
- Protein: 3g
- Fiber: 1g

237. Moms Baking Powder Biscuits

"This is the recipe my mom always made. I like to use the butter flavored shortening, but you can use regular. Amount of biscuits you get depends on how big around you make them and the thickness. My daughter likes me to make smaller ones."

Serving: 24 | Prep: 15 m | Cook: 15 m | Ready in: 30 m

Ingredients

- 2 cups all-purpose flour
- 2 1/2 teaspoons baking powder
- 3/4 teaspoon salt
- 5 tablespoons shortening
- 3/4 cup milk

Direction

- Preheat oven to 450 degrees F (230 degrees C).
- In a bowl mix the flour, baking powder and salt. Add the shortening and mix until in little pieces. Add milk a little at a time and mix until it forms a ball.
- Roll out on floured board to 1/4 inch to 1/2 inch thick. Cut out in desired size and dip in melted shortening. Place biscuits on an ungreased baking sheet.
- Bake at 450 degrees F (230 degrees C) for 12 to 15 minutes.
- Variation: For shortcakes add 2 tablespoons for sugar to the dough and roll dough out to 1/2 inch thick.

Nutrition Information

- Calories: 66 calories
- Total Fat: 2.9 g
- Cholesterol: < 1 mg
- Sodium: 127 mg
- Total Carbohydrate: 8.4 g
- Protein: 1.3 g

238. Monkey Biscuits

The dear friend who shared this recipe has since passed away, but I think of her every time I prepare this sweet bread. Maple syrup provides a saucy caramel flavor. I enjoy developing original recipes or altering others to suit my tastes.

Serving: 1 loaf. | Prep: 15 m | Cook: 25 m | Ready in: 40 m

Ingredients

- 2 tubes (7-1/2 ounces each) refrigerated buttermilk biscuits
- 1 cup packed brown sugar
- 1 teaspoon ground cinnamon
- 1 teaspoon ground nutmeg
- 1/2 cup butter, melted
- 1/2 cup chopped nuts
- 1/2 cup maple syrup

Direction

- Cut each biscuit into quarters. In a small bowl, combine brown sugar, cinnamon and nutmeg. Dip biscuits in butter, then roll in sugar mixture. Layer half the biscuits in a 10-in. fluted pan; sprinkle with half the nuts. Repeat layers. Pour syrup over top.
- Bake at 350 degrees for 25-30 minutes or until golden brown. Immediately invert onto a serving platter. Serve warm. Refrigerate leftovers.

Nutrition Information

- Calories: 185 calories
- Total Fat: 8g
- Cholesterol: 15mg
- Sodium: 178mg
- Total Carbohydrate: 27g
- Protein: 2g
- Fiber: 0 g

239. Monkey Bread Biscuits

These rolls get their name because the first rise happens overnight in the refrigerator. The next day, just shape, let rise again, and bake.--Dana Johnson, Scottsdale, Arizona

Serving: 1 dozen. | Prep: 10 m | Cook: 10 m | Ready in: 20 m

Ingredients

- 1 tube (16.3 ounces) large refrigerated flaky biscuits
- 3 tablespoons butter, melted
- 1 garlic clove, minced
- 1/2 teaspoon Italian seasoning
- 1/4 cup grated Parmesan cheese
- Additional Italian seasoning

Direction

- Preheat oven to 425 degrees. Separate biscuits; cut each into six pieces. In a large bowl, combine butter, garlic and Italian seasoning; add biscuit pieces and toss to coat.

- Place four pieces in each of 12 greased muffin cups. Sprinkle with cheese and additional Italian seasoning. Bake 8-10 minutes or until golden brown. Serve warm.

Nutrition Information

- Calories: 159 calories
- Total Fat: 9g
- Cholesterol: 9mg
- Sodium: 418mg
- Total Carbohydrate: 16g
- Protein: 3g
- Fiber: 1g

240. Never Fail Biscuits

"These biscuits are a never fail recipe, they're easy to make and everyone enjoys them. "

Serving: 4 | Prep: 10 m | Cook: 10 m | Ready in: 20 m

Ingredients

- 2 cups all-purpose flour
- 1/2 teaspoon salt
- 4 teaspoons baking powder
- 1/2 teaspoon cream of tartar
- 2 teaspoons white sugar
- 1/2 cup butter, chilled and diced
- 3/4 cup milk

Direction

- Preheat oven to 450 degrees F (230 degrees C).
- In a large bowl, sift together dry ingredients. Cut in butter until mixture resembles coarse oatmeal. Make a well in the center of the dry mixture and pour in the milk. Stir until dough begins to pull together then turn out onto a lightly floured surface.
- Press dough together and then roll out until 3/4 inch thick. Cut into 2 inch round biscuits and place on an ungreased baking sheet.
- Bake in preheated oven for 10 minutes, or until golden.

Nutrition Information

- Calories: 465 calories
- Total Fat: 24.5 g
- Cholesterol: 65 mg
- Sodium: 834 mg
- Total Carbohydrate: 53.1 g
- Protein: 8.2 g

241. Nutty Cream Cheese Biscuits

These nutty biscuits are worth every bit of the time they take to prepare. Their rich taste and creamy texture make requests for seconds routine. --Claudia Beene, Bossier, Louisiana

Serving: about 1-1/2 dozen. | Prep: 25 m | Cook: 20 m | Ready in: 45 m

Ingredients

- 2 tubes (10 ounces each) refrigerated biscuits
- 6 ounces cream cheese
- 1/2 cup sugar
- 1 teaspoon ground cinnamon
- 1/4 teaspoon each ground cloves, nutmeg and allspice
- 6 tablespoons butter, melted
- 1 cup chopped pecans

Direction

- Roll each biscuit into a 3-1/2-in. to 4-in. circle. Cut cream cheese into 20 equal cubes; place one cube in the center of each biscuit. Combine sugar, cinnamon, cloves, nutmeg and allspice; sprinkle 1/2 teaspoonful over each biscuit. Set remaining sugar mixture aside. Moisten edges of dough with water; fold over cheese and press edges with a fork to seal.
- Pour 2 tablespoons butter each into two 9-in. round baking pans; sprinkle 1 tablespoon of reserved sugar mixture into each. Dip one side of each biscuit remaining butter. Arrange in pans, forming a pinwheel pattern, with butter side up. Sprinkle pecans and remaining sugar mixture on top. Bake at 375 degrees for 20-25

minutes or until golden brown. Serve warm. Refrigerate leftovers.

Nutrition Information

- Calories: 169 calories
- Total Fat: 13g
- Cholesterol: 15mg
- Sodium: 202mg
- Total Carbohydrate: 13g
- Protein: 2g
- Fiber: 1g

Nutrition Information

- Calories: 217 calories
- Total Fat: 8g
- Cholesterol: 14mg
- Sodium: 309mg
- Total Carbohydrate: 32g
- Protein: 4g
- Fiber: 1g

242. Nutty Sweet Potato Biscuits

Back in the 1920's and '30's Mom always had something good for us to eat when we got home from school. Her wood range had an apron right by the firebox, and Mom often left a plate of these warm wonderful biscuits waiting for us. What a treat! --Mrs. India Thacker, Clifford, Virginia

Serving: 18 servings. | Prep: 15 m | Cook: 15 m | Ready in: 30 m

Ingredients

- 2-3/4 cups all-purpose flour
- 4 teaspoons baking powder
- 1-1/4 teaspoons salt
- 1/2 teaspoon ground cinnamon
- 1/2 teaspoon ground nutmeg
- 3/4 cup chopped nuts
- 2 cups mashed sweet potatoes
- 3/4 cup sugar
- 1/2 cup butter, melted
- 1 teaspoon vanilla extract

Direction

- In a large bowl, combine flour, baking powder, salt, cinnamon, nutmeg and nuts. In another bowl, combine sweet potatoes, sugar, butter and vanilla; add to flour mixture and mix well.
- Turn onto a lightly floured surface; knead slightly. Roll dough to 1/2-in. thickness. Cut with a 2-1/2-in. biscuit cutter and place on lightly greased baking sheets. Bake at 450 degrees for 12 minutes or until golden brown.

243. Oatcakes

"Originally a Scottish recipe. Very little sugar and no white flour. Easy to make and a wonderful addition to breakfast."

Serving: 12 | Prep: 25 m | Cook: 20 m | Ready in: 45 m

Ingredients

- 3 3/4 cups rolled oats
- 1 cup whole wheat flour
- 1 teaspoon white sugar
- 1 1/4 teaspoons salt
- 1/2 teaspoon baking soda
- 1/2 cup cold butter, cubed
- 1/4 cup hot water, or as needed

Direction

- Preheat oven to 375 degrees F (190 degrees C). Line a heavy baking sheet with parchment paper.
- Mix oats, whole wheat flour, sugar, salt, and baking soda together in a bowl. Rub in butter with your fingers until mixture is chunky. Pour in enough water to form a thick dough.
- Spread a thin layer of oats and whole wheat flour on a flat work surface. Turn out dough and pat to an even thickness. Cut into circles using the rim of a drinking glass. Transfer to the prepared baking sheet.
- Bake in the preheated oven until golden brown, 20 to 30 minutes.

Nutrition Information

- Calories: 199 calories
- Total Fat: 9.5 g
- Cholesterol: 20 mg
- Sodium: 351 mg
- Total Carbohydrate: 24.7 g
- Protein: 4.8 g

244. Oatmeal Biscuits

This recipe has been in the family for generations, and my sister and I make these biscuits often for our families. When I bake them first thing in the morning, the house soon smells delicious.

Serving: 15 biscuits. | Prep: 15 m | Cook: 15 m | Ready in: 30 m

Ingredients

- 2 cups all-purpose flour
- 1/2 cup packed brown sugar
- 2 teaspoons baking powder
- 1 teaspoon baking soda
- 1 teaspoon salt
- 1/2 cup shortening
- 1-1/4 cups quick-cooking oats
- 3/4 cup milk

Direction

- In a large bowl, combine the flour, brown sugar, baking powder, baking soda and salt. Cut in shortening until mixture resembles coarse crumbs. Stir in oats and milk just until moistened.
- Turn onto a lightly floured surface. Roll out to 3/4-in. thickness. Cut with a floured 2-in. biscuit cutter. Place 1 in. apart on an ungreased baking sheet. Bake at 375 degrees for 15-20 minutes or until lightly browned. Serve warm.

Nutrition Information

- Calories: 180 calories

- Total Fat: 7g
- Cholesterol: 2mg
- Sodium: 304mg
- Total Carbohydrate: 25g
- Protein: 3g
- Fiber: 1g

245. OldFashioned Biscuits

Fresh-from-the-oven biscuits can be yours in no time. Serve them with the omelet here or a steaming mug of coffee or tea. Either way, you'll love every bite!

Serving: 4 biscuits. | Prep: 20 m | Cook: 15 m | Ready in: 35 m

Ingredients

- 1/2 cup all-purpose flour
- 1/2 cup cake flour
- 1 teaspoon baking powder
- 1 teaspoon sugar
- 1/4 teaspoon salt
- 1/8 teaspoon baking soda
- 3/4 ounce cold reduced-fat cream cheese
- 1 tablespoon cold butter
- 1/4 cup plus 1/2 teaspoon buttermilk, divided

Direction

- In a small bowl, combine the flours, baking powder, sugar, salt and baking soda. Cut in cream cheese and butter until mixture resembles coarse crumbs. Stir in 1/4 cup buttermilk just until moistened. Turn onto a lightly floured surface; knead 5-6 times.
- Pat or roll out to 1/2-in. thickness; cut with a floured 2-in. biscuit cutter.
- Place 2 in. apart on a baking sheet coated with cooking spray. Brush with remaining buttermilk. Bake at 400 degrees for 12-15 minutes or until golden brown. Serve warm.

Nutrition Information

- Calories: 167 calories
- Total Fat: 4g
- Cholesterol: 12mg

- Sodium: 355mg
- Total Carbohydrate: 27g
- Protein: 4g
- Fiber: 1g

246. OldFashioned Buttermilk Biscuits

My family gobbles up these biscuits, which are low in fat, cholesterol and sugar. I almost always make these now instead of my old shortening-based recipe. --Wendy Masters, Grand Valley, Ontario

Serving: 8 biscuits. | Prep: 10 m | Cook: 10 m | Ready in: 20 m

Ingredients

- 1-3/4 cups all-purpose flour
- 2 teaspoons baking powder
- 1/2 teaspoon baking soda
- 1/2 teaspoon sugar
- 1/4 teaspoon salt
- 2/3 cup buttermilk
- 2 tablespoons canola oil
- 1 tablespoon reduced-fat sour cream

Direction

- In a large bowl, combine the flour, baking powder, baking soda, sugar and salt. Combine the buttermilk, oil and sour cream; stir into flour mixture just until moistened. Turn onto a lightly floured surface; knead 8-10 times.
- Pat or roll out to 1/2-in. thickness; cut with a floured 2-1/2-in. biscuit cutter. Place 2 in. apart on an ungreased baking sheet. Bake at 400 degrees for 8-12 minutes or until lightly golden brown. Serve warm.

Nutrition Information

- Calories: 142 calories
- Total Fat: 4g
- Cholesterol: 1mg
- Sodium: 276mg

- Total Carbohydrate: 22g
- Protein: 4g
- Fiber: 1g

247. Onion Cheddar Biscuits

"These biscuits are seriously addictive! I make a batch and freeze them - my husband microwaves one for breakfast every morning." Elaine Sweet, Dallas, TX

Serving: 6 biscuits. | Prep: 25 m | Cook: 15 m | Ready in: 40 m

Ingredients

- 1/4 cup finely chopped sweet onion
- 4 tablespoons cold butter, divided
- 1/4 cup white balsamic vinegar
- 1 cup all-purpose flour
- 1 tablespoon sugar
- 1-1/2 teaspoons baking powder
- 1/4 teaspoon garlic salt
- 1/4 teaspoon pepper
- 1/8 teaspoon cayenne pepper
- 1/2 cup shredded cheddar cheese
- 2 green onions, chopped
- 1/4 cup buttermilk

Direction

- In a small skillet, sauté sweet onion in 1 tablespoon butter until tender. Add vinegar; cook and stir until liquid is evaporated. Cool.
- In a small bowl, combine the flour, sugar, baking powder and seasonings. Cut in remaining butter until mixture resembles coarse crumbs. Add the onion mixture, cheese and green onions. Stir in buttermilk just until moistened.
- Turn onto a lightly floured surface; knead 6-8 times. Pat or roll out to 1/2-in. thickness; cut with a floured 2-1/2-in. biscuit cutter. Place 2 in. apart on a greased baking sheet. Bake at 400 degrees for 12-15 minutes or until golden brown. Serve warm.

Nutrition Information

- Calories: 199 calories
- Total Fat: 11g
- Cholesterol: 30mg
- Sodium: 301mg
- Total Carbohydrate: 21g
- Protein: 5g
- Fiber: 1g

248. Onion Cheese Biscuits

"I received the recipe for these pretty biscuits from a neighbor," relates Joann Alexander of Center, Texas. "She called me 10 years later to ask for the recipe because she lost her copy. She was so glad she'd shared it with me!"

Serving: 6 biscuits. | Prep: 15 m | Cook: 15 m | Ready in: 30 m

Ingredients

- 1/2 cup milk
- 1 egg
- 1 tablespoon butter, melted
- 1-1/2 cups biscuit/baking mix
- 3/4 cup shredded cheddar cheese, divided
- 1/2 cup finely chopped onion
- 1 tablespoon poppy seeds

Direction

- In a bowl, combine the milk, egg and butter. Add biscuit mix, 1/2 cup cheese and onion. Spoon into six greased muffin cups. Sprinkle with poppy seeds and remaining cheese.
- Bake at 400 degrees for 12-14 minutes or until a toothpick comes out clean. Cool for 5 minutes before removing from pan to a wire rack.

Nutrition Information

- Calories: 227 calories
- Total Fat: 13g
- Cholesterol: 58mg
- Sodium: 503mg

- Total Carbohydrate: 22g
- Protein: 7g
- Fiber: 1g

249. Onion Herb Biscuits

These fluffy well-seasoned biscuits make a pleasant accompaniment to almost any meal.

Serving: 1 dozen. | Prep: 20 m | Cook: 15 m | Ready in: 35 m

Ingredients

- 2 cups all-purpose flour
- 1 tablespoon baking powder
- 1 tablespoon minced fresh thyme or 1 teaspoon dried thyme
- 1 teaspoon dried savory
- 1/2 teaspoon salt
- 1/4 teaspoon baking soda
- 1/4 teaspoon pepper
- 1-1/2 cups reduced-fat sour cream
- 2 tablespoons olive oil
- 1/4 cup thinly sliced green onions
- 1 tablespoon butter, melted

Direction

- In a large bowl, combine the flour, baking powder, thyme, savory, salt, baking soda and pepper. Combine sour cream and oil. Stir sour cream mixture into dry ingredients just until blended and mixture holds together. Stir in green onions.
- Turn onto a lightly floured surface; gently knead three or four times. Roll dough to 3/4 in. thickness; cut with a floured 2-1/2 in. biscuit cutter. Place 1 in. apart on ungreased baking sheet.
- Brush lightly with butter. Bake at 400 degrees for 14-18 minutes or until lightly browned. Serve warm.

Nutrition Information

- Calories: 144 calories
- Total Fat: 6g

- Cholesterol: 13mg
- Sodium: 277mg
- Total Carbohydrate: 18g
- Protein: 4g
- Fiber: 1g

250. Onion Poppy Seed Biscuits

Perfect alongside a salad or casserole, these buttermilk biscuits are ready in no time. Golden on the outside, tender on the inside, they offer a mild onion flavor with every bite.
— Test Kitchen

Serving: 1 dozen. | Prep: 20 m | Cook: 10 m | Ready in: 30 m

Ingredients

- 1 medium onion, finely chopped
- 2 cups all-purpose flour
- 1 teaspoon baking powder
- 1 teaspoon brown sugar
- 3/4 teaspoon poppy seeds
- 1/2 teaspoon salt
- 1/2 teaspoon baking soda
- 1/4 cup cold butter, cubed
- 1 cup buttermilk

Direction

- In a small nonstick skillet coated with cooking spray, sauté the onion until tender; set aside. In a large bowl, combine the flour, baking powder, brown sugar, poppy seeds, salt and baking soda. Cut in butter until mixture resembles coarse crumbs. Stir in onions. Stir in buttermilk just until moistened.
- Turn dough onto a lightly floured surface; knead 6-8 times. Pat to 1/2-in. thickness; cut with a floured 2-1/2-in. biscuit cutter. Place 2 in. apart on baking sheets coated with cooking spray.
- Bake at 450 degrees for 9-12 minutes or until golden brown. Serve warm.

Nutrition Information

- Calories: 125 calories
- Total Fat: 4g
- Cholesterol: 11mg
- Sodium: 245mg
- Total Carbohydrate: 18g
- Protein: 3g
- Fiber: 1g

251. Oniony Wheat Biscuits

"I've had this recipe in my files for more than 10 years and make these sweet-savory biscuits often," writes Bernice Janowski from her kitchen in Stevens Point, Wisconsin. "They taste great and complement all kinds of meals."

Serving: 10 biscuits. | Prep: 30 m | Cook: 10 m | Ready in: 40 m

Ingredients

- 1 tablespoon butter
- 2 teaspoons brown sugar
- 1 sweet onion, halved and thinly sliced
- DOUGH:
- 1 cup all-purpose flour
- 3/4 cup whole wheat flour
- 2 tablespoons brown sugar
- 1 teaspoon baking powder
- 3/4 teaspoon rubbed sage
- 1/2 teaspoon salt
- 1/2 teaspoon baking soda
- 3 tablespoons cold butter
- 1 egg
- 1 cup (8 ounces) plain yogurt

Direction

- In a large nonstick skillet coated with cooking spray, melt butter. Stir in brown sugar until blended; add onion. Cook over medium heat for 15-20 minutes or until onion is golden brown, stirring frequently. Set aside.
- In a large bowl, combine the flours, brown sugar, baking powder, sage, salt and baking

soda. Cut in butter until mixture resembles coarse crumbs. Combine egg and yogurt; stir into crumb mixture just until combined (dough will be sticky). Stir in a third of the onion mixture.

- Drop by 1/4 cupfuls 2 in. apart onto a baking sheet coated with cooking spray. Gently press remaining onion mixture onto dough. Bake at 425 degrees for 10-15 minutes or until golden brown. Serve warm.

Nutrition Information

- Calories: 158 calories
- Total Fat: 6g
- Cholesterol: 37mg
- Sodium: 287mg
- Total Carbohydrate: 22g
- Protein: 4g
- Fiber: 2g

252. Orange Biscuits

These biscuits are a special treat with a ham dinner, but they're also delicious just by themselves. They're often requested by my five children and seven grandchildren. I've been enjoying them since the 1940's. --Winifred Brown, Wilmette, Illinois

Serving: 1 dozen. | Prep: 25 m | Cook: 15 m | Ready in: 40 m

Ingredients

- 1/2 cup orange juice
- 3/4 cup sugar, divided
- 1/4 cup butter
- 2 teaspoons grated orange zest
- 2 cups all-purpose flour
- 1 tablespoon baking powder
- 1/2 teaspoon salt
- 1/4 cup shortening
- 3/4 cup milk
- Melted butter
- 1/2 teaspoon ground cinnamon

Direction

- In a saucepan, combine orange juice, 1/2 cup sugar, butter and orange zest. Cook and stir over medium heat for 2 minutes. Divide among 12 muffin cups; set aside.
- In a large bowl, combine flour, baking powder and salt. Cut in shortening until mixture resembles coarse crumbs. With a fork, stir in milk until mixture forms a ball. On a lightly floured surface, knead the dough 1 minute. Roll into a 9-in. square, about 1/2-in. thick. Brush with melted butter.
- Combine the cinnamon and remaining sugar; sprinkle over butter. Roll up. Cut into 12 slices, about 3/4 in. thick. Place slices, cut side down, over orange mixture in muffin cups. Bake at 450 degrees for 12-16 minutes. Cool for 2-3 minutes; remove from pan.

Nutrition Information

- Calories: 209 calories
- Total Fat: 9g
- Cholesterol: 12mg
- Sodium: 245mg
- Total Carbohydrate: 30g
- Protein: 3g
- Fiber: 1g

253. Orange Rosemary Biscuits

The appealing orange and rosemary flavor of these flaky, tender biscuits complements oven-roasted turkey. They bake up beautifully every time.--Lorraine Caland, Thunder Bay, Ontario

Serving: 1 dozen. | Prep: 15 m | Cook: 10 m | Ready in: 25 m

Ingredients

- 2 cups all-purpose flour
- 4 teaspoons grated orange zest
- 1 tablespoon baking powder
- 1 tablespoon minced fresh rosemary or 1 teaspoon dried rosemary

- 1/2 teaspoon salt
- 1/2 cup cold butter, cubed
- 2 tablespoons orange juice
- 1 cup plus 1 tablespoon buttermilk, divided

Direction

- Place the flour, orange zest, baking powder, rosemary and salt in a food processor; cover and pulse to blend. Add butter; cover and pulse until mixture resembles coarse crumbs. Add orange juice and 1 cup buttermilk and pulse just until moistened. Turn onto a lightly floured surface; knead 8-10 times.
- Pat or roll out to 1/2-in. thickness; cut with a floured 2-1/2-in. biscuit cutter. Place 1 in. apart on a greased baking sheet. Brush with remaining buttermilk. Bake at 425 degrees for 8-12 minutes or until golden brown. Serve warm.

Nutrition Information

- Calories: 153 calories
- Total Fat: 8g
- Cholesterol: 21mg
- Sodium: 275mg
- Total Carbohydrate: 17g
- Protein: 3g
- Fiber: 1g

254. Paleo Biscuits

"Here is the recipe and they are super yummy. I even cut them open and grilled while I was preparing my zucchini scrambled eggs! I made a yummy blueberry jam and decided to serve with paleo biscuits."

Serving: 12 | Prep: 15 m | Cook: 15 m | Ready in: 30 m

Ingredients

- 2 1/2 cups blanched almond flour
- 1 teaspoon baking soda
- 3/4 teaspoon sea salt
- 1/4 cup coconut oil, melted and cooled
- 2 large eggs at room temperature, beaten
- 1 tablespoon raw honey

Direction

- Preheat oven to 350 degrees F (175 degrees C). Line a baking sheet with parchment paper.
- Mix almond flour, baking soda, and sea salt together in a bowl; stir in coconut oil until fully incorporated. Stir eggs and honey into almond flour mixture until a dough ball forms. Scoop dough using an ice cream scoop and arrange dough scoops in the parchment paper. Lightly press each piece of dough to create a biscuit shape.
- Bake in the preheated oven until biscuits are lightly browned, about 15 minutes.

Nutrition Information

- Calories: 57 calories
- Total Fat: 5.5 g
- Cholesterol: 31 mg
- Sodium: 227 mg
- Total Carbohydrate: 1.5 g
- Protein: 1.1 g

255. Paprika Cheese Biscuits

My husband, Tom, loves these biscuit's cheddar flavor. They're so tender, I eat them as a snack.--Melody Smaller, Fowler, Colorado

Serving: 8 biscuits. | Prep: 10 m | Cook: 10 m | Ready in: 20 m

Ingredients

- 2-1/4 cups biscuit/baking mix
- 1/2 cup shredded cheddar cheese
- 2/3 cup milk
- 1 tablespoon butter, melted
- 1/2 teaspoon paprika

Direction

- In a large bowl, combine the biscuit mix and cheese. With a fork, stir in milk just until moistened. Turn onto a floured surface; knead

10 times. Roll dough to 1/2-in. thickness; cut with a 2-1/2-in. biscuit cutter.

- Place on an ungreased baking sheet. Brush with butter; sprinkle with paprika. Bake at 450 degrees for 8-10 minutes or until golden brown.

Nutrition Information

- Calories: 188 calories
- Total Fat: 9g
- Cholesterol: 14mg
- Sodium: 492mg
- Total Carbohydrate: 22g
- Protein: 5g
- Fiber: 1g

256. Parmesan Chive Biscuits

"I'm an emergency room doctor, and in my free time, I love to create new recipes like this one," says Sonali Ruder of New York, New York. "I hope you enjoy these tender, flaky biscuits as much as my husband and I do!"

Serving: 8 biscuits. | Prep: 20 m | Cook: 10 m | Ready in: 30 m

Ingredients

- 1/4 cup 2% milk
- 3 tablespoons beaten egg, divided
- 1 cup all-purpose flour
- 3/4 teaspoon baking powder
- 1/4 teaspoon salt
- 1/8 teaspoon pepper
- 6 tablespoons cold butter, cubed
- 2 tablespoons minced chives
- 1 teaspoon water
- 1 tablespoon shredded Parmesan cheese

Direction

- In a small bowl, combine milk and 2 tablespoons egg; set aside. In another bowl, combine the flour, baking powder, salt and pepper. Cut in butter until mixture resembles coarse crumbs. Stir in milk mixture just until

moistened. Stir in chives. Turn onto a lightly floured surface; knead 8-10 times.

- Pat or roll out to 1/2-in. thickness; cut with a floured 2-1/2-in. biscuit cutter. Place 2 in. apart on a baking sheet coated with cooking spray. Combine remaining egg and water; brush over biscuits. Sprinkle with cheese.
- Bake at 425 degrees for 8-12 minutes or until golden brown. Serve warm.

Nutrition Information

- Calories: 147 calories
- Total Fat: 10g
- Cholesterol: 48mg
- Sodium: 194mg
- Total Carbohydrate: 12g
- Protein: 3g
- Fiber: 0 g

257. Parmesan Basil Biscuits

Rise to the occasion and serve these light flavorful biscuits the next time you invite guests to dinner. The olive oil, Parmesan cheese and basil make the golden gems so tasty, they don't even need butter! The recipe comes from our Test Kitchen.

Serving: 1 dozen. | Prep: 20 m | Cook: 20 m | Ready in: 40 m

Ingredients

- 2-1/2 cups all-purpose flour
- 1/4 cup shredded Parmesan cheese
- 2 tablespoons minced fresh basil or 2 teaspoons dried basil
- 2-1/2 teaspoons baking powder
- 1/2 teaspoon baking soda
- 1/2 teaspoon salt
- 1/4 teaspoon pepper
- 1 cup buttermilk
- 3 tablespoons olive oil

Direction

- In a large bowl, combine the flour, cheese, basil, baking powder, baking soda, salt and pepper. Stir in buttermilk and oil just until moistened.
- Turn onto a lightly floured surface; gently knead three times. Roll dough to 1/2-in. thickness; cut with a floured 2-1/2-in. biscuit cutter. Place 1 in. apart on an ungreased baking sheet.
- Bake at 400 degrees for 16-18 minutes or until lightly browned. Serve warm.

Nutrition Information

- Calories: 129 calories
- Total Fat: 4g
- Cholesterol: 2mg
- Sodium: 301mg
- Total Carbohydrate: 19g
- Protein: 4g
- Fiber: 1g

258. Parmesan Sweet Cream Biscuits

Sweet cream biscuits were the first kind I mastered. Since the ingredients are so simple, I can scale the recipe up or down. In fact, I've actually memorized it! --Helen Nelander, Boulder Creek, California

Serving: about 1 dozen | Prep: 10 m | Cook: 15 m | Ready in: 25 m

Ingredients

- 2 cups all-purpose flour
- 1/3 cup grated Parmesan cheese
- 2 teaspoons baking powder
- 1/2 teaspoon salt
- 1-1/2 cups heavy whipping cream

Direction

- Preheat oven to 400 degrees. Whisk together first four ingredients. Add cream; stir just until moistened.
- Turn dough onto a lightly floured surface; knead gently 6-8 times. Roll or pat dough to 1/2-in. thickness; cut with a floured 2-3/4-in. biscuit cutter. Place 1 in. apart on an ungreased baking sheet.
- Bake until light golden brown, 12-15 minutes. Serve warm.

Nutrition Information

- Calories: 187 calories
- Total Fat: 12g
- Cholesterol: 36mg
- Sodium: 227mg
- Total Carbohydrate: 17g
- Protein: 4g
- Fiber: 1g

259. PearNut Biscuits

Pears bring a mild sweetness to these tender biscuits, while chopped pecans lend a little crunch. These are great for an on-the-go breakfast. --Mary Ann Dell, Phoenixville, Pennsylvania

Serving: 10 biscuits. | Prep: 20 m | Cook: 15 m | Ready in: 35 m

Ingredients

- 1-3/4 cups all-purpose flour
- 1/3 cup packed brown sugar
- 2 teaspoons baking powder
- 3/4 teaspoon salt
- 3 tablespoons cold butter
- 1 egg
- 1/2 cup half-and-half cream
- 1 cup chopped peeled ripe pears
- 1/4 cup chopped pecans

Direction

- In a large bowl, combine the flour, brown sugar, baking powder and salt. Cut in butter until mixture resembles coarse crumbs. Whisk egg and cream; stir into crumb mixture just until moistened. Fold in pears and pecans. Drop by 1/4 cupfuls onto an ungreased baking sheet.
- Bake at 400 degrees for 15-18 minutes or until golden brown. Serve warm.

Nutrition Information

- Calories: 191 calories
- Total Fat: 8g
- Cholesterol: 36mg
- Sodium: 307mg
- Total Carbohydrate: 27g
- Protein: 4g
- Fiber: 1g

260. Pecan Pumpkin Biscuits

Our two daughters love munching on these rich pecan-studded biscuits for breakfast. I make dozens and serve them piping-hot with butter and honey.

Serving: 1 dozen. | Prep: 15 m | Cook: 15 m | Ready in: 30 m

Ingredients

- 2 cups all-purpose flour
- 1/4 cup sugar
- 4 teaspoons baking powder
- 1/2 teaspoon salt
- 1/2 teaspoon ground cinnamon
- 1/2 teaspoon ground nutmeg
- 1/2 cup cold butter
- 1/3 cup chopped pecans, toasted
- 2/3 cup canned pumpkin
- 1/3 cup half-and-half cream

Direction

- In a large bowl, combine the first six ingredients. Cut in butter until mixture resembles coarse crumbs. Stir in pecans. Combine pumpkin and cream; stir into dry ingredients. Turn onto a floured surface; knead four to six times. Roll to 1/2-in. thickness; cut with a 2-1/2-in. biscuit cutter. Place on a greased baking sheet. Bake at 400 degrees for 12-15 minutes or until golden brown. Serve warm.

Nutrition Information

- Calories: 194 calories
- Total Fat: 11g
- Cholesterol: 24mg
- Sodium: 313mg
- Total Carbohydrate: 22g
- Protein: 3g
- Fiber: 1g

261. Pepperoni Drop Biscuits

Sandra Buchanan uses garlic powder, Italian seasoning, sliced pepperoni and cheddar cheese to whip up a savory sensation in her Bath, New York kitchen. "These biscuits go great with spaghetti, macaroni and cheese or breaded fish," she says.

Serving: 2 dozen. | Prep: 10 m | Cook: 20 m | Ready in: 30 m

Ingredients

- 2 cups biscuit/baking mix
- 3/4 cup milk
- 3 tablespoons butter, melted
- 1/2 teaspoon garlic powder
- 1/2 teaspoon Italian seasoning
- 1 package (3-1/2 ounces) sliced pepperoni, finely chopped
- 2/3 cup shredded cheddar cheese

Direction

- In a bowl, combine biscuit mix, milk, butter, garlic powder and Italian seasoning. Stir in pepperoni and cheese just until combined. Drop by heaping tablespoonfuls 2 in. apart onto ungreased baking sheets. Bake at 400 degrees for 16-18 minutes or until golden brown. Serve warm.

Nutrition Information

- Calories: 89 calories
- Total Fat: 6g
- Cholesterol: 12mg
- Sodium: 239mg
- Total Carbohydrate: 7g
- Protein: 2g
- Fiber: 0 g

262. Pillow Potato Biscuits

I developed this recipe one evening while making "ordinary" biscuits. I had half a cup of potato flakes left in the box and I just added them to the dough. The biscuits came out of the oven as light and airy as pillows!

Serving: 12-18 biscuits, depending on thickness and size. | Prep: 25 m | Cook: 15 m | Ready in: 40 m

Ingredients

- 1/2 cup instant mashed potato flakes
- 1 teaspoon sugar
- 2 tablespoons butter, softened
- 1/2 cup hot water
- 1/3 cup cold water
- 3 cups biscuit/baking mix
- Milk for biscuit tops, optional

Direction

- In a bowl, combine the potato flakes, sugar, butter and hot water. Add cold water and biscuit mix, stirring until well-blended. Add more cold water if necessary to form a soft dough.
- Turn onto a lightly floured surface; knead 10 times. Roll dough to 1/2-in. to 3/4-in.-thickness; cut with 2-in. biscuit cutter.
- Place on an ungreased baking sheet; brush with milk if desired. Bake at 450 degrees for 13-14 minutes or until lightly browned.

Nutrition Information

- Calories: 100 calories
- Total Fat: 4g
- Cholesterol: 3mg
- Sodium: 269mg
- Total Carbohydrate: 14g
- Protein: 2g
- Fiber: 0 g

263. Pina Colada Biscuits

This recipe is quick to make and tastes great. You'll think you're on a tropical vacation! --Carolyn Piette, Johnston, Rhode Island

Serving: 1 dozen. | Prep: 20 m | Cook: 10 m | Ready in: 30 m

Ingredients

- 2-1/2 cups biscuit/baking mix
- 2 tablespoons sugar
- 1/4 cup cold butter, cubed
- 1/4 cup 2% milk
- 1 large egg
- 1/2 teaspoon vanilla extract
- 1/2 cup unsweetened pineapple tidbits, well drained
- 1/2 cup sweetened shredded coconut
- 1/4 cup chopped macadamia nuts

Direction

- Preheat oven 450 degrees. In a large bowl, whisk biscuit mix and sugar. Cut in butter until mixture resembles coarse crumbs. In another bowl, whisk milk, egg and vanilla; stir into crumb mixture just until moistened. Stir in remaining ingredients.
- Turn onto a lightly floured surface; knead gently 8-10 times. Pat or roll dough to 1/2-in. thickness; cut with a floured 2-1/2-in. biscuit cutter. Place 1 in. apart on an ungreased baking sheet. Bake 7-9 minutes or until golden brown. Serve warm.

Nutrition Information

- Calories:
- Total Fat: g
- Cholesterol: mg
- Sodium: mg
- Total Carbohydrate: g
- Protein: g
- Fiber: g

264. Pineapple Biscuits

Refrigerated biscuits hurry along preparation of these breakfast buns from Carol Henderson of Stephenville, Texas. The pineapple topping has just four ingredients and is a snap to stir together.

Serving: 10 servings. | Prep: 15 m | Cook: 10 m | Ready in: 25 m

Ingredients

- 1/2 cup packed brown sugar
- 1/4 cup butter, softened
- 1 can (8 ounces) crushed pineapple, drained
- 1 teaspoon ground cinnamon
- 1 tube (12 ounces) refrigerated biscuits

Direction

- In a bowl, combine the brown sugar and butter; stir in the pineapple and cinnamon. Spoon into 10 greased muffin cups. Place one biscuit in each prepared cup. Bake at 425 degrees for 10 minutes or until golden brown. Let stand for 5 minutes before inverting onto a serving platter.

Nutrition Information

- Calories: 207 calories
- Total Fat: 10g
- Cholesterol: 12mg
- Sodium: 374mg
- Total Carbohydrate: 28g
- Protein: 2g
- Fiber: 1g

265. Pizza Biscuits

For fast appetizers or after-school munchies, fix a batch of these zippy bites from Angie Marquart of Bellville, Ohio. They're covered with onion, seasoned tomato sauce and mozzarella cheese. Add whatever pizza toppings you like.

Serving: 9 servings. | Prep: 10 m | Cook: 22 m | Ready in: 32 m

Ingredients

- 1 tablespoon butter, melted
- 1/2 cup tomato sauce
- 1/4 cup chopped onion
- 1 tablespoon canola oil
- 1 garlic clove, minced
- 1/2 teaspoon dried basil
- 1/2 teaspoon dried oregano
- 1 tube (7-1/2 ounces) refrigerated buttermilk biscuits
- 1/3 cup shredded part-skim mozzarella cheese

Direction

- Pour butter into a 9-in. square baking dish; set aside. In a bowl, combine the tomato sauce, onion, oil, garlic, basil and oregano. Cut each biscuit into four wedges; dip into tomato mixture.
- Place in prepared pan; pour any remaining tomato mixture over top. Sprinkle with mozzarella cheese. Bake at 400 degrees for 18-22 minutes or until golden brown. Serve warm.

Nutrition Information

- Calories: 99 calories
- Total Fat: 4g
- Cholesterol: 6mg
- Sodium: 317mg
- Total Carbohydrate: 13g
- Protein: 3g
- Fiber: 0 g

266. Pizza Drop Biscuits

"Blend delicious cheese drop biscuits with some pizza ingredients, and presto! Simple biscuits that kids and adults will love!"

Serving: 18 | Prep: 15 m | Cook: 15 m | Ready in: 30 m

Ingredients

- 3 cups all-purpose flour
- 1 1/2 tablespoons baking powder
- 1 1/4 teaspoons garlic powder, divided
- 1/2 teaspoon salt
- 1/4 teaspoon ground white pepper
- 1/4 cup shortening
- 1 cup milk
- 1/2 cup shredded Cheddar cheese
- 12 slices pepperoni, diced
- 1/4 cup melted butter

Direction

- Preheat oven to 450 degrees F (230 degrees C). Lightly grease a baking sheet.
- Mix flour, baking powder, 3/4 teaspoon garlic powder, salt, and white pepper together in a bowl.
- Cut shortening into flour mixture with a knife or pastry blender until the mixture is slightly lumpy. Stir milk, Cheddar cheese, and pepperoni into flour mixture until well blended. Drop 2-inch balls onto the prepared baking sheet.
- Bake in the preheated oven until golden, 12 to 15 minutes.
- Stir butter and remaining 1/2 teaspoon garlic powder together in a small bowl; brush onto biscuits.

Nutrition Information

- Calories: 151 calories
- Total Fat: 7.5 g
- Cholesterol: 13 mg
- Sodium: 252 mg
- Total Carbohydrate: 17.1 g
- Protein: 3.7 g

267. PlumOat Drop Biscuits

"These easy biscuits get a flavor boost from plump dried plums."

Serving: 12 | Prep: 20 m | Cook: 10 m | Ready in: 30 m

Ingredients

- 2 tablespoons white sugar
- 1/2 teaspoon ground cinnamon
- 1 1/3 cups all-purpose flour
- 1 1/3 cups rolled oats
- 1 tablespoon baking powder
- 1/4 teaspoon salt
- 3 tablespoons butter
- 3/4 cup chopped pitted prunes (dried plums)
- 1 cup fat-free milk

Direction

- Preheat oven to 450 degrees F (230 degrees C). Grease a baking sheet.
- Combine sugar and cinnamon together in a bowl. Mix flour, oats, baking powder, 1 tablespoon cinnamon-sugar mixture, and salt together in a separate bowl. Cut butter into flour mixture using a pastry blender until mixture resembles coarse crumbs; fold in prunes.
- Make a well in the center of the flour mixture; add milk to the well. Stir mixture with a fork just until dough is moistened. Drop dough into 12 mounds, about 1/4 cup each, on the prepared baking sheet. Sprinkle remaining cinnamon-sugar over each dough mound.
- Bake in the preheated oven until biscuits are golden brown, 10 to 12 minutes. Serve immediately.

Nutrition Information

- Calories: 151 calories
- Total Fat: 3.7 g
- Cholesterol: 8 mg
- Sodium: 201 mg
- Total Carbohydrate: 26.9 g
- Protein: 3.6 g

268. Poppy Onion Biscuits

"A recipe that has been in our family for years."

Serving: 12 | Prep: 15 m | Cook: 20 m | Ready in: 35 m

Ingredients

- 2 large onions, grated
- 1 teaspoon white sugar
- 1 egg
- 3/4 cup vegetable oil
- 1/4 cup warm water
- 4 teaspoons poppy seeds
- 1 teaspoon baking powder
- 1/2 teaspoon salt
- 1/2 teaspoon ground black pepper
- 2 cups flour

Direction

- Preheat oven to 425 degrees F (220 degrees C).
- Lightly grease a baking sheet or line with baking parchment.
- Mix onions, sugar, egg, vegetable oil, and warm water in a large bowl with an electric mixer until well combined.
- Mix the baking powder, salt, pepper, and poppy seeds into the onion mixture.
- Beat the flour into the onion mixture in batches with the mixer set to Low speed until incorporated into a dough.
- Drop dough by the tablespoon onto the prepared baking sheet.
- Bake in the preheated oven until golden brown on top, 20 to 30 minutes.

Nutrition Information

- Calories: 219 calories
- Total Fat: 14.7 g
- Cholesterol: 16 mg
- Sodium: 145 mg
- Total Carbohydrate: 19 g
- Protein: 3.1 g

269. Poppy Seed Biscuits

In her Emerald Park, Saskatchewan home, Diäne Molberg uses convenient baking mix to stir up these pleasant-tasting biscuits. "The subtly sweet seeded treats are a good accompaniment to soup or a main-dish salad," she Note:s.

Serving: about 1 dozen. | Prep: 15 m | Cook: 10 m | Ready in: 25 m

Ingredients

- 1/4 cup 2% milk
- 2 tablespoons honey
- 1/2 cup cream-style cottage cheese
- 2-1/4 cups biscuit/baking mix
- 1 tablespoon poppy seeds

Direction

- In a blender, combine the milk, honey and cottage cheese. Cover and process until smooth. In a large bowl, combine biscuit mix and poppy seeds. Stir in cottage cheese mixture just until blended.
- Turn onto a floured surface; pat to 1/2-in. thickness. Cut with a 2-1/2-in. biscuit cutter.
- Place on an ungreased baking sheet. Bake at 425 degrees for 8-10 minutes or until golden brown. Cool for 1 minute before removing to wire rack. Serve warm.

Nutrition Information

- Calories: 119 calories
- Total Fat: 2g
- Cholesterol: 1mg
- Sodium: 323mg
- Total Carbohydrate: 21g
- Protein: 3g
- Fiber: 0 g

270. Potato Biscuits

THE potatoes in this recipe make these biscuits tender and moist.

Serving: 6 biscuits. | Prep: 15 m | Cook: 10 m | Ready in: 25 m

Ingredients

- 1 cup all-purpose flour
- 1-1/2 teaspoons brown sugar
- 1 teaspoon baking powder
- 1/4 teaspoon baking soda
- 1/4 teaspoon salt
- 1/2 cup mashed potatoes (without added milk and butter)
- 1/2 cup buttermilk
- 1 tablespoon butter, melted
- 1-1/2 teaspoons honey

Direction

- In a small bowl, combine the flour, brown sugar, baking powder, baking soda and salt. In another bowl, combine the potatoes, buttermilk, butter and honey; stir into dry ingredients just until moistened.
- Turn onto a lightly floured surface; knead 8-10 times. Pat or roll out to 1/2-in. thickness; cut with a floured 2-1/2-in. biscuit cutter. Place 1 in. apart on an ungreased baking sheet.
- Bake at 425 degrees for 8-12 minutes or until golden brown. Serve warm.

Nutrition Information

- Calories: 123 calories
- Total Fat: 2g
- Cholesterol: 6mg
- Sodium: 257mg
- Total Carbohydrate: 22g
- Protein: 3g
- Fiber: 1g

271. Potato Drop Biscuits

When you don't have time to make biscuit dough from scratch and cut out the biscuits, you can rely on this four-ingredient recipe.

Serving: 1 dozen. | Prep: 10 m | Cook: 10 m | Ready in: 20 m

Ingredients

- 2-1/4 cups biscuit/baking mix
- 1/3 cup mashed potato flakes
- 2/3 cup 2% milk
- 2 tablespoons sour cream

Direction

- In a large bowl, combine biscuit mix and potato flakes. In a small bowl, whisk milk and sour cream. Stir into dry ingredients just until moistened.
- Drop by heaping tablespoonfuls onto a greased baking sheet. Bake at 400 degrees for 10-12 minutes or until tops begin to brown. Serve warm.

Nutrition Information

- Calories: 112 calories
- Total Fat: 4g
- Cholesterol: 4mg
- Sodium: 295mg
- Total Carbohydrate: 16g
- Protein: 2g
- Fiber: 0 g

272. Praline Biscuits

"These upside-down biscuits have an appealing nut topping that adds a special touch to a company brunch," says Merrill Powers of Spearville, Kansas. Best of all, they bake in just minutes.

Serving: 1 dozen. | Prep: 20 m | Cook: 10 m | Ready in: 30 m

Ingredients

- 1/2 cup butter, melted
- 1/2 cup packed brown sugar

- 36 pecan halves
- Ground cinnamon
- 2 cups biscuit/baking mix
- 1/3 cup unsweetened applesauce
- 1/3 cup 2% milk

Direction

- Grease 12 muffin cups. In each cup, place 2 teaspoons brown sugar, three pecan halves and a dash cinnamon. In a large bowl, combine the biscuit mix, applesauce and milk just until moistened.
- Spoon into muffin cups. Bake at 450 degrees for 10 minutes. Immediately invert onto a serving platter. Serve warm.

Nutrition Information

- Calories: 220 calories
- Total Fat: 14g
- Cholesterol: 21mg
- Sodium: 336mg
- Total Carbohydrate: 23g
- Protein: 2g
- Fiber: 1g

273. Prosciutto Cheddar Breakfast Biscuits

When my family visits, I love to make my nephew Robbie happy by making any breakfast with pork and cheese. I created this as a twist on the traditional breakfast sandwich. --Kelly Boe, Whiteland, Indiana

Serving: 6 servings. | Prep: 30 m | Cook: 15 m | Ready in: 45 m

Ingredients

- 2-1/3 cups biscuit/baking mix
- 1/2 cup 2% milk
- 3 tablespoons butter, melted
- 1 to 2 tablespoons minced fresh chives
- EGGS:
- 6 large eggs
- 2 tablespoons 2% milk
- 1/4 teaspoon salt

- 2 ounces thinly sliced prosciutto or deli ham, cut into strips
- 2 green onions, chopped
- 1 tablespoon butter
- 1/2 cup shredded cheddar cheese

Direction

- Preheat oven to 425 degrees. In a bowl, combine biscuit mix, milk, melted butter and chives; mix just until moistened.
- Turn dough onto a lightly floured surface; knead gently 8-10 times. Pat or roll to 3/4-in. thickness; cut with a floured 2-1/2-in. biscuit cutter. Place 2 in. apart on an ungreased baking sheet. Bake 12-14 minutes or until golden brown.
- Meanwhile, in a large bowl, whisk eggs, milk and salt. Place a large skillet over medium heat. Add prosciutto and green onions; cook until prosciutto begins to brown, stirring occasionally. Stir in butter until melted. Add egg mixture; cook and stir until eggs are thickened and no liquid egg remains. Stir in cheese; remove from heat.
- Split warm biscuits in half. Fill with egg mixture.

Nutrition Information

- Calories: 397 calories
- Total Fat: 24g
- Cholesterol: 252mg
- Sodium: 1062mg
- Total Carbohydrate: 31g
- Protein: 15g
- Fiber: 1g

274. Pub Peanut Muffins

"What is better than beer and peanuts? Having the perfect combination in a sweet muffin! For extra yummy flavor, serve warm with peanut butter or nut butter spread."

Serving: 15 | Prep: 10 m | Cook: 25 m | Ready in: 35 m

Ingredients

- 4 cups all-purpose flour
- 1/2 cup white sugar
- 1 1/2 teaspoons baking powder
- 1 1/2 teaspoons salt
- 2 cups pale ale or lager beer
- 1 cup chopped peanuts
- 2 tablespoons butter, melted

Direction

- Preheat the oven to 350 degrees F (175 degrees C). Grease the cups of a muffin tin.
- In a large bowl, stir together the flour, sugar, baking powder, and salt. Pour in the beer and stir until evenly moistened. The dough will be slightly sticky. Stir in peanuts. Fill muffin cups 3/4 full with the batter and spoon about 1/2 teaspoon of butter over the top of each one.
- Bake for 25 minutes in the preheated oven, or until browned and firm. Cool in the pan for about 5 minutes before removing and cooling on a wire rack.

Nutrition Information

- Calories: 234 calories
- Total Fat: 6.7 g
- Cholesterol: 4 mg
- Sodium: 294 mg
- Total Carbohydrate: 35.5 g
- Protein: 6 g

275. PullApart Herb Biscuits

Serve any main dish with these biscuits from Nancy Zimmerman of Cape May Court House, New Jersey. She writes, "This easy-to-prepare bread incorporates many different flavors including garlic, cheese and various herbs. And it bakes up golden and aromatic."

Serving: 5 servings. | Prep: 10 m | Cook: 10 m | Ready in: 20 m

Ingredients

- 1 tube (12 ounces) refrigerated buttermilk biscuits
- 1/4 cup butter, melted
- 2 tablespoons grated Parmesan cheese
- 1 tablespoon sesame seeds
- 1 teaspoon minced garlic
- 1 teaspoon dried parsley flakes
- 1 teaspoon dried basil
- 1/2 teaspoon dried oregano
- 1/2 teaspoon dried thyme

Direction

- Separate biscuits and cut into quarters. In an ungreased 9-in. round baking pan, combine the remaining ingredients. Add biscuits and toss to coat.
- Bake at 450 degrees for 8-12 minutes or until golden brown. Invert onto a serving platter. Serve warm.

Nutrition Information

- Calories:
- Total Fat: g
- Cholesterol: mg
- Sodium: mg
- Total Carbohydrate: g
- Protein: g
- Fiber: g

276. Pumpkin and Maple Biscuits

"These are tender, moist biscuits with a subtle and mellow taste and a bright saffron-yellow color. Even my son who hates pumpkin will eat these."

Serving: 8 | Prep: 5 m | Cook: 15 m | Ready in: 20 m

Ingredients

- 2 1/2 cups self-rising flour
- 1 cup canned pumpkin
- 2/3 cup sour cream
- 1/2 teaspoon maple flavoring
- 2 tablespoons maple syrup
- 2 tablespoons butter-flavored shortening, melted

Direction

- Preheat oven to 400 degrees F (200 degrees C). Lightly grease a baking sheet.
- Place the flour in a large bowl. Make a well in the center of the flour. Place the pumpkin, sour cream, maple flavoring, and syrup in the well. Mix the pumpkin mixture into the flour to make the dough until stiff. Roll the dough on a lightly-floured surface. Cut into 8 biscuits. Dip each biscuit into the melted shortening and place the biscuits on the baking sheet with the side that was dipped in shortening facing up.
- Bake in preheated oven until tops are golden brown, 12 to 15 minutes.

Nutrition Information

- Calories: 232 calories
- Total Fat: 7.7 g
- Cholesterol: 8 mg
- Sodium: 581 mg
- Total Carbohydrate: 35.7 g
- Protein: 4.8 g

277. Pumpkin Biscuits

"A staple in our holiday bread basket. Originally submitted to ThanksgivingRecipe.com."

Serving: 36

Ingredients

- 2 1/2 cups all-purpose flour
- 3 tablespoons packed brown sugar
- 1 tablespoon baking powder
- 1/2 teaspoon salt
- 1/4 teaspoon ground nutmeg
- 1/4 teaspoon ground cinnamon
- 1/4 teaspoon ground ginger
- 1/2 cup butter, sliced
- 2 cups pumpkin puree

Direction

- Preheat oven to 400 degrees F (205 degrees C). Butter one large cookie sheet.
- Stir together the flour, brown sugar, baking powder, salt, nutmeg, cinnamon and ginger. Cut in the butter with a pastry blender until the mixture resembles coarse crumbs. Stir in the pumpkin and mix to form a soft dough.
- On a lightly floured surface pat the dough out to 1/2 inch thick. Cut out biscuits with a round 2 inch cutter. Place biscuits on the prepared cookie sheet.
- Bake at 400 degrees F (205 degrees C) for 15 to 20 minutes. Serve warm from the oven.

Nutrition Information

- Calories: 62 calories
- Total Fat: 2.7 g
- Cholesterol: 7 mg
- Sodium: 92 mg
- Total Carbohydrate: 8.5 g
- Protein: 1 g

278. Pumpkin Patch Biscuits

I got smart and started making double batches of these moist, fluffy biscuits to meet the demand. My dad loves their pumpkiny goodness and requests them for Christmas, Father's Day and his birthday. --Liza Taylor, Seattle, Washington

Serving: 6 biscuits. | Prep: 20 m | Cook: 20 m | Ready in: 40 m

Ingredients

- 1-3/4 cups all-purpose flour
- 1/4 cup packed brown sugar
- 2-1/2 teaspoons baking powder
- 1/2 teaspoon salt
- 1/4 teaspoon baking soda
- 1/2 cup plus 1-1/2 teaspoons cold butter, divided
- 3/4 cup canned pumpkin
- 1/3 cup buttermilk

Direction

- In a large bowl, combine the flour, brown sugar, baking powder, salt and baking soda. Cut in 1/2 cup butter until mixture resembles coarse crumbs. Combine pumpkin and buttermilk; stir into crumb mixture just until moistened.
- Turn onto a lightly floured surface; knead 8-10 times. Pat or roll out to 1-in. thickness; cut with a floured 2-1/2-in. biscuit cutter. Place 1 in. apart on a greased baking sheet.
- Bake at 425 degrees for 18-22 minutes or until golden brown. Melt remaining butter; brush over biscuits. Serve warm.

Nutrition Information

- Calories: 328 calories
- Total Fat: 17g
- Cholesterol: 44mg
- Sodium: 609mg
- Total Carbohydrate: 40g
- Protein: 5g
- Fiber: 2g

279. Pumpkin Pecan Biscuits

"Pumpkin and pecans is an irresistible combination. The good thing about these biscuits is that they can easily be transformed from sweet to savory by cutting down on brown sugar or putting no sugar at all. Perfect to serve on Thanksgiving."

Serving: 5 | Prep: 15 m | Cook: 17 m | Ready in: 1 h 2 m

Ingredients

- 1/4 cup pecans
- 1/2 cup all-purpose flour
- 1/2 cup whole wheat flour
- 1 1/2 teaspoons baking powder
- 1/2 teaspoon salt
- 6 tablespoons cold butter, cut into small cubes
- 1/4 cup cold water
- 1/4 cup dark brown sugar
- 1 cup pumpkin puree
- 1 teaspoon vegetable oil

Direction

- Preheat oven to 350 degrees F (175 degrees C). Spread pecans on a baking sheet.
- Toast pecans in the preheated oven until golden brown and fragrant, about 5 minutes. Chop coarsely.
- Increase oven temperature to 425 degrees F (220 degrees C). Brush a large rimmed baking sheet with oil.
- Mix all-purpose flour, whole wheat flour, baking powder, and salt together in a bowl. Rub butter into the mixture until it reaches a crumbly consistency.
- Stir water and brown sugar together in a bowl. Blend into crumbly mixture. Stir in pumpkin puree and fold in pecans. Wrap dough in plastic wrap.
- Chill dough in the freezer for 10 minutes.
- Divide dough into 5 pieces and shape into balls. Flatten slightly and place 1 inch apart on the prepared baking sheet.
- Bake in the preheated oven until puffed and golden brown, 12 to 15 minutes. Transfer to a

wire rack and cool completely, about 20 minutes.

Nutrition Information

- Calories: 317 calories
- Total Fat: 19.5 g
- Cholesterol: 37 mg
- Sodium: 599 mg
- Total Carbohydrate: 34.2 g
- Protein: 4.2 g

280. Quick Biscuits

Quick Biscuits from Diane Hixon of Niceville, Florida make a satisfying accompaniment to the meal. "I never made biscuits until I tried this two-ingredient recipe," Diane explains. "Now my husband wants biscuits all the time!"

Serving: 9 biscuits. | Prep: 15 m | Cook: 10 m | Ready in: 25 m

Ingredients

- 2 cups self-rising flour
- 1 cup heavy whipping cream

Direction

- In a large bowl, combine the flour and cream. Turn out onto a floured surface; knead for 5 minutes or until no longer sticky. On a floured surface, roll dough to a 1/2-in. thickness. Cut into 3-in. biscuits.
- Place on a greased baking sheet. Bake at 450 degrees for 8 to 10 minutes.

Nutrition Information

- Calories: 180 calories
- Total Fat: 10g
- Cholesterol: 36mg
- Sodium: 330mg
- Total Carbohydrate: 20g
- Protein: 3g
- Fiber: 0 g

281. Quick Cheddar Garlic Biscuits

"Warm cheesy garlic biscuits!"

Serving: 5 | Prep: 10 m | Cook: 10 m | Ready in: 20 m

Ingredients

- 2 cups biscuit mix
- 1 cup shredded mild Cheddar cheese
- 2/3 cup milk
- 1/4 cup butter
- 1/4 teaspoon garlic powder

Direction

- Preheat an oven to 450 degrees F (230 degrees C). Grease a baking sheet.
- Mix biscuit mix, Cheddar cheese, and milk together in a bowl using a wooden spoon until batter is soft and doughy, 30 seconds. Drop spoonfuls of batter onto the prepared baking sheet.
- Bake in the preheated oven until biscuits are lightly browned and cooked through, 8 to 10 minutes.
- Heat butter and garlic powder in a saucepan over low heat until melted, about 5 minutes. Brush garlic butter over cooked biscuits.

Nutrition Information

- Calories: 385 calories
- Total Fat: 24.6 g
- Cholesterol: 51 mg
- Sodium: 824 mg
- Total Carbohydrate: 31.5 g
- Protein: 10.2 g

282. Quick Cheese Biscuits

Cheddar cheese adds a burst of sunny flavor to the flaky biscuits Donna Engel bakes in her Portsmouth, Rhode Island kitchen.

Serving: 1-1/2 dozen. | Prep: 10 m | Cook: 10 m | Ready in: 20 m

Ingredients

- 2 cups buttermilk baking mix
- 2/3 cup milk
- 1/2 cup shredded cheddar cheese
- 2 tablespoons butter, melted
- 1/2 teaspoon garlic powder

Direction

- In a bowl, stir in the biscuit mix, milk and cheese just until moistened. Drop by tablespoonfuls onto an ungreased baking sheet. Mix butter and garlic powder; brush over biscuits. Bake at 475 degrees for 8 to 10 minutes or until golden brown. Serve warm.

Nutrition Information

- Calories: 82 calories
- Total Fat: 4g
- Cholesterol: 8mg
- Sodium: 204mg
- Total Carbohydrate: 9g
- Protein: 2g
- Fiber: 0 g

283. Quick n Easy Blueberry Oat Biscuits

"A healthy, fast, and tasty way to use up leftover Bisquick® mix --- which is just what I did upon returning from a canoe/camping trip from which we were able to bring home bags of wild blueberries. Especially nice alongside a cheese soup."

Serving: 12 | Prep: 15 m | Cook: 8 m | Ready in: 23 m

Ingredients

- 2 cups baking mix (such as Bisquick®)
- 3/4 cup rolled oats
- 1/2 cup skim milk
- 1 tablespoon hemp seeds (optional)
- 1 cup blueberries
- 2 tablespoons light butter, melted
- 1 tablespoon brown sugar

Direction

- Preheat oven to 450 degrees F (230 degrees C).
- Combine baking mix, oats, milk, and hemp seeds in a bowl; stir until dough forms a ball. Fold in blueberries until evenly distributed.
- Drop heaping teaspoonfuls of dough onto an ungreased baking sheet.
- Bake in the preheated oven until golden brown, 8 to 10 minutes. Brush each biscuit with melted butter; sprinkle with brown sugar.

Nutrition Information

- Calories: 128 calories
- Total Fat: 4.8 g
- Cholesterol: 3 mg
- Sodium: 273 mg
- Total Carbohydrate: 19.4 g
- Protein: 2.8 g

284. Raisin Tea Biscuits

"Moist, lightly sweet biscuits are just perfect for breakfast or a cup of tea in the afternoon. This is as close as I could get to the store bakery version. My husband and kids loved these just as much as the store bought biscuits. We make a lactose free version with vanilla soy milk and margarine, but have made the milk variety for others. Recipe works perfectly in both options."

Serving: 8 | Prep: 15 m | Cook: 15 m | Ready in: 30 m

Ingredients

- 2/3 cup raisins
- 1 cup hot water
- 3 1/4 cups all-purpose flour
- 3 tablespoons white sugar
- 1 tablespoon baking powder
- 1/2 teaspoon salt
- 3/4 cup cold butter, cut into pieces
- 1 cup milk
- 1 egg
- 1 tablespoon water

Direction

- Preheat an oven to 375 degrees F (190 degrees C). Soak raisins in water for 10 minutes; drain and set aside. Line a baking sheet with parchment paper.
- Whisk together the flour, sugar, baking powder, and salt in a mixing bowl. Cut in the butter with a knife or pastry cutter until the mixture resembles coarse crumbs. Stir milk into the flour mixture until moistened. Add the drained raisins. Turn the dough out onto a lightly floured surface and pat or roll the dough out into a 3/4 to 1-inch thick round. Cut dough with a biscuit cutter and place onto the prepared baking sheet. Beat the egg with 1 tablespoon water in a small bowl. Brush egg mixture on each biscuit.
- Bake in the preheated oven until golden brown, about 15 minutes.

Nutrition Information

- Calories: 416 calories
- Total Fat: 19 g
- Cholesterol: 69 mg
- Sodium: 474 mg
- Total Carbohydrate: 55 g
- Protein: 7.5 g

285. Ranch Biscuits

I jazz up biscuit mix with ranch salad dressing mix, then brush the golden bites with garlic butter after baking. I bake several dozen at once and store them in the freezer. The parsley-flecked biscuits go well with any entree.--Christi Gillentine, Tulsa, Oklahoma

Serving: 9 biscuits. | Prep: 15 m | Cook: 10 m | Ready in: 25 m

Ingredients

- 2 cups biscuit/baking mix
- 4 teaspoons dry ranch salad dressing mix
- 2/3 cup milk
- 2 tablespoons butter, melted
- 1 teaspoon dried parsley flakes
- 1/8 teaspoon garlic powder

Direction

- In a large bowl, stir the biscuit mix, salad dressing mix and milk until combined. Drop 2 in. apart onto a greased baking sheet.
- Bake at 425 degrees for 10-15 minutes or until golden brown. In a small bowl, combine the butter, parsley and garlic powder; brush over warm biscuits. Serve warm.

Nutrition Information

- Calories: 150 calories
- Total Fat: 7g
- Cholesterol: 8mg
- Sodium: 641mg
- Total Carbohydrate: 19g
- Protein: 3g
- Fiber: 0 g

286. Ranch Eggs n Biscuits

In Jefferson City, Missouri, Melinda Kimlinger relies on tender homemade biscuits topped with poached eggs and a spicy sauce to wake up her family's taste buds. "My teenage son would eat the whole batch if I'd let him," she says.

Serving: 6 servings (12 biscuits). | Prep: 30 m | Cook: 10 m | Ready in: 40 m

Ingredients

- 2 cups all-purpose flour
- 5 teaspoons baking powder
- 2 teaspoons sugar
- 1 teaspoon salt
- 1/2 teaspoon cream of tartar
- 1/2 cup cold butter, cubed
- 3/4 cup milk
- 1/2 pound bacon, diced
- 1/3 cup chopped onion
- 1 teaspoon chili powder
- 2 cups picante sauce
- 2 tablespoons minced fresh cilantro
- 6 eggs

Direction

- In a bowl, combine the first five ingredients. Cut in butter until mixture resembles coarse crumbs. With a fork, stir in milk until the mixture forms a ball. Turn onto a floured surface; knead 8-10 times. Roll to 1/2-in. thickness; cut out 12 biscuits with a 2-in. biscuit cutter. Place on an ungreased baking sheet. Bake at 450 degrees for 10-12 minutes or until golden brown.
- Meanwhile, in a large skillet, cook bacon until almost crisp; drain. Add onion and chili powder; cook until onion is tender. Stir in picante sauce and cilantro. Make six wells in picante mixture; break an egg into each. Cover and cook over medium heat until eggs are completely set. Serve over warm biscuits.

Nutrition Information

- Calories: 488 calories
- Total Fat: 28g
- Cholesterol: 268mg
- Sodium: 1510mg
- Total Carbohydrate: 42g
- Protein: 16g
- Fiber: 1g

287. Red Lobster Biscuits Gluten Free

"This is one of my favorite recipes and it's gluten free!"

Serving: 12 | Prep: 10 m | Cook: 10 m | Ready in: 30 m

Ingredients

- Biscuits:
- 2 cups gluten-free all-purpose baking flour
- 1 tablespoon baking powder
- 1 teaspoon salt
- 1 teaspoon dried parsley
- 1/2 teaspoon onion powder
- 1/2 teaspoon garlic powder
- 2/3 cup whole milk
- 1/3 cup vegetable oil
- 3/4 cup shredded Cheddar cheese
- Brushing:
- 1/4 cup dried parsley
- 2 tablespoons melted butter
- 1/2 teaspoon garlic powder

Direction

- Preheat oven to 450 degrees F (230 degrees C). Line a baking sheet with aluminum foil.
- Whisk flour, baking powder, salt, 1 teaspoon parsley, onion powder, and 1/2 teaspoon garlic powder together in a bowl. Add milk and vegetable oil; stir until smooth. Mix in Cheddar cheese until dough is combined. Roll dough into 2-inch balls and place 2-inches apart on prepared baking sheet.
- Bake in the preheated oven until golden brown, 10 to 12 minutes.
- Stir 1/4 cup parsley, melted butter, and 1/2 teaspoon garlic powder together in a bowl.

Brush butter mixture onto hot biscuits; let biscuits cool 10 to 15 minutes.

Nutrition Information

- Calories: 186 calories
- Total Fat: 11.6 g
- Cholesterol: 14 mg
- Sodium: 343 mg
- Total Carbohydrate: 18 g
- Protein: 4.6 g

baking until golden brown, about 5 minutes more.

Nutrition Information

- Calories: 379 calories
- Total Fat: 22.1 g
- Cholesterol: 90 mg
- Sodium: 796 mg
- Total Carbohydrate: 34 g
- Protein: 11.1 g

288. Red Lobster Cheddar Biscuits

"I made these with baked potato soup and loved it. Great addition! I gave them to a friend and he said they tasted just like the ones at Red Lobster®. The recipe will yield more if made into smaller biscuits. They are best served fresh out of the oven."

Serving: 6 | Prep: 10 m | Cook: 15 m | Ready in: 25 m

Ingredients

- 2 cups all-purpose flour
- 1 cup shredded Cheddar cheese
- 1 tablespoon baking powder
- 1 teaspoon salt
- 1/2 teaspoon garlic powder
- 2/3 cup milk
- 1/3 cup butter
- 1 large egg
- 2 tablespoons melted butter

Direction

- Preheat oven to 400 degrees F (200 degrees C). Butter a baking sheet.
- Combine flour, Cheddar cheese, baking powder, salt, and garlic powder in a bowl.
- Combine milk, 1/3 cup butter, and egg in a separate bowl. Mix into the flour mixture until chunky; be careful not to over-mix the batter.
- Drop batter by tablespoonfuls onto the prepared baking sheet.
- Bake in the preheated oven for 10 minutes. Brush melted butter on top and continue

289. Red Pepper Biscuits

"Great with stew or soup!"

Serving: 12

Ingredients

- 2 3/4 cups baking mix
- 1/2 teaspoon crushed red pepper flakes
- 3/4 teaspoon garlic powder
- 1 cup milk
- 1 cup shredded Cheddar cheese
- 2 tablespoons butter, melted

Direction

- Preheat oven to 425 degrees F (220 degrees C).
- Combine biscuit mix, pepper, and 1/2 teaspoon garlic powder in a large bowl. With a fork, stir in milk and cheese until mixture forms a soft dough. Drop by 1/4 cupfuls onto greased cookie sheet.
- Combine butter and remaining 1/4 teaspoon garlic powder, and brush on top of biscuits.
- Bake for 10 to 12 minutes, or until golden brown.

Nutrition Information

- Calories: 158 calories
- Total Fat: 5.8 g
- Cholesterol: 17 mg
- Sodium: 610 mg
- Total Carbohydrate: 21.2 g

- Protein: 5.4 g

290. Rich Parsley Biscuits

"These honey-flavored biscuits are delectable," assures Margaret Wilt of Ridley Park, Pennsylvania. They'd be a perfect treat at brunch or alongside soup at lunch or dinner.

Serving: 16 biscuits. | Prep: 20 m | Cook: 10 m | Ready in: 30 m

Ingredients

- 2-1/4 cups all-purpose flour
- 3 teaspoons baking powder
- 1/4 teaspoon baking soda
- 4 ounces cold reduced-fat cream cheese
- 4-1/2 teaspoons cold reduced-fat butter
- 2/3 cup reduced-sodium chicken broth
- 1/2 cup minced fresh parsley
- 1/2 cup honey

Direction

- In a large bowl, combine the flour, baking powder and baking soda. Cut in cream cheese and butter until mixture resembles coarse crumbs. Stir in the broth, parsley and honey just until moistened.
- Turn onto a lightly floured surface; knead 8-10 times. Pat or roll out to 1/2-in. thickness; cut with a floured 2-1/2-in. biscuit cutter.
- Place 2 in. apart on a baking sheet coated with cooking spray. Bake at 450 degrees for 8-10 minutes or until golden brown. Serve warm.

Nutrition Information

- Calories: 123 calories
- Total Fat: 2g
- Cholesterol: 7mg
- Sodium: 159mg
- Total Carbohydrate: 23g
- Protein: 3g
- Fiber: 1g

291. Rise n Shine Biscuits

"These biscuits come out nice and sweet and fluffy--and they couldn't be easier!" Note:s Diane Hixon of Niceville, Florida. Adjust the sugar to your liking, she suggests. You're sure to like the price of only 8 cent; each.

Serving: 9 biscuits. | Prep: 10 m | Cook: 10 m | Ready in: 20 m

Ingredients

- 1/3 cup club soda
- 1/3 cup sour cream
- 5 teaspoons sugar
- 2 cups biscuit/baking mix

Direction

- In a bowl, combine the club soda, sour cream and sugar. Add biscuit mix, stirring just until moistened. Drop dough by 1/3 cupfuls 2 in. apart onto a greased baking sheet. Bake at 450 degrees for 10-12 minutes or until golden brown.

Nutrition Information

- Calories: 136 calories
- Total Fat: 6g
- Cholesterol: 6mg
- Sodium: 342mg
- Total Carbohydrate: 19g
- Protein: 2g
- Fiber: 0 g

292. Rolled Buttermilk Biscuits

I scribbled down this recipe when our family visited the Cooperstown Farm Museum more than 25 years ago. I must have gotten it right, because these biscuits turn out great every time. --Patricia Kile, Elizabeth, Pennsylvania

Serving: 8 biscuits. | Prep: 20 m | Cook: 15 m | Ready in: 35 m

Ingredients

- 2 cups all-purpose flour
- 3 teaspoons baking powder
- 1/2 teaspoon baking soda
- 1/4 teaspoon salt
- 3 tablespoons cold butter
- 3/4 to 1 cup buttermilk
- 1 tablespoon fat-free milk

Direction

- In a large bowl, combine the flour, baking powder, baking soda and salt; cut in butter until mixture resembles coarse crumbs. Stir in enough buttermilk just to moisten dough.
- Turn onto a lightly floured surface; knead 3-4 times. Pat or roll to 3/4-in. thickness. Cut with a floured 2-1/2-in. biscuit cutter. Place on a baking sheet coated with cooking spray.
- Brush with milk. Bake at 450 degrees for 12-15 minutes or until golden brown.

Nutrition Information

- Calories: 164 calories
- Total Fat: 5g
- Cholesterol: 13mg
- Sodium: 382mg
- Total Carbohydrate: 25g
- Protein: 4g
- Fiber: 1g

293. Rosemary Biscuits

"Seasoned with rosemary, these light and tender biscuits are extra special," says Jacqueline Graves of Lawrenceville, Georgia. "And with just four ingredients, they're a snap to make."

Serving: 8 servings. | Prep: 20 m | Cook: 10 m | Ready in: 30 m

Ingredients

- 3 ounces reduced-fat cream cheese, cubed
- 1-3/4 cups reduced-fat biscuit/baking mix
- 1/2 cup fat-free milk
- 2 teaspoons minced fresh rosemary or 3/4 teaspoon dried rosemary, crushed

Direction

- In a large bowl, cut cream cheese into baking mix until crumbly. Stir in milk and rosemary just until moistened.
- Turn dough onto a lightly floured surface; knead 10 times. Roll out into a 6-in. square. Cut into four 3-in. squares; cut each square diagonally in half.
- Place on a baking sheet coated with cooking spray. Bake at 400 degrees for 10-12 minutes or until golden brown. Serve warm.

Nutrition Information

- Calories: 133 calories
- Total Fat: 4g
- Cholesterol: 8mg
- Sodium: 355mg
- Total Carbohydrate: 20g
- Protein: 4g
- Fiber: 0 g

294. Rustic Garden Herb Biscuits

The rosemary butter takes warm biscuits to another level. I use herbs from the garden but dried work, too. --Michelle Gauer, Spicer, Minnesota

Serving: 12 biscuits (1/4 cup rosemary butter). | Prep: 25 m | Cook: 25 m | Ready in: 50 m

Ingredients

- 3-3/4 cups all-purpose flour
- 6 tablespoons sugar
- 3 teaspoons baking powder
- 2 teaspoons dried minced onion
- 2 teaspoons minced fresh basil
- 2 teaspoons minced fresh parsley
- 1 teaspoon salt
- 1 teaspoon snipped fresh dill
- 1 garlic clove, minced
- 3/4 teaspoon baking soda
- 1/2 teaspoon minced fresh rosemary
- 1 cup cold butter, cubed
- 3/4 cup shredded Monterey Jack cheese
- 1-1/2 cups buttermilk
- 1/4 cup chopped roasted sweet red peppers
- ROSEMARY BUTTER:
- 1/4 cup butter, softened
- 1 teaspoon honey
- 1/2 garlic clove, minced
- Dash minced fresh rosemary

Direction

- Preheat oven to 350 degrees. In a large bowl, whisk the first 11 ingredients. Cut in butter until mixture resembles coarse crumbs. Stir in cheese. Add buttermilk and peppers; stir just until moistened.
- Drop mixture by 1/3 cupfuls into greased muffin cups. Bake 25-30 minutes or until golden brown. Cool 5 minutes before removing from pan to a wire rack.
- In a small bowl, mix remaining ingredients until blended. Serve warm biscuits with rosemary butter.

Nutrition Information

- Calories: 377 calories
- Total Fat: 22g
- Cholesterol: 58mg
- Sodium: 599mg
- Total Carbohydrate: 39g
- Protein: 7g
- Fiber: 1g

295. Rye Biscuits

With a yield of only four biscuits, this recipe from our Test Kitchen delivers fresh-baked goods without a lot of leftovers. The moist and flavorful bites come together in a mere 15 minutes.

Serving: 4 biscuits. | Prep: 5 m | Cook: 10 m | Ready in: 15 m

Ingredients

- 1/3 cup all-purpose flour
- 1/4 cup rye flour
- 1 tablespoon brown sugar
- 1 teaspoon baking powder
- 1/4 teaspoon caraway seeds
- 1/8 teaspoon salt
- 2 tablespoons cold butter
- 1 egg
- 1 tablespoon half-and-half cream

Direction

- In a small bowl, combine the first six ingredients. Cut in butter until mixture resembles coarse crumbs. Stir in egg and cream just until moistened.
- Drop batter into four mounds 2 in. apart on a baking sheet coated with cooking spray. Bake at 400 degrees for 10-12 minutes or until golden brown, immediately remove to a wire rack. Serve warm.

Nutrition Information

- Calories: 148 calories
- Total Fat: 8g
- Cholesterol: 70mg
- Sodium: 209mg

- Total Carbohydrate: 17g
- Protein: 3g
- Fiber: 1g

296. Rye Drop Biscuits

"My husband, Ken, and I like these rich, rugged, melt-in-your mouth biscuits with any meal," says Nancy Zimmerman (right with Ken) from Cape May Court House, New Jersey. "They're so easy to make since you don't have to knead them or cut them out."

Serving: 4 biscuits. | Prep: 20 m | Cook: 0 m | Ready in: 20 m

Ingredients

- 1/3 cup all-purpose flour
- 1/4 cup rye flour
- 1 tablespoon brown sugar
- 1 teaspoon baking powder
- 1/4 teaspoon dried parsley flakes
- 1/8 teaspoon salt
- 1/4 cup cold butter
- 1 egg
- 1 tablespoon milk

Direction

- In a small bowl, combine the flours, brown sugar, baking powder, parsley and salt. Cut in butter until mixture resembles coarse crumbs. Stir in the egg and milk just until combined.
- Drop by 1/4 cupfuls 2 in. apart onto a greased baking sheet. Bake at 400 degrees for 7-10 minutes or until golden brown. Remove from pan to a wire rack. Serve warm.

Nutrition Information

- Calories: 195 calories
- Total Fat: 13g
- Cholesterol: 84mg
- Sodium: 309mg
- Total Carbohydrate: 17g
- Protein: 3g
- Fiber: 1g

297. Sadies Buttermilk Biscuits

"This country fair award-winning recipe was perfected by my grandmother on the northern Canadian prairies. Sadie's advice - leave little chunks of lard the size of peas when cutting the flour in. Can be served at breakfast, lunch, or dinner."

Serving: 18 | Prep: 20 m | Cook: 12 m | Ready in: 32 m

Ingredients

- 4 cups all-purpose flour
- 1 teaspoon salt
- 1 teaspoon baking soda
- 1 teaspoon cream of tartar
- 4 teaspoons baking powder
- 1 cup lard
- 2 cups buttermilk

Direction

- Preheat oven to 450 degrees F (230 degrees C).
- Whisk together flour, salt, baking soda, cream of tartar, and baking powder. Cut lard into flour mixture using a pastry blender until crumbly; stir in buttermilk. Turn mixture onto a floured surface and knead just a few times to form a moist dough.
- Roll dough out 1-inch thick; cut biscuits with a cookie cutter or round glass. Place biscuits on an ungreased baking sheet.
- Bake in the preheated oven until tops are golden, about 12 minutes.

Nutrition Information

- Calories: 216 calories
- Total Fat: 11.9 g
- Cholesterol: 12 mg
- Sodium: 337 mg
- Total Carbohydrate: 22.9 g
- Protein: 3.8 g

298. Sage Cornmeal Biscuits

My family loves these outstanding savory biscuits with eggs and sausage at breakfast or with meat at dinner. They bake up light and tender and have just the right amount of sage. --Mary Kincaid, Bostic, North Carolina

Serving: 10 biscuits. | Prep: 20 m | Cook: 10 m | Ready in: 30 m

Ingredients

- 1-1/2 cups all-purpose flour
- 1/2 cup cornmeal
- 3 teaspoons baking powder
- 1/2 to 3/4 teaspoon rubbed sage
- 1/2 teaspoon salt
- 1/3 cup shortening
- 3/4 cup milk

Direction

- In a large bowl, combine the first five ingredients. Cut in shortening until mixture resembles coarse crumbs. Stir in milk just until moistened.
- Turn onto a lightly floured surface. Roll to 3/4-in. thickness; cut with a floured 2-in. biscuit cutter. Place 2 in. apart on an ungreased baking sheet. Bake at 450 degrees for 10-12 minutes or until browned. Serve warm.

Nutrition Information

- Calories: 163 calories
- Total Fat: 7g
- Cholesterol: 2mg
- Sodium: 248mg
- Total Carbohydrate: 21g
- Protein: 3g
- Fiber: 1g

299. Sage Scented Cornmeal Biscuits

The sage-infused biscuit dough can be mixed and formed about an hour before baking; set it aside in the refrigerator. Serve alongside roast chicken or turkey.

Serving: 12 | Cook: 25 m | Ready in: 40 m

Ingredients

- 1½ cups all-purpose flour
- ½ cup cornmeal, preferably stone-ground
- 1 tablespoon chopped fresh sage, or 1 teaspoon dried rubbed sage
- 1 tablespoon baking powder
- 1 teaspoon sugar
- ½ teaspoon baking soda
- ¼ teaspoon salt
- 3 tablespoons reduced-fat cream cheese, (Neufchâtel)
- 2 tablespoons cold butter, cut into small pieces
- 1 cup buttermilk
- 1 large egg, lightly beaten, mixed with 1 tablespoon water

Direction

- Preheat oven to 425°F. Lightly oil a baking sheet or coat it with cooking spray.
- Stir together flour, cornmeal, sage, baking powder, sugar, baking soda and salt in a mixing bowl. Cut in cream cheese and butter with two knives or your fingers until you have lumps the size of peas. Stir in buttermilk until just combined. Do not overmix or the biscuits will be tough.
- Turn the dough out onto a floured surface and pat into a circle about 9 inches in diameter. Cut into 12 wedges with a sharp knife. Transfer the wedges to the prepared baking sheet. Brush them lightly with some of the egg mixture. Bake until they are firm to the touch and very lightly browned, 10 to 12 minutes. Serve warm.

Nutrition Information

- Calories: 116 calories
- Total Fat: 3 g

- Saturated Fat: 2 g
- Cholesterol: 23 mg
- Sodium: 297 mg
- Total Carbohydrate: 18 g
- Protein: 4 g
- Fiber: 1 g
- Sugar: 2 g

300. Sausage Cheese Biscuits

These breakfast-in-a-biscuit goodies will appeal to the young...and the young at heart. It's one of my favorite recipes because it doesn't require any special ingredients. -- Marlene Neideigh, Myrtle Point, Oregon

Serving: 10 servings. | Prep: 15 m | Cook: 15 m | Ready in: 30 m

Ingredients

- 1 tube (12 ounces) refrigerated buttermilk biscuits
- 1 package (8 ounces) frozen Jones All Natural Fully Cooked Sausage Links, thawed
- 2 large eggs, beaten
- 1/2 cup shredded cheddar cheese
- 3 tablespoons chopped green onions

Direction

- Preheat oven to 400 degrees. Roll out each biscuit into a 5-in. circle; place each in an ungreased muffin cup. Cut sausages into fourths; brown in a skillet. Drain. Divide sausages among cups.
- In a small bowl, combine eggs, cheese and onions; spoon into cups. Bake 13-15 minutes or until browned.

Nutrition Information

- Calories: 227 calories
- Total Fat: 16g
- Cholesterol: 57mg
- Sodium: 548mg
- Total Carbohydrate: 16g
- Protein: 8g
- Fiber: 0 g

301. Sausage Gravy with Biscuits

"This is one of our favorite quick dishes," writes Alyce Wyman of Pembina, North Dakota. "My husband and I used to winter in Florida and after a day of gold, it was always a cinch to prepare this satisfying meal with a tossed salad."

Serving: 2 servings. | Prep: 25 m | Cook: 0 m | Ready in: 25 m

Ingredients

- 2 individually frozen biscuits
- 1/4 pound Jones No Sugar Pork Sausage Roll sausage
- 3 tablespoons all-purpose flour
- 1/4 teaspoon salt, optional
- 1/4 teaspoon Italian seasoning
- 1/4 teaspoon rubbed sage
- 1/8 teaspoon garlic powder
- 1/8 teaspoon pepper
- 1-1/2 cups 2% milk

Direction

- Bake biscuits according to package directions. Meanwhile, crumble sausage into a small skillet. Cook over medium heat until no longer pink; drain. Stir in flour and seasonings until blended. Gradually add milk. Bring to a boil; cook and stir for 2 minutes or until thickened. Split biscuits in half; serve with sausage gravy.

Nutrition Information

- Calories: 444 calories
- Total Fat: 22g
- Cholesterol: 44mg
- Sodium: 1105mg
- Total Carbohydrate: 42g
- Protein: 21g
- Fiber: 1g

302. Sausage n Egg Biscuits

Why pay restaurant prices when you can make it yourself at home? This savory breakfast sandwich is so simple, you can whip it up on a weekday morning.

Serving: 2 servings. | Prep: 10 m | Cook: 10 m | Ready in: 20 m

Ingredients

- 1/2 cup Quick Baking Mix
- 2 tablespoons water
- 2 eggs
- 1 teaspoon minced chives
- 2 frozen Jones All Natural Fully Cooked Sausage Patties
- 2 slices process American cheese

Direction

- In a small bowl, combine baking mix and water just until moistened. Turn onto a lightly floured surface; knead 8-10 times. Pat or roll out to 1/2-in. thickness; cut with a floured 3-in. biscuit cutter.
- Place on an ungreased baking sheet. Bake at 425 degrees for 8-12 minutes or until golden brown.
- Meanwhile, in a small bowl, whisk eggs and chives. Heat a small nonstick skillet coated with cooking spray over medium heat. Add egg mixture; cook and stir until set. Heat sausage patties according to package directions.
- To assemble, split each biscuit; layer with a cheese slice, sausage patty and scrambled eggs. Replace tops.

Nutrition Information

- Calories: 405 calories
- Total Fat: 28g
- Cholesterol: 244mg
- Sodium: 822mg
- Total Carbohydrate: 22g
- Protein: 16g
- Fiber: 1g

303. Savory AlmondButtermilk Biscuits

Chock-full of almonds, these biscuits are an updated version of a Southern classic. With their crunchy character, they always garnered praise from patrons at Dairy Hollow House, the inn I ran with my husband, Ned. The inn is now a non-profit retreat for writers. It provides them with the solitude they need to create.--Almond Board of California, x, California

Serving: 1 dozen. | Prep: 20 m | Cook: 10 m | Ready in: 30 m

Ingredients

- 3 tablespoons butter, divided
- 1 small onion, finely chopped
- 2 garlic cloves, minced
- 2 cups all-purpose flour
- 1 tablespoon baking powder
- 1 teaspoon salt
- 1/2 teaspoon baking soda
- 1/3 cup shortening
- 1 cup buttermilk
- 1/2 cup coarsely chopped almonds, toasted
- 2 tablespoons minced fresh parsley
- 1-1/2 teaspoons minced fresh sage or 1/2 teaspoon dried sage
- 1-1/2 teaspoons minced fresh rosemary or 1/2 teaspoon dried rosemary, crushed
- 1-1/2 teaspoons minced fresh thyme or 1/2 teaspoon dried thyme

Direction

- In a skillet, melt 1 tablespoon butter; sauté onion and garlic until tender. Cool completely. Combine the flour, baking powder, salt and baking soda. Cut in shortening until mixture resembles coarse crumbs. Add the buttermilk, almonds, parsley, sage, rosemary, thyme and onion mixture; stir just until mixed.
- Turn onto a floured surface; knead lightly for 1 minute. On a floured surface, roll dough to a 1/2-in. thickness. Cut with a 2-in. round biscuit cutter. Place on an ungreased baking sheet. Bake at 450 degrees for 10 to 15 minutes

or until golden brown. Melt remaining butter and brush over warm biscuits.

Nutrition Information

- Calories: 193 calories
- Total Fat: 11g
- Cholesterol: 8mg
- Sodium: 401mg
- Total Carbohydrate: 19g
- Protein: 4g
- Fiber: 1g

304. Savory Biscuits

Shredded cheese and a sprinkling of herbs give refrigerated biscuits great flavor. This is one of my favorite bread recipes.

Serving: 20 biscuits. | Prep: 10 m | Cook: 25 m | Ready in: 35 m

Ingredients

- 2 tubes (12 ounces each) refrigerated buttermilk biscuits
- 1/2 cup shredded Monterey Jack cheese
- 1/2 cup shredded cheddar cheese
- 3 tablespoons butter, melted
- 3/4 teaspoon dried basil
- 1/4 teaspoon dried oregano
- 1/8 teaspoon dill weed
- 1/8 teaspoon garlic powder

Direction

- Separate each tube of biscuits into 10 biscuits; place in a single layer in a greased 11x7-in. baking pan. Sprinkle with cheeses. Drizzle with butter; sprinkle with seasonings. Bake at 350 degrees for 25-30 minutes or until golden brown. Serve warm.

Nutrition Information

- Calories: 77 calories
- Total Fat: 4g

- Cholesterol: 10mg
- Sodium: 195mg
- Total Carbohydrate: 8g
- Protein: 3g
- Fiber: 0 g

305. Savory Drop Biscuits

The addition of cheese and green chilies makes these mouthwatering biscuits wonderfully moist. They're a fabulous accompaniment to soup and stew.

Serving: 2 dozen. | Prep: 10 m | Cook: 10 m | Ready in: 20 m

Ingredients

- 2-1/2 cups biscuit/baking mix
- 1 cup shredded cheddar cheese
- 1 can (4 ounces) chopped green chilies, drained
- 1 teaspoon chili powder
- 1/2 teaspoon garlic powder
- 1/2 teaspoon onion powder
- 2/3 cup whole milk

Direction

- In a medium bowl, combine the first six ingredients; mix well. Stir in milk just until moistened. Drop by tablespoonfuls 2 in. apart onto ungreased baking sheets. Bake at 450 degrees for 10 - 12 minutes or until golden brown. Serve warm.

Nutrition Information

- Calories: 74 calories
- Total Fat: 3g
- Cholesterol: 6mg
- Sodium: 209mg
- Total Carbohydrate: 9g
- Protein: 2g
- Fiber: 0 g

306. School Day Biscuits

A sweet buttery coating disguises convenient refrigerator biscuits in this recipe form Dixie Terry of Goreville, Illinois. "With a houseful of children and now grandchildren, these cinnamony treats have become a classic for breakfast or a snack," she relates.

Serving: 10 biscuits. | Prep: 10 m | Cook: 0 m | Ready in: 10 m

Ingredients

- 1/2 cup packed brown sugar
- 1 teaspoon ground cinnamon
- 1 tube (12 ounces) refrigerated buttermilk biscuits
- 1/4 cup butter, melted

Direction

- In a small bowl, combine brown sugar and cinnamon. Separate biscuits; dip the top of each in butter, then in cinnamon-sugar. Place sugared side up on an ungreased baking sheet. Bake at 400 degrees for 6-8 minutes or until golden brown. Serve warm.

Nutrition Information

- Calories: 164 calories
- Total Fat: 5g
- Cholesterol: 12mg
- Sodium: 341mg
- Total Carbohydrate: 27g
- Protein: 3g
- Fiber: 0 g

307. Shamrock Biscuits

Just the right mix of seasonings flavors these simple-to-fix-biscuits baked by the CT home economists. Garlic, Parmesan cheese and oregano add a tasty twist to standard refrigerated dough. And using a cookie cutter to form shamrocks gives the a festive flair for gatherings all through spring.

Serving: 10 biscuits. | Prep: 15 m | Cook: 15 m | Ready in: 30 m

Ingredients

- 1 tube (16.3 ounces) large refrigerated flaky biscuits
- 1/4 cup butter, melted
- 2 tablespoons grated Parmesan cheese
- 1 garlic clove, minced
- 1/4 teaspoon dried oregano

Direction

- Cut biscuits into shamrock shapes with a 2-in. cookie cutter or knife; discard trimmings. Place biscuits on an ungreased baking sheet.
- Bake at 375 degrees for 11-15 minutes or until golden brown. Combine remaining ingredients; brush over warm biscuits.

Nutrition Information

- Calories:
- Total Fat: g
- Cholesterol: mg
- Sodium: mg
- Total Carbohydrate: g
- Protein: g
- Fiber: g

308. Shmunkys Colby Jack Cheddar Biscuits

"These biscuits have an amazing aroma and taste that will turn any grump into a jolly lad! They are crispy on the outside, yet soft and puffy in the center. They freeze well too, for making large batches. This recipe is best when hand made, so try not to be tempted by your mixers. Trust me, it will pay off in the end. Buy block cheese and grate it by hand for best quality. I use a medium size grate. I do NOT recommend using fine grated cheeses."

Serving: 8 | Prep: 15 m | Cook: 20 m | Ready in: 35 m

Ingredients

- 1 teaspoon olive oil
- 2 cups all-purpose flour
- 1 tablespoon baking powder
- 1 1/2 teaspoons dried parsley
- 1/8 teaspoon ground thyme
- 1 teaspoon salt
- 1 teaspoon white sugar
- 1 cup shredded Colby-Monterey Jack cheese
- 1/4 cup shredded white Cheddar cheese
- 6 tablespoons butter
- 1 cup 2% milk

Direction

- Preheat oven to 400 degrees F (200 degrees C). Using olive oil, grease a baking sheet.
- With a fork, mix together the flour, baking powder, parsley, thyme, salt, sugar, Colby-Monterey Jack cheese, and white Cheddar cheese together in a bowl. Cut the butter into the flour mixture in coarse chunks, then use the fork to further cut the butter into the flour-cheese mixture until the mixture resembles coarse crumbs. Lightly stir in the milk just until the dough holds together.
- Drop the batter by heaping 1/8-cup measuring cup onto the prepared baking sheet, and bake in the preheated oven until risen and golden brown, 20 to 30 minutes.

Nutrition Information

- Calories: 293 calories
- Total Fat: 16.8 g
- Cholesterol: 45 mg
- Sodium: 701 mg
- Total Carbohydrate: 26.9 g
- Protein: 9 g

309. Simple Sweet Potato Biscuits

Only four ingredients make these moist biscuits a snap to prepare. "I modified my grandma's recipe to make it shorter and quicker," says Pam Bouillion of Rayne, Louisiana. "They're my husband's favorites."

Serving: about 1 dozen. | Prep: 15 m | Cook: 10 m | Ready in: 25 m

Ingredients

- 2-1/2 cups biscuit/baking mix
- 1-1/2 cups canned sweet potatoes
- 6 tablespoons milk
- 1/3 cup butter, melted

Direction

- Preheat oven to 425 degrees. Place biscuit mix in a large bowl. In a small bowl, mash sweet potatoes; stir in milk and butter. Stir into biscuit mix just until moistened.
- Drop by heaping tablespoonfuls 2 in. apart onto a greased baking sheet. Bake 8-10 minutes or until golden brown. Serve warm.

Nutrition Information

- Calories: 132 calories
- Total Fat: 7g
- Cholesterol: 11mg
- Sodium: 287mg
- Total Carbohydrate: 16g
- Protein: 2g
- Fiber: 1g

310. SkyHigh Biscuits

"When I think of food and summer, I think of our county fair in July. My three sons and I have competed in a lot of 4-H cooking contests. I enter 15 or more food items every year in the open show. My recipe for Sky-High Biscuits (below) never fails to win a ribbon. They're moist, high and flaky, with a wonderful wheat flavor."

Serving: 1 dozen. | Prep: 20 m | Cook: 10 m | Ready in: 30 m

Ingredients

- 2 cups all-purpose flour
- 1 cup whole wheat flour
- 2 tablespoons sugar
- 4-1/2 teaspoons baking powder
- 3/4 teaspoon cream of tartar
- 1/2 teaspoon salt
- 3/4 cup cold butter, cubed
- 1 egg
- 1 cup milk

Direction

- In a bowl, combine the first six ingredients. Cut in butter until crumble. Combine egg and milk; stir into crumb mixture just until moistened. Turn onto a floured surface; knead 10-15 times. Roll out to 1-in. thickness; cut with a 2-1/2-in. biscuit cutter. Place on a greased baking sheet. Bake at 450 degrees for 10-15 minutes or until golden brown.

Nutrition Information

- Calories: 237 calories
- Total Fat: 13g
- Cholesterol: 51mg
- Sodium: 380mg
- Total Carbohydrate: 26g
- Protein: 5g
- Fiber: 2g

311. Soft Sweet Potato Biscuits

This was one of my great-grandmother's favorite recipes. I'm 87, so you can bet this recipe has stood the test of time! I like to make these biscuits often during winter since they're a good complement to any hearty meal...very tasty when served hot with butter!

Serving: 1-1/2 dozen. | Prep: 15 m | Cook: 15 m | Ready in: 30 m

Ingredients

- 2 cups self-rising flour
- 1/8 teaspoon salt
- 1/2 cup shortening
- 1 cup mashed sweet potatoes
- 4 to 5 tablespoons 2% milk

Direction

- In a large bowl, combine flour and salt. Cut in shortening and sweet potatoes until mixture resembles coarse crumbs. Stir in enough milk just until dough clings together. Knead lightly on a floured surface.
- Roll dough to 1/2-in. thickness. Cut with a 2-in. biscuit cutter and place on a lightly greased baking sheet. Bake at 450 degrees for 12 minutes or until golden brown. Serve warm.

Nutrition Information

- Calories: 115 calories
- Total Fat: 6g
- Cholesterol: 0 mg
- Sodium: 180mg
- Total Carbohydrate: 14g
- Protein: 2g
- Fiber: 1g

312. Sour Cream Chive Biscuits

Chives add a nice, mild onion flavor to just about any dish, be it soup, dip, baked potato or buttery spread. They really are a nice touch in these biscuits from Priscilla Gilbert of Indian Harbour Beach, Florida.

Serving: 16 biscuits. | Prep: 10 m | Cook: 10 m | Ready in: 20 m

Ingredients

- 3 cups biscuit/baking mix
- 3 tablespoons minced chives
- 2/3 cup water
- 2/3 cup sour cream

Direction

- Preheat oven to 450 degrees. In a large bowl, combine biscuit mix and chives. Stir in water and sour cream just until moistened.
- Drop by heaping tablespoonfuls onto a baking sheet coated with cooking spray. Bake 8-10 minutes or until lightly browned. Serve warm.

Nutrition Information

- Calories: 112 calories
- Total Fat: 5g
- Cholesterol: 7mg
- Sodium: 287mg
- Total Carbohydrate: 14g
- Protein: 2g
- Fiber: 0 g

313. Sour Cream and Scallion Drop Biscuits

All that sour cream keeps these biscuits super moist and tender – they reheat well, even after sitting out for hours (pop back into 350°F oven for 5 minutes).

Serving: Makes 8 | Prep: 15 m | Cook: 30 m

Ingredients

- 2 cups all-purpose flour
- 2 teaspoons baking powder
- 2 teaspoons kosher salt
- 1 teaspoon sugar
- 1/2 teaspoon baking soda
- 1/2 cup unsalted butter, melted, cooled, divided
- 4 scallions, thinly sliced
- 1 1/2 cups sour cream
- Hungarian hot paprika (for serving)

Direction

- Preheat oven to 400°F. Whisk flour, baking powder, salt, sugar, and baking soda in a large bowl. Drizzle in 6 Tbsp. butter and mix lightly with your hands just to distribute butter. Make a well in center of bowl and add scallions and sour cream. Mix with a wooden spoon until no dry spots remain and mixture forms a shaggy dough.
- Using 2 spoons, drop 1/2-cupfuls of dough onto a parchment-lined baking sheet, spacing at least 1 1/2" apart, or into a 12" cast-iron skillet, arranging so sides of biscuits are just touching (you should have 8). Brush tops with remaining 2 Tbsp. butter; sprinkle with paprika. Bake biscuits until tops and bottoms are golden brown on top and bottom, 12–15 minutes.
- Per 4 servings (2 each): Calories (kcal) 630 Fat (g) 39 Saturated Fat (g) 25 Cholesterol (mg) 120 Carbohydrates (g) 55 Dietary Fiber (g) 3 Total Sugars (g) 5 Protein (g) 10 Sodium (mg) 1370

314. Sour Cream Biscuits

"These biscuits are light and fluffy. Delicious!"

Serving: 12 | Prep: 10 m | Cook: 12 m | Ready in: 22 m

Ingredients

- 2 cups all-purpose flour
- 1/2 teaspoon salt
- 1/2 teaspoon baking soda
- 3 teaspoons baking powder
- 3/4 cup sour cream

- 1 1/2 tablespoons water

Direction

- Mix together flour, salt, baking soda, and baking powder. Add sour cream and mix to a soft dough. Add additional water if necessary.
- With well-floured hands shape dough into round biscuit shapes. Bake at 450 degrees F (230 degrees C) for 12 minutes.

Nutrition Information

- Calories: 107 calories
- Total Fat: 3.2 g
- Cholesterol: 6 mg
- Sodium: 279 mg
- Total Carbohydrate: 16.8 g
- Protein: 2.6 g

315. Sour Cream n Chive Biscuits

I grow chives in my front yard and like to use them in as many recipes as I can. These moist, tender biscuits are delectable as well as attractive.--Lucile H. Proctor, Panguitch, Utah

Serving: 12-15 biscuits. | Prep: 15 m | Cook: 15 m | Ready in: 30 m

Ingredients

- 2 cups all-purpose flour
- 1 tablespoon baking powder
- 1/2 teaspoon salt
- 1/4 teaspoon baking soda
- 1/3 cup shortening
- 3/4 cup sour cream
- 1/4 cup milk
- 1/4 cup minced chives

Direction

- In a large bowl, combine dry ingredients. Cut in shortening until mixture resembles coarse crumbs. With a fork, stir in sour cream, milk and chives until the mixture forms a ball.

- On a lightly floured surface, knead five to six times. Roll to 3/4-in. thickness; cut with a 2-in. biscuit cutter. Place on an ungreased baking sheet.
- Bake at 350 degrees for 12-15 minutes or until golden brown. Serve warm.

Nutrition Information

- Calories: 126 calories
- Total Fat: 7g
- Cholesterol: 9mg
- Sodium: 188mg
- Total Carbohydrate: 13g
- Protein: 2g
- Fiber: 0 g

316. Sour Cream Pan Biscuits

These golden brown biscuits makes a convenient meal accompaniment since they bake at the same temperature and for about as long as the chicken. They're fluffy and tender on the inside with just a hint of sweetness.--Jennifer Hoeft, Thorndale, Texas

Serving: 6 servings. | Prep: 5 m | Cook: 20 m | Ready in: 25 m

Ingredients

- 2 cups biscuit/baking mix
- 1 teaspoon sugar
- 1/2 cup club soda
- 3 tablespoons sour cream

Direction

- In a small bowl, combine all ingredients; stir just until moistened. Drop into six mounds in a 9-in. round baking pan coated with cooking spray.
- Bake at 400 degrees for 20 minutes or until golden brown. Serve warm.

Nutrition Information

- Calories: 164 calories
- Total Fat: 3g

- Cholesterol: 3mg
- Sodium: 474mg
- Total Carbohydrate: 29g
- Protein: 4g
- Fiber: 1g

317. Sour CreamLeek Biscuits

These biscuits are a wonderful pairing for soups. I've made them with all-purpose white flour as well as whole wheat, and both work equally well. --Bonnie Appleton, Canterbury, Connecticut

Serving: about 1 dozen. | Prep: 15 m | Cook: 15 m | Ready in: 30 m

Ingredients

- 1/3 cup cold unsalted butter, divided
- 1-1/2 cups finely chopped leeks (white portion only)
- 2 cups white whole wheat flour
- 2-1/2 teaspoons baking powder
- 1/2 teaspoon salt
- 1/4 teaspoon baking soda
- 3/4 cup reduced-fat sour cream
- 1/4 cup water

Direction

- Preheat oven to 400 degrees. In a small skillet over medium heat, melt 1 tablespoon butter. Add leeks; cook until tender, 6-7 minutes. Cool.
- Whisk together flour, baking powder, salt and baking soda. Cut in remaining butter until mixture resembles coarse crumbs. Stir in leeks, sour cream and water just until moistened. Turn onto a lightly floured surface; knead 8-10 times.
- Pat or roll out to 1/2-in. thickness; cut with a floured 2-1/2-in. biscuit cutter. Place biscuits 2 in. apart on an ungreased baking sheet; bake until golden brown, 12-16 minutes. Serve warm.

Nutrition Information

- Calories: 166 calories
- Total Fat: 7g
- Cholesterol: 20mg
- Sodium: 241mg
- Total Carbohydrate: 20g
- Protein: 4g
- Fiber: 3g

318. Sourdough Drop Biscuits

"You may choose which sourdough starter to use."

Serving: 18 | Prep: 5 m | Cook: 15 m | Ready in: 20 m

Ingredients

- 1 cup sourdough starter
- 1/3 cup vegetable oil
- 3/4 teaspoon baking soda
- 1/4 teaspoon salt
- 1 cup all-purpose flour

Direction

- Sift flour, salt, and soda together into a large bowl. Mix starter with oil, and stir into the sifted ingredients. Drop dough by tablespoons onto an ungreased baking sheet.
- Bake at 350 degrees F (175 degrees C) for 10 to 15 minutes. Serve warm.

Nutrition Information

- Calories: 81 calories
- Total Fat: 4.2 g
- Cholesterol: < 1 mg
- Sodium: 88 mg
- Total Carbohydrate: 9.2 g
- Protein: 1.6 g

319. South Georgia Biscuits

"These are traditional hand-formed South Georgia biscuits as made by my family for generations. Unlike most recipes, these biscuits are formed entirely by hand, not rolled and cut. Once you master the technique, you can make them very quickly and will find the texture and appearance to be much better than rolled biscuits."

Serving: 12 | Prep: 10 m | Cook: 12 m | Ready in: 22 m

Ingredients

- 2 1/2 cups all-purpose flour
- 1 tablespoon baking powder
- 1 teaspoon salt
- 1/2 cup shortening
- 1 cup whole milk

Direction

- Preheat the oven to 450 degrees F (220 degrees C).
- In a large bowl, stir together the flour, baking powder and salt. Cut in shortening with a pastry blender or by rubbing between your fingers until the lumps are smaller than peas. Pour in the milk all at once, and stir with a large spoon until dough is evenly moist. It should be sticky.
- Flour your hands, and knead the dough lightly for 3 or 4 turns, adding just enough flour so that it doesn't stick to your hands. Let the dough rest for a minute or two.
- With well-floured hands, pinch off pieces of dough (about 12) and pat lightly into balls. Don't over work the dough. Place about 2 inches apart on ungreased baking sheets. With floured knuckles, press each ball down to about 1/2 inch thickness.
- Bake for 11 to 12 minutes in the preheated oven, until browned on the bottom. Serve hot with butter.

Nutrition Information

- Calories: 183 calories
- Total Fat: 9.5 g
- Cholesterol: 2 mg
- Sodium: 286 mg
- Total Carbohydrate: 21 g
- Protein: 3.3 g

320. Southern Biscuits with Mayonnaise

"A tender, old-fashioned Southern biscuit recipe from my mother-in-law. Grab your cast iron skillet, and you are ready to make these tasty biscuits!"

Serving: 12 | Prep: 15 m | Cook: 20 m | Ready in: 45 m

Ingredients

- 2/3 cup buttermilk
- 2 tablespoons vegetable oil
- 3 tablespoons mayonnaise
- 2 cups self-rising flour

Direction

- In a large bowl mix together the buttermilk, oil, and mayonnaise. Gradually stir in the flour and mix until all ingredients are combined.
- Turn dough out onto a well-floured surface. If dough is sticky knead in a little extra flour. Pat the dough out to about a 1/2-inch thickness. Use a biscuit cutter to cut dough into pieces. Place into an oiled cast iron skillet. Allow biscuits to rest in the pan for 10 minutes.
- Bake in a preheated 425 degree F (220 degrees C) until nicely browned, about 20 minutes.

Nutrition Information

- Calories: 124 calories
- Total Fat: 5.4 g
- Cholesterol: 2 mg
- Sodium: 298 mg
- Total Carbohydrate: 16.2 g
- Protein: 2.5 g

321. Southern Buttermilk Biscuits

The recipe for these four-ingredient biscuits has been handed down for many generations. --Fran Thompson, Tarboro, North Carolina

Serving: 8 biscuits. | Prep: 15 m | Cook: 15 m | Ready in: 30 m

Ingredients

- 1/2 cup cold butter, cubed
- 2 cups self-rising flour
- 3/4 cup buttermilk
- Melted butter

Direction

- In a large bowl, cut butter into flour until mixture resembles coarse crumbs. Stir in buttermilk just until moistened. Turn onto a lightly floured surface; knead 3-4 times. Pat or lightly roll to 3/4-in. thickness. Cut with a floured 2-1/2-in. biscuit cutter.
- Place on a greased baking sheet. Bake at 425 degrees until golden brown, 11-13 minutes. Brush tops with butter. Serve warm.

Nutrition Information

- Calories:
- Total Fat: 11 g
- Cholesterol: 28 mg
- Sodium: 451 mg
- Total Carbohydrate: 22 g
- Protein: 4 g
- Fiber: 1 g fiber

322. Southern Eggs and Biscuits

To me, nothing beats the flavor of Southern cooking, especially for breakfast! The rich flavor of these eggs served over homemade biscuits is a hearty way to start the day. -- Ruth Ward, Lexington, Tennessee

Serving: 6-8 servings. | Prep: 30 m | Cook: 25 m | Ready in: 55 m

Ingredients

- 10 hard-boiled large eggs, sliced
- 1 pound sliced bacon, diced
- 1/3 cup all-purpose flour
- 1/4 teaspoon salt
- 1/8 teaspoon pepper
- 4 cups milk
- 2 cups cubed process cheese (Velveeta)
- BISCUITS:
- 1/2 cup shortening
- 3 cups self-rising flour
- 1-1/4 cups buttermilk

Direction

- Place eggs in a greased 13-in. x 9-in. baking dish. In a large skillet, cook bacon until crisp. Drain, reserving 1/4 cup drippings. Sprinkle bacon over eggs.
- Whisk the flour, salt and pepper into reserved drippings until smooth. Gradually add milk. Bring to a boil. Cook and stir for 2 minutes or until thickened and bubbly. Stir in cheese until melted; pour over eggs.
- For biscuits, cut shortening into flour until mixture resembles coarse crumbs. Stir in buttermilk; gently knead six to eight times. Roll out on a lightly floured surface to 1/2-in. thickness. Cut with a 2-1/2-in. biscuit cutter and place on a greased baking sheet.
- Bake biscuits and eggs at 400 degrees for 25 minutes or until biscuits are golden brown. Serve eggs over biscuits.

Nutrition Information

- Calories: 667 calories
- Total Fat: 39g
- Cholesterol: 317mg

- Sodium: 1426mg
- Total Carbohydrate: 47g
- Protein: 29g
- Fiber: 1g

323. Southern Gal Biscuits

When I got married, I made sure to copy this recipe of my mom's. I'm glad I did...it's become one of my husband's favorites. We especially like to eat them smothered with homemade country sausage gravy.

Serving: about 1 dozen. | Prep: 25 m | Cook: 15 m | Ready in: 40 m

Ingredients

- 2 cups all-purpose flour
- 2 tablespoons sugar
- 4 teaspoons baking powder
- 1/2 teaspoon salt
- 1/2 teaspoon cream of tartar
- 1/2 cup shortening
- 1 egg
- 2/3 cup milk

Direction

- In a bowl, combine flour, sugar, baking powder, salt and cream of tartar. Cut in shortening until mixture resembles fine crumbs. In a small bowl, beat egg and milk; stir into dry ingredients just until moistened. Turn onto a lightly floured surface; roll to 1/2-in. thickness. Cut with a 2-1/2-in. biscuit cutter. Bake at 400 degrees for 12-15 minutes or until golden brown.

Nutrition Information

- Calories: 172 calories
- Total Fat: 9g
- Cholesterol: 20mg
- Sodium: 244mg
- Total Carbohydrate: 19g
- Protein: 3g
- Fiber: 1g

324. Spelt Biscuits

"I have made these biscuits for health nuts and non healthy eaters alike, but there are never leftovers. These are heavier on account of the spelt flour, but the nutty whole grain flavor is divine. Best when served fresh out of the oven, eaten with butter and honey or jam."

Serving: 6 | Prep: 10 m | Cook: 12 m | Ready in: 22 m

Ingredients

- 2 cups spelt flour
- 1 tablespoon baking powder
- 1 teaspoon salt
- 6 tablespoons butter
- 2/3 cup milk

Direction

- Preheat the oven to 450 degrees F (220 degrees C).
- In a large bowl, stir together the flour, baking powder and salt. Cut in the butter until the mixture resembles coarse crumbs. Gradually stir in milk until dough pulls away from the sides of the bowl. You may need to adjust the amount of milk. Pat out on a floured surface to about 1 inch thick. Cut into biscuits and place on a baking sheet.
- Bake in the preheated oven for 12 to 15 minutes, until the bottoms are golden brown.

Nutrition Information

- Calories: 250 calories
- Total Fat: 12.7 g
- Cholesterol: 33 mg
- Sodium: 726 mg
- Total Carbohydrate: 29.9 g
- Protein: 6.3 g

325. Spiced Biscuits

From Mechanicsville, Maryland, Elaine Green shares the recipe for mildly spiced biscuits that taste best served warm. They rely on convenient baking mix and orange yogurt, so they're virtually fuss-free.

Serving: 16 biscuits. | Prep: 15 m | Cook: 15 m | Ready in: 30 m

Ingredients

- 3 cups reduced-fat biscuit/baking mix
- 3 tablespoons sugar
- 1/2 teaspoon ground ginger
- 2 tablespoons cold butter
- 3/4 cup (6 ounces) orange yogurt
- 1/4 cup plus 1 tablespoon egg substitute, divided

Direction

- In a bowl, combine the biscuit mix, sugar and ginger. Cut in butter until the mixture resembles coarse crumbs. With a fork, stir in yogurt and 1/4 cup egg substitute until mixture forms a ball.
- Turn onto a floured surface; knead 5-6 times. Roll out to 1/2-in. thickness; cut with a 2-1/2-in. biscuit cutter. Place on an ungreased baking sheet. Brush tops with remaining egg substitute.
- Bake at 425 degrees for 14-16 minutes or until golden brown.

Nutrition Information

- Calories: 123 calories
- Total Fat: 3g
- Cholesterol: 1mg
- Sodium: 289mg
- Total Carbohydrate: 21g
- Protein: 3g
- Fiber: 0 g

326. Spiced Sweet Potato Biscuits

A pumpkin cookie cutter can be used for sweet treats and for savory biscuits as well. These biscuits are a fun addition to any meal in fall. --Flo Burtnett, Gage, Oklahoma

Serving: 1 dozen. | Prep: 25 m | Cook: 10 m | Ready in: 35 m

Ingredients

- 1-1/2 cups all-purpose flour
- 2 teaspoons baking powder
- 1/2 teaspoon salt
- 1/4 teaspoon ground cinnamon
- 1/8 teaspoon ground nutmeg
- 1/3 cup cold butter, cubed
- 1 cup cold mashed sweet potatoes (prepared without milk or butter)
- 1/3 cup milk
- 1 large egg, lightly beaten
- 1/2 teaspoon sugar

Direction

- In a large bowl, combine the first five ingredients. Cut in butter until crumbly. Combine sweet potato and milk; stir into crumb mixture just until moistened. Turn onto a floured surface; knead 10-15 times. Roll out to 1/2-in. thickness; cut with a floured 2-1/2-in. pumpkin-shaped cookie cutter or biscuit cutter.
- Place 2 in. apart on a greased baking sheet. Brush with egg; sprinkle with sugar. Bake at 425 degrees for 10-12 minutes or until golden brown. Serve warm.

Nutrition Information

- Calories: 141 calories
- Total Fat: 6g
- Cholesterol: 32mg
- Sodium: 229mg
- Total Carbohydrate: 19g
- Protein: 3g
- Fiber: 1g

327. Sriracha Biscuits

"I bought self-rising flour by accident, so I decided to make the best of the situation. I could make regular biscuits, but regular biscuits are boring. What could make biscuits more interesting? The answer was in the side door of my refrigerator: Sriracha!"

Serving: 6 | Prep: 5 m | Cook: 15 m | Ready in: 20 m

Ingredients

- 2 1/4 cups self-rising flour
- 1 cup half-and-half
- 1/2 cup vegetable oil
- 1 tablespoon Sriracha hot sauce, or more to taste
- 1 tablespoon melted butter, or to taste (optional)
- salt to taste (optional)

Direction

- Preheat oven to 425 degrees F (220 degrees C).
- Stir flour, half-and-half, vegetable oil, and Sriracha sauce together in a bowl to form a lumpy dough. Roll dough into 2-inch balls and place on a baking sheet.
- Bake biscuits in the preheated oven until golden brown, about 15 minutes. Brush melted butter and sprinkle salt on top of each biscuit.

Nutrition Information

- Calories: 397 calories
- Total Fat: 25.2 g
- Cholesterol: 20 mg
- Sodium: 731 mg
- Total Carbohydrate: 36.8 g
- Protein: 5.8 g

328. Sticky Apple Biscuits

Instead of the typical drop or cut biscuits, this hearty version is rolled up like a cinnamon roll. Tender apples, crunchy pecans and sweet honey make these a wonderful breakfast treat.

Serving: 1 dozen. | Prep: 20 m | Cook: 20 m | Ready in: 40 m

Ingredients

- 1/4 cup honey
- 1/4 cup packed brown sugar
- 2 tablespoons butter, melted
- 2 tablespoons water
- 1/3 cup pecan halves
- BISCUIT:
- 2 cups all-purpose flour
- 2 teaspoons baking powder
- 1/2 teaspoon salt
- 1/2 teaspoon ground cinnamon
- 3 tablespoons shortening
- 3 tablespoons cold butter
- 2/3 cup milk
- 1/2 cup diced peeled tart apple
- FILLING:
- 3 tablespoons butter, softened
- 2 tablespoons applesauce
- 1 tablespoon honey
- 1/4 cup packed brown sugar
- 3 tablespoons raisins

Direction

- In a small bowl, combine the honey, brown sugar, butter and water. Divide among 12 greased muffin cups. Sprinkle with pecans; set aside.
- In a large bowl, combine the flour, baking powder, salt and cinnamon. Cut in shortening and butter until mixture resembles coarse crumbs. Stir in milk and apple just until moistened.
- Turn onto a floured surface. Pat into a 10-in. x 8-in. rectangle, about 1/2 in. thick. Spread with butter, then applesauce; drizzle with honey. Sprinkle with brown sugar and raisins. Roll up, jelly-roll style, starting with a long

side. Cut into 12 biscuits. Place, cut side down, over pecan mixture in muffin cups.

- Bake at 425 degrees for 20-25 minutes or until golden brown. Cool for 1 minute before inverting onto a serving platter. Serve warm.

Nutrition Information

- Calories: 271 calories
- Total Fat: 13g
- Cholesterol: 22mg
- Sodium: 253mg
- Total Carbohydrate: 36g
- Protein: 3g
- Fiber: 1g

329. Sugar and Spice Biscuits

Serve these low-fat biscuits for breakfast or brunch. Family and guests will love the sweet flavor and the pretty fan shapes.

Serving: 12 | Prep: 15 m | Ready in: 25 m

Ingredients

- 2 cups all-purpose flour
- 4 teaspoons baking powder
- ½ teaspoon cream of tartar
- ¼ teaspoon salt
- ¼ cup shortening
- ¾ cup fat-free milk
- 2 tablespoons granulated sugar
- 1 teaspoon ground cinnamon

Direction

- Grease twelve 2- ½-inch muffin cups; set aside. In a large bowl, stir together flour, baking powder, cream of tartar, and salt. Using a pastry blender, cut in shortening until mixture resembles coarse crumbs. Make a well in the center; add milk. Stir just until dough clings together.
- Turn dough out onto a lightly floured surface. Knead by folding and gently pressing dough for 10 to 12 strokes or until dough is nearly smooth. Divide dough in half. Roll one portion

into a 12x10-inch rectangle. In a small bowl combine the sugar and cinnamon. Sprinkle some of the sugar mixture over the rectangle.

- Cut rectangle into five 12x2-inch strips. Stack the strips on top of each other. Cut into six 2-inch-square stacks. Place each stack, cut side down, in a prepared muffin cup. Repeat with remaining dough and sugar mixture.
- Bake in a 450°F oven for 10 to 12 minutes or until golden. Serve warm. Makes 12 biscuits.

Nutrition Information

- Calories: 121 calories
- Total Fat: 4 g
- Saturated Fat: 1 g
- Sodium: 190 mg
- Total Carbohydrate: 18 g
- Protein: 3 g
- Fiber: 1 g
- Sugar: 1 g

330. SugarCrusted Sweet Potato Biscuits

"Drop biscuits are sweetened with mashed sweet potato and a bit of brown sugar with an extra sprinkle on top for a pretty sugar coating."

Serving: 12 | Prep: 15 m | Cook: 17 m | Ready in: 35 m

Ingredients

- Crisco® Original No-Stick Cooking Spray
- 2 cups Martha White® Self-Rising Flour
- 4 tablespoons brown sugar, divided
- 3 tablespoons Crisco® All-Vegetable Shortening
- 2/3 cup milk
- 1/2 cup mashed canned sweet potato or mashed cooked sweet potato
- 1/3 cup sour cream

Direction

- Heat oven to 400 degrees F. Spray cookie sheet with no-stick cooking spray. Combine flour and 2 tablespoons of the brown sugar in medium bowl; mix well. Cut in shortening with pastry blender or fork until mixture resembles coarse crumbs.
- Combine milk, sweet potato and sour cream in small bowl; blend well. Add to flour mixture all at once, stirring just until moistened (if dough is too dry, add additional milk 1 teaspoon at a time, until dry ingredients are moistened). Drop dough by 1/4 cupfuls onto prepared cookie sheet. Sprinkle with remaining 2 tablespoons brown sugar.
- Bake 15 to 20 minutes or until biscuits are golden brown. Immediately remove from cookie sheet. Serve warm.

Nutrition Information

- Calories: 149 calories
- Total Fat: 5 g
- Cholesterol: 4 mg
- Sodium: 272 mg
- Total Carbohydrate: 23.1 g
- Protein: 2.9 g

---

331. SunDried Tomato Cheese Biscuits

On busy weeknights, I whip up these biscuits-especially when we're eating Italian. By the time the pasta's done cooking, they're golden brown and ready to serve. — Lisa Huff, Clive, Iowa

Serving: 6 biscuits. | Prep: 10 m | Cook: 10 m | Ready in: 20 m

Ingredients

- 1-1/2 cups biscuit/baking mix
- 1/3 cup shredded part-skim mozzarella cheese
- 1/4 cup grated Parmesan cheese
- 1 teaspoon Italian seasoning

- 1/4 teaspoon onion powder
- 1/4 teaspoon garlic powder
- 1/2 cup buttermilk
- 3 tablespoons oil-packed sun-dried tomatoes, drained and finely chopped
- 1-1/2 teaspoons butter, melted

Direction

- In a large bowl, combine the biscuit mix, cheeses, Italian seasoning, onion powder and garlic powder. Stir in buttermilk and tomatoes just until moistened.
- Drop by 1/4 cupfuls 2 in. apart onto a greased baking sheet. Bake at 425 degrees for 8-12 minutes or until golden brown. Brush with butter. Serve warm.

Nutrition Information

- Calories: 178 calories
- Total Fat: 8g
- Cholesterol: 10mg
- Sodium: 496mg
- Total Carbohydrate: 21g
- Protein: 6g
- Fiber: 1g

---

332. Sunshine Biscuits

These golden biscuits really bring sunshine to my breakfast table, especially on cold winter mornings when they're served with butter and molasses.

Serving: 1 dozen. | Prep: 25 m | Cook: 10 m | Ready in: 35 m

Ingredients

- 2 cups all-purpose flour
- 1 cup cornmeal
- 2 tablespoons sugar
- 4-1/2 teaspoons baking powder
- 3/4 teaspoon cream of tartar
- 1/2 teaspoon salt
- 3/4 cup cold butter
- 1 egg, lightly beaten

- 1 cup milk

Direction

- In a bowl, combine flour cornmeal, sugar, baking powder, cream of tartar and salt. Cut in butter until mixture resembles coarse crumbs. Combine egg and milk; stir into flour mixture just until moistened. Let stand 5 minutes.
- Turn onto a floured surface; knead for about 1 minute. Pat or roll out to 3/4-in, thickness; cut with a 3-in. biscuit cutter. Place on a greased baking sheet. Bake at 450 degrees for 10-12 minutes.

Nutrition Information

- Calories: 246 calories
- Total Fat: 13g
- Cholesterol: 51mg
- Sodium: 380mg
- Total Carbohydrate: 28g
- Protein: 4g
- Fiber: 1g

333. Super Quick Biscuit Squares

"These biscuits bake up golden brown on the outside and light fluffy inside. They're perfect slathered with butter, honey, and/or jelly. Sometimes we top them with a rich, thick chicken gravy for a top notch chicken and biscuits dinner."

Serving: 6 | Prep: 10 m | Cook: 10 m | Ready in: 20 m

Ingredients

- 2 cups all-purpose flour
- 1 tablespoon baking powder
- 1 teaspoon salt
- 2/3 cup milk
- 1/3 cup vegetable oil

Direction

- Preheat oven to 450 degrees F (230 degrees C). Lightly grease a baking sheet.
- Combine flour, baking powder, and salt in a bowl. Stir milk and oil into flour mixture until

just moistened. Gently knead until dough comes together, 8 to 10 times.
- Turn dough out onto a flat surface and roll to a 3/4-inch thick rectangle. Cut dough in half lengthwise and cut each half into thirds crosswise. Transfer each biscuit to the prepared baking sheet.
- Bake in preheated oven until gold brown, 10 to 12 minutes.

Nutrition Information

- Calories: 274 calories
- Total Fat: 13.2 g
- Cholesterol: 2 mg
- Sodium: 567 mg
- Total Carbohydrate: 33.5 g
- Protein: 5.2 g

334. Super Simple Biscuits

"This super simple recipe will have warm biscuits on your table in a jiffy! Best served warm... add some Cheddar cheese and garlic powder if you like. Yummm!"

Serving: 6 | Prep: 5 m | Cook: 30 m | Ready in: 35 m

Ingredients

- 1 cup self-rising flour
- 1/2 cup butter, softened
- 1/2 cup sour cream

Direction

- Preheat an oven to 350 degrees F (175 degrees C).
- Stir the flour, butter, and sour cream together in a bowl until blended. Scoop the batter into ungreased cupcake tins.
- Bake in the preheated oven until puffed and golden brown, 20 to 30 minutes.

Nutrition Information

- Calories: 250 calories
- Total Fat: 19.6 g

- Cholesterol: 49 mg
- Sodium: 384 mg
- Total Carbohydrate: 16.3 g
- Protein: 2.8 g

335. Sweet Cream Biscuits

People are surprised that these three-ingredient biscuits have such a wonderful homemade flavor.

Serving: 1 dozen. | Prep: 25 m | Cook: 10 m | Ready in: 35 m

Ingredients

- 2 cups biscuit/baking mix
- 2/3 cup heavy whipping cream
- 2 tablespoons sugar

Direction

- In a large bowl, combine the biscuit mix, cream and sugar; stir just until moistened.
- Turn onto lightly floured surface; knead 8-10 times. Pat or roll out to 1/2-in. thickness; cut with a floured 2-1/2-in. biscuit cutter.
- Place 2 in. apart on a lightly greased baking sheet. Bake at 450 degrees for 10-12 minutes or until golden brown. Remove to a wire rack. Serve warm.

Nutrition Information

- Calories: 135 calories
- Total Fat: 8g
- Cholesterol: 18mg
- Sodium: 257mg
- Total Carbohydrate: 15g
- Protein: 2g
- Fiber: 0 g

336. Sweet Potato and Black Pepper Biscuits

"Sweet and peppery biscuits, great for ham sandwiches with a little honey mustard. You can substitute pumpkin or winter squash for the sweet potato."

Serving: 12 | Prep: 15 m | Cook: 12 m | Ready in: 27 m

Ingredients

- 2 cups all-purpose flour
- 2 teaspoons baking powder
- 1 teaspoon white sugar
- 1/2 teaspoon ground black pepper
- 1/2 teaspoon baking soda
- 1/4 teaspoon salt
- 3/4 cup butter
- 1 cup cold mashed sweet potatoes
- 2 tablespoons heavy cream

Direction

- Preheat oven to 425 degrees F (220 degrees C).
- Whisk flour, baking powder, sugar, pepper, baking soda, and salt together in a large mixing bowl. Cut butter into the flour mixture with a pastry cutter or fork until the mixture resembles coarse crumbs. Stir sweet potatoes and cream into the flour mixture until the dough is soft.
- Turn the dough out onto a lightly floured work surface; knead the dough, turning over about 5 times. Roll to about 1/2-inch thick. Cut 2-inch circles out of dough and arrange on a baking sheet.
- Bake in preheated oven until lightly browned, 12 to 15 minutes.

Nutrition Information

- Calories: 210 calories
- Total Fat: 12.7 g
- Cholesterol: 34 mg
- Sodium: 281 mg
- Total Carbohydrate: 21.5 g
- Protein: 2.8 g

337. Sweet Potato Biscuits

"This recipe makes a wonderfully light and fluffy biscuit. A great way to use up those leftover mashed sweet potatoes. Makes a delicious sandwich with a slice ham, or simply topped with butter."

Serving: 8 | Prep: 5 m | Cook: 15 m | Ready in: 20 m

Ingredients

- 1 cup all-purpose flour
- 3 teaspoons baking powder
- 2 teaspoons white sugar
- 1 teaspoon salt
- 2 tablespoons shortening
- 3/4 cup mashed sweet potatoes
- 1/4 cup milk

Direction

- Preheat the oven to 400 degrees F (200 degrees C).
- In a medium bowl, stir together the flour, baking powder, sugar and salt. Cut in the shortening until pieces of shortening are pea-sized or smaller. Mix in the sweet potatoes, and enough of the milk to make a soft dough.
- Turn dough out onto a floured surface, and roll or pat out to 1/2 inch thickness. Cut into circles using a biscuit cutter or a drinking glass. Place biscuits 1 inch apart onto a greased baking sheet.
- Bake for 12 to 15 minutes in the preheated oven, or until golden brown.

Nutrition Information

- Calories: 118 calories
- Total Fat: 3.6 g
- Cholesterol: < 1 mg
- Sodium: 447 mg
- Total Carbohydrate: 19.2 g
- Protein: 2.3 g

338. Sweet Potato Biscuits with Honey Butter

We often think of sweet potatoes in a supporting role as a side dish, mashed, baked whole, cubed and roasted. Here's another thought--why not give them a starring role for breakfast when made into biscuits? Served with cinnamon-honey butter, they're all kinds of awesome. --Cathy Bell, Joplin, Missouri

Serving: 10 biscuits (about 1/2 cup honey butter). | Prep: 20 m | Cook: 10 m | Ready in: 30 m

Ingredients

- 2 cups all-purpose flour
- 4 teaspoons sugar
- 3 teaspoons baking powder
- 1 teaspoon salt
- 1 teaspoon ground cinnamon
- 1/2 teaspoon ground nutmeg
- 1/4 cup shortening
- 1 cup mashed sweet potatoes
- 1/2 cup half-and-half cream
- HONEY BUTTER:
- 1/2 cup butter, softened
- 2 tablespoons honey
- 1 teaspoon ground cinnamon

Direction

- In a small bowl, combine the first six ingredients. Cut in shortening until mixture resembles coarse crumbs. Combine sweet potatoes and cream; stir into crumb mixture just until moistened. Turn onto a lightly floured surface; gently knead 8-10 times.
- Pat or roll out to 1/2-in. thickness; cut with a floured 2-1/2-in. biscuit cutter. Place 1 in. apart on a greased baking sheet.
- Bake at 400 degrees for 9-11 minutes or until golden brown. Meanwhile, in a small bowl, beat the butter, honey and cinnamon until blended. Serve with warm biscuits.

Nutrition Information

- Calories: 277 calories
- Total Fat: 15g
- Cholesterol: 30mg

- Sodium: 436mg
- Total Carbohydrate: 31g
- Protein: 4g
- Fiber: 2g

339. Swiss Onion Drop Biscuits

In Hebron, Indiana, Edna Hoffman stirs up a big batch of these tender drop biscuits made with whole wheat flour. They're yummy spread with butter alongside a bowl of soup or a luncheon salad.

Serving: 2 dozen. | Prep: 15 m | Cook: 15 m | Ready in: 30 m

Ingredients

- 2 cups all-purpose flour
- 3/4 cup whole wheat flour
- 1 tablespoon sugar
- 3 teaspoons baking powder
- 3/4 teaspoon onion salt
- 1/2 teaspoon baking soda
- 1/2 cup cold butter
- 1 cup shredded Swiss cheese
- 1/3 cup thinly sliced green onions
- 2 large eggs
- 3/4 cup plus 2 tablespoons buttermilk

Direction

- In a large bowl, combine the flours, sugar, baking powder, onion salt and baking soda. Cut in butter until mixture resembles coarse crumbs. Stir in the cheese and onions. Combine eggs and buttermilk; stir into cheese mixture just until moistened.
- Drop by tablespoonfuls 2 in. apart onto greased baking sheets. Bake at 425 degrees for 12-15 minutes or until golden brown. Serve warm.

Nutrition Information

- Calories: 113 calories
- Total Fat: 6g
- Cholesterol: 32mg

- Sodium: 198mg
- Total Carbohydrate: 12g
- Protein: 4g
- Fiber: 1g

340. Tea Biscuits

"A quick tea time treat. Serve warm, buttered, and with jam or honey."

Serving: 20

Ingredients

- 2 cups all-purpose flour
- 4 teaspoons baking powder
- 1 teaspoon salt
- 1/2 cup shortening
- 3/4 cup milk

Direction

- Preheat oven to 400 degrees F (205 degrees C). Grease a baking sheet.
- Combine flour, baking powder, and salt. Cut shortening in until mixture has a fine crumb texture. Stir in milk with a fork to make a soft dough. Knead 8 to 10 times, and then roll out to a thickness of at least 1/2 inch. Cut into rounds with a cookie or biscuit cutter. Place on cookie sheet, and allow to rest for a few minutes.
- Bake for 12 to 15 minutes. Serve warm.

Nutrition Information

- Calories: 96 calories
- Total Fat: 5.4 g
- Cholesterol: < 1 mg
- Sodium: 218 mg
- Total Carbohydrate: 10.2 g
- Protein: 1.6 g

341. Teddy Bear Biscuits

"Children can't resist helping to assemble these cute cinnamony bears before baking," remarks Catherine Berra Bleem of Walsh, Illinois. "Refrigerated biscuit dough makes them easy, convenient and fun!"

Serving: 3 bears. | Prep: 10 m | Cook: 10 m | Ready in: 20 m

Ingredients

- 1 tube (7-1/2 ounces) refrigerated buttermilk biscuits (10 biscuits)
- 1 egg, lightly beaten
- 2 tablespoons sugar
- 1/4 teaspoon ground cinnamon
- 9 miniature semisweet chocolate chips

Direction

- For each bear, shape one biscuit into an oval for the body and place on a greased baking sheet. Cut one biscuit into four pieces; shape into balls for arms and legs. Place next to body.
- Cut one biscuit into two small pieces and one large pieces; shape into head and ears and place above body. Brush with egg. Combine sugar and cinnamon; sprinkle over bears.
- Bake at 425 degrees for 8-10 minutes (the one remaining biscuit can be baked with the bears) or until golden brown. Place chocolate chips on head for eyes and nose while the biscuits are still warm.

Nutrition Information

- Calories:
- Total Fat: g
- Cholesterol: mg
- Sodium: mg
- Total Carbohydrate: g
- Protein: g
- Fiber: g

342. Teenas Overnight Southern Buttermilk Biscuits

"I'm a Southern girl and these are the ultimate buttermilk biscuits. They're easy to make and, the best part is, you put the dough in the fridge the night before to let them rise extra high!"

Serving: 12 | Prep: 20 m | Cook: 15 m | Ready in: 8 h 35 m

Ingredients

- 4 cups self-rising flour
- 2 tablespoons white sugar
- 2/3 cup shortening
- 2 cups buttermilk

Direction

- Sift together the flour and sugar in a large bowl. Cut in the shortening until the mixture has a fine crumb or cornmeal texture. Stir in the buttermilk with a fork until a soft dough forms.
- Turn the dough out onto a floured surface, pulling off any pieces sticking inside the bowl. Gather dough into a ball and knead about 20 times, until smooth and elastic. Wrap in plastic wrap and refrigerate overnight.
- Preheat oven to 425 degrees F (220 degrees C).
- Working on a floured surface, roll or pat the dough out to 1 inch thickness. Cut into rounds with a 2 inch biscuit cutter, or the floured rim of a glass, by pressing straight down and up. Twisting the cutter will prevent the biscuits from rising as high. Place biscuits about 1 inch apart on an ungreased baking sheet, and allow to rest a few minutes.
- Bake in preheated oven until lightly brown, 12 to 15 minutes. Cool on a wire rack. Serve warm.

Nutrition Information

- Calories: 273 calories
- Total Fat: 12.2 g
- Cholesterol: 2 mg
- Sodium: 572 mg
- Total Carbohydrate: 35 g

- Protein: 5.5 g

343. Tender Biscuits for Two

These quick and easy rolls are lower in fat but not flavor. They'll dress up any weeknight meal. — Ane Burke, Bella Vista, Arkansas

Serving: 2 biscuits. | Prep: 15 m | Cook: 15 m | Ready in: 30 m

Ingredients

- 1/3 cup self-rising flour
- 1 tablespoon grated Parmesan cheese
- 1/8 teaspoon garlic salt
- 3 tablespoons reduced-fat cream cheese
- 3 tablespoons fat-free milk
- 1 tablespoon fat-free plain yogurt

Direction

- In a small bowl, combine the flour, Parmesan cheese and garlic salt. Cut in cream cheese until mixture resembles coarse crumbs. Stir in milk and yogurt just until moistened.
- Drop by scant 1/3 cupfuls 2 in. apart onto a baking sheet coated with cooking spray. Bake at 400 degrees for 12-15 minutes or until golden brown. Serve warm.

Nutrition Information

- Calories: 142 calories
- Total Fat: 5g
- Cholesterol: 18mg
- Sodium: 497mg
- Total Carbohydrate: 17g
- Protein: 6g
- Fiber: 0 g

344. Tender Potato Biscuits

"These tender potato biscuits are great to use up those leftover mashed potatoes! We like them for breakfast, lunch or dinner!"

Serving: 8 | Prep: 10 m | Cook: 20 m | Ready in: 30 m

Ingredients

- 2 1/2 cups all-purpose flour
- 2 tablespoons baking powder
- 1 teaspoon salt
- 1/4 cup sugar
- 1/4 cup butter or margarine
- 1 1/2 cups leftover mashed potatoes
- 1 egg, beaten
- 1/3 cup cold water
- 1/3 cup milk
- 2 tablespoons milk, or as needed

Direction

- Preheat the oven to 450 degrees F (230 degrees C).
- In a medium bowl, stir together the flour, baking powder, salt, and sugar. Cut in butter, until pieces of butter are no larger than peas. Use a fork to stir in mashed potatoes, breaking them up into chunks. Make a well in the mixture, and pour in egg, water and milk. Stir into a loose dough using the fork.
- Turn dough out onto a floured surface, and knead for 6 or 8 times so the dough holds together. Pat the dough out to about 3/4 inch thickness, and cut into circles with a biscuit cutter or drinking glass. Place biscuits onto an ungreased baking sheet. Brush the tops with 2 tablespoons milk.
- Bake for 15 to 20 minutes in the preheated oven, or until bottoms are golden.

Nutrition Information

- Calories: 279 calories
- Total Fat: 8.7 g
- Cholesterol: 40 mg
- Sodium: 730 mg
- Total Carbohydrate: 44.1 g
- Protein: 6.1 g

- Fiber: 1g

345. Tender Sweet Potato Biscuits

Whoever said biscuits were boring never tasted these. We love their rich flavor. These tender treats are great with a meal or as a snack with honey butter.

Serving: 1-1/2 dozen. | Prep: 25 m | Cook: 10 m | Ready in: 35 m

Ingredients

- 2 cups self-rising flour
- 1/4 cup packed brown sugar
- 1 teaspoon ground cinnamon
- 1 teaspoon ground ginger
- 7 tablespoons cold butter, divided
- 3 tablespoons shortening
- 1 cup mashed sweet potatoes
- 6 tablespoons 2% milk

Direction

- In a large bowl, combine the flour, brown sugar, cinnamon and ginger. Cut in 4 tablespoons butter and shortening until mixture resembles coarse crumbs.
- In a small bowl, combine sweet potatoes and milk; stir into crumb mixture just until moistened. Turn onto a lightly floured surface; knead 10 times.
- Pat or roll out to 1/2-in. thickness; cut with a floured 2-1/2-in. biscuit cutter. Place 2-in. apart on ungreased baking sheets.
- Melt remaining butter; brush over dough. Bake at 425 degrees for 10-12 minutes or until golden brown. Remove from pans to wire racks. Serve warm.

Nutrition Information

- Calories: 136 calories
- Total Fat: 7g
- Cholesterol: 13mg
- Sodium: 211mg
- Total Carbohydrate: 18g
- Protein: 2g

346. TexMex Biscuits

I love cooking with green chilies because they add so much flavor to ordinary dishes. Once while making a pot of chili, I had some green chilies left over and mixed them into my biscuit dough, creating this recipe. The fresh-from-the-oven treats are a wonderful accompaniment to soup or chili. - Angie Trolz, Jackson, Michigan

Serving: about 1 dozen. | Prep: 10 m | Cook: 10 m | Ready in: 20 m

Ingredients

- 2 cups biscuit/baking mix
- 2/3 cup 2% milk
- 1 cup (4 ounces) finely shredded cheddar cheese
- 1 can (4 ounces) chopped green chilies, drained

Direction

- In a large bowl, combine biscuit mix and milk until a soft dough forms. Stir in cheese and chilies. Turn onto a floured surface; knead 10 times. Roll out to 1/2-in. thickness; cut with a 2-1/2-in. biscuit cutter.
- Place on an ungreased baking sheet. Bake at 450 degrees for 8-10 minutes or until golden brown. Serve warm.

Nutrition Information

- Calories: 125 calories
- Total Fat: 6g
- Cholesterol: 12mg
- Sodium: 353mg
- Total Carbohydrate: 14g
- Protein: 4g
- Fiber: 1g

347. TomatoBasil Drop Biscuits

I grow fresh basil in my garden each summer. I use it in almost everything I cook. It really gets your taste buds going.--Shirley A. Glaab, Hattiesburg, Mississippi

Serving: about 1-1/2 dozen. | Prep: 25 m | Cook: 0 m | Ready in: 25 m

Ingredients

- 1/2 cup finely chopped green onions
- 1 tablespoon olive oil
- 3/4 cup chopped fresh tomato, drained
- 1/4 cup minced fresh basil or 4 teaspoons dried basil
- 2 cups all-purpose flour
- 1 tablespoon baking powder
- 1 teaspoon salt
- 1/4 teaspoon coarsely ground black pepper
- 1/3 cup shortening
- 2/3 cup 2% milk

Direction

- In a small skillet, sauté onions in oil until tender. Add tomato; cook 1 minute longer. Remove from the heat; stir in basil. Cool slightly.
- In a large bowl, combine the flour, baking powder, salt and pepper. Cut in shortening until the mixture resembles coarse crumbs. Stir in milk and tomato mixture just until combined.
- Drop by heaping teaspoonfuls 2 in. apart onto greased baking sheets. Bake at 425 degrees for 10-12 minutes or until golden brown. Remove to wire racks. Serve warm.

Nutrition Information

- Calories: 90 calories
- Total Fat: 4g
- Cholesterol: 1mg
- Sodium: 203mg
- Total Carbohydrate: 12g
- Protein: 2g
- Fiber: 1g

348. Touch of Honey Biscuits

Honey lends just a hint of sweetness to these light and tender dinner biscuits from Donna Jeffers of Petersburg, West Virginia (with her husband, Paul, right). "Our friend Joan gave us this recipe, so when my husband or I make them, we always call them Joan's Biscuits," Donna relates.

Serving: 4 biscuits. | Prep: 15 m | Cook: 10 m | Ready in: 25 m

Ingredients

- 1 cup all-purpose flour
- 1-1/2 teaspoons baking powder
- 1/4 teaspoon salt
- 1/4 teaspoon cream of tartar
- 1/4 cup cold butter
- 1/3 cup milk
- 1 teaspoon honey

Direction

- In a large bowl, combine the flour, baking powder, salt and cream of tartar; cut in butter until crumbly. Stir in milk and honey just until moistened.
- Turn onto a floured surface; knead gently 8-10 times. Roll out to 3/4-in. thickness; cut with a floured 2-1/2-in. biscuit cutter. Place 1 in. apart on a greased baking sheet. Bake at 450 degrees for 10-15 minutes or until golden brown.

Nutrition Information

- Calories: 232 calories
- Total Fat: 12g
- Cholesterol: 33mg
- Sodium: 424mg
- Total Carbohydrate: 26g
- Protein: 4g
- Fiber: 1g

349. Triple Herbed Biscuits

As if the tenderness and flakiness of these biscuits wasn't reason enough to fall in love with them, the robust herb flavor is! Serve them with any number of main dishes, or just enjoy one all by itself. — Roblynn Hunnisett, Guelph, Ontario

Serving: 8 biscuits. | Prep: 20 m | Cook: 15 m | Ready in: 35 m

Ingredients

- 1-1/2 cups all-purpose flour
- 1/2 cup All-Bran
- 2 tablespoons sugar
- 2 tablespoons minced fresh parsley
- 1 tablespoon baking powder
- 1 tablespoon minced fresh thyme
- 1-1/2 teaspoons minced fresh rosemary
- 1/4 teaspoon salt
- 1/2 cup cold butter
- 1 egg
- 2/3 cup plus 2 teaspoons 2% milk, divided

Direction

- In a large bowl, combine the first eight ingredients. Cut in butter until mixture resembles coarse crumbs. Whisk egg and 2/3 cup milk; stir into flour mixture just until moistened. Turn onto a floured surface and knead 10 times.
- Pat or roll out to 3/4-in. thickness; cut with a floured 2-1/2-in. biscuit cutter. Place on a greased baking sheet. Brush tops with remaining milk. Bake at 425 degrees for 12-15 minutes or until golden brown. Serve warm.

Nutrition Information

- Calories: 229 calories
- Total Fat: 13g
- Cholesterol: 58mg
- Sodium: 334mg
- Total Carbohydrate: 25g
- Protein: 5g
- Fiber: 2g

350. Upside Down Orange Biscuits

From Mendota, Illinois, Kim Marie Van Rheenen guarantees that "The aroma of these baking is enough to get even the soundest sleeper out of bed!"

Serving: 1 dozen. | Prep: 20 m | Cook: 20 m | Ready in: 40 m

Ingredients

- 2 cups all-purpose flour
- 1 tablespoon baking powder
- 1/2 teaspoon salt
- 3 tablespoons shortening
- 3/4 cup whole milk
- 2 tablespoons butter, softened
- 1/4 cup sugar
- 1 teaspoon ground cinnamon
- TOPPING:
- 1/2 cup sugar
- 1/2 cup orange juice
- 3 tablespoons butter, melted
- 2 teaspoons grated orange zest

Direction

- In a large bowl, combine flour, baking powder and salt; cut in shortening until mixture resembles coarse crumbs. Stir in milk just until moistened. Turn onto a lightly floured surface; knead gently 10-12 times.
- Roll into a 15x12-in. rectangle. Spread with butter. Combine the sugar and cinnamon; sprinkle over butter. Roll up jelly-roll style, starting from the short side. Cut into 12 equal slices. Place, cut side down, in a greased 9-in. round baking pan.
- Combine topping ingredients; pour over biscuits. Bake at 450 degrees for 20-25 minutes or until lightly browned. Cool in pan 5 minutes; invert onto a platter and serve warm.

Nutrition Information

- Calories: 208 calories
- Total Fat: 8g
- Cholesterol: 15mg
- Sodium: 255mg
- Total Carbohydrate: 30g

- Protein: 3g
- Fiber: 1g

351. Vegan Biscuits

"These biscuits are vegan, moist, delicious and easy to make!"

Serving: 12 | Prep: 10 m | Cook: 15 m | Ready in: 25 m

Ingredients

- 3 cups flour
- 1 1/2 tablespoons baking powder
- 1 1/2 teaspoons salt
- 6 tablespoons coconut oil, softened
- 1 cup hemp milk

Direction

- Preheat oven to 350 degrees F (175 degrees C).
- Combine flour, baking powder, and salt in a bowl. Fluff with a fork until mixture is evenly distributed. Drop in chunks of coconut oil. Mix by hand, breaking chunks apart, until dough is crumbly. Stir in hemp milk; do not over-knead.
- Place dough on a lightly floured surface and roll it out to about 1/2-inch thickness. Cut into biscuit-size squares using a round cookie cutter.
- Bake in the preheated oven until fluffy and lightly golden, about 15 minutes. And then eat them all! Just kidding. You should share... a few.

Nutrition Information

- Calories: 185 calories
- Total Fat: 7.5 g
- Cholesterol: 0 mg
- Sodium: 485 mg
- Total Carbohydrate: 26 g
- Protein: 3.5 g

352. Vegan Sweet Potato Biscuits

"These are incredible! You would never know they have no butter in them! Drizzle with honey or pure maple syrup if desired."

Serving: 12 | Prep: 20 m | Cook: 20 m | Ready in: 40 m

Ingredients

- 1 sweet potato
- 1/2 cup white whole wheat flour
- 1/2 cup whole wheat flour
- 1 tablespoon baking powder
- 2 teaspoons white sugar
- 1/2 teaspoon baking soda
- 1/2 teaspoon salt
- 1/2 teaspoon ground cinnamon
- 2 tablespoons coconut oil
- 1/4 cup cashew milk, or more as needed

Direction

- Prick sweet potato all over with a fork. Microwave on high in 2-minute intervals until tender, turning halfway through, 8 to 10 minutes. Cool sweet potato until easily handled.
- Preheat oven to 375 degrees F (190 degrees C). Line a baking sheet with parchment paper.
- Mix white whole wheat flour, whole wheat flour, baking powder, sugar, baking soda, salt, and cinnamon together in a large bowl. Cut in coconut oil with a pastry cutter until mixture is the size of peas.
- Peel sweet potato and mash coarsely with a fork. Measure out 3/4 cup mashed sweet potato and mix into the flour mixture. Pour in cashew milk and mix until dough is just sticky.
- Dust a flat work surface with flour. Turn out dough and knead 5 to 6 times to bring it together. Pat out to 1/2-inch thickness. Cut into rounds with a biscuit cutter. Place 1 inch apart on the lined baking sheet.
- Bake biscuits in the preheated oven until bottoms are golden brown, 12 to 16 minutes.

Nutrition Information

- Calories: 79 calories
- Total Fat: 2.5 g
- Cholesterol: 0 mg
- Sodium: 285 mg
- Total Carbohydrate: 13.5 g
- Protein: 1.7 g

353. Vegan Whole Wheat Biscuits

"Yummy whole grain biscuits made without any animal products."

Serving: 12 | Prep: 15 m | Cook: 10 m | Ready in: 25 m

Ingredients

- 2 cups whole wheat pastry flour
- 4 teaspoons baking powder
- 1 tablespoon stevia powder
- 3/4 teaspoon salt
- 1/4 cup coconut oil, at room temperature
- 1 cup almond milk

Direction

- Preheat oven to 450 degrees F (230 degrees C).
- Mix flour, baking powder, stevia powder, and salt in a bowl. Cut in coconut oil with a pastry cutter or knife until mixture resembles coarse crumbs. Stir in almond milk until dough is just moistened.
- Turn dough out onto a lightly floured surface; knead gently 8 to 10 times. Pat or roll the dough out into a 3/4 inch thick round. Cut circles with a 2 1/2-inch biscuit cutter and arrange biscuits on a baking sheet.
- Bake in preheated oven until lightly browned, 8 to 10 minutes.

Nutrition Information

- Calories: 102 calories
- Total Fat: 5.1 g
- Cholesterol: 0 mg
- Sodium: 321 mg
- Total Carbohydrate: 13.5 g
- Protein: 2.1 g

354. Wheat Biscuits

I'VE HAD this recipe in my file for a long time. I love cooking and baking and am always creating something new by experimenting with recipes. I thought the substitution of whole wheat flour gave these biscuits a little different taste.
-Edna Hoffman, Hebron, Indiana

Serving: 4 biscuits. | Prep: 10 m | Cook: 20 m | Ready in: 30 m

Ingredients

- 1/3 cup all-purpose flour
- 1/3 cup whole wheat flour
- 1 tablespoon sugar
- 3/4 teaspoon baking powder
- 1/4 teaspoon baking soda
- 1/4 teaspoon salt
- 2 tablespoons cold butter
- 1/4 cup buttermilk

Direction

- In a small bowl, combine the first six ingredients. Cut in butter until crumbly. Stir in buttermilk just until moistened.
- Turn onto a floured surface; knead 6-8 times. Pat or roll out to 1-in. thickness; cut with a 2-1/2-in. biscuit cutter. Place on a greased baking sheet. Bake at 375 degrees for 18-20 minutes or until lightly browned.

Nutrition Information

- Calories: 140 calories
- Total Fat: 6g
- Cholesterol: 16mg
- Sodium: 376mg
- Total Carbohydrate: 19g
- Protein: 3g
- Fiber: 1g

355. Whipped Cream Biscuits

Since there is no shortening to cut in, these light, airy biscuits are quick and easy to make. Time the baking so that they're out of the oven when you sit down to eat. -Linda Murrow, Aurora, Colorado

Serving: 5 biscuits. | Prep: 10 m | Cook: 10 m | Ready in: 20 m

Ingredients

- 1 cup all-purpose flour
- 1-1/2 teaspoons baking powder
- 1/4 teaspoon salt
- 1/2 cup heavy whipping cream, whipped

Direction

- In a bowl, combine the flour, baking powder and salt. Stir in cream. Turn dough onto a floured surface; knead 10 times. Roll to 3/4-in. thickness; cut with a 2-1/4-in. round biscuit cutter.
- Place on an ungreased baking sheet. Bake at 425 degrees for 10 minutes or until lightly browned. Serve warm.

Nutrition Information

- Calories: 173 calories
- Total Fat: 9g
- Cholesterol: 33mg
- Sodium: 248mg
- Total Carbohydrate: 20g
- Protein: 3g
- Fiber: 1g

356. White Lily Light and Fluffy Biscuits

"These light and versatile biscuits come together so easily and are ready to eat in no time."

Serving: 12 | Prep: 10 m | Cook: 12 m | Ready in: 25 m

Ingredients

- 2 cups White Lily® Enriched Bleached Self-Rising Flour or White Lily® Enriched Unbleached Self-Rising Flour
- 1/4 cup Crisco® All-Vegetable Shortening
- 3/4 cup buttermilk
- 2 tablespoons butter, melted (optional)

Direction

- Heat oven to 475 degrees F.
- Place flour in large bowl. Cut in shortening with pastry blender or 2 knives until crumbs are the size of peas. Add buttermilk, stirring with fork just until flour is moistened.
- Turn dough onto lightly floured surface. Knead gently 5 to 6 times, just until a smooth dough is formed. Roll dough into a 7-inch circle that is 3/4- to 1-inch thick. Cut out 7 to 8 biscuits using a floured 2-inch biscuit cutter. Place on baking sheet, about 1-inch apart. (For softer biscuits, arrange so that edges almost touch.) Shape dough scraps into a ball. Pat out until 3/4-inch thick. Cut out additional biscuits.
- Bake 8 to 10 minutes or until golden brown. Remove from oven. Brush with butter, if desired.

Nutrition Information

- Calories: 126 calories
- Total Fat: 6.1 g
- Cholesterol: 6 mg
- Sodium: 263 mg
- Total Carbohydrate: 15.4 g
- Protein: 1.9 g

357. Whole Wheat Biscuits

This quick and easy recipe adds a special touch to everyday meals. See if you don't get a lot of compliments when you serve these biscuits fresh from the oven.

Serving: about 1 dozen. | Prep: 15 m | Cook: 10 m | Ready in: 25 m

Ingredients

- 1-1/2 cups all-purpose flour
- 1/2 cup whole wheat flour
- 2 tablespoons sugar
- 1 tablespoon baking powder
- 1/2 teaspoon cream of tartar
- 1/4 teaspoon salt
- 1/2 cup shortening
- 1 egg
- 1/2 cup milk
- 1 tablespoon butter, melted

Direction

- In a bowl, combine flours, sugar, baking powder, cream of tartar and salt. Cut in shortening until mixture resembles coarse crumbs. Beat egg and milk; stir into dry ingredients until a ball forms.
- Turn onto a floured surface, knead 5-6 times. Roll to 1/2-in. thickness; brush with butter. Cut with a 2-in. biscuit cutter. Place on an ungreased baking sheet. Bake at 450 degrees for 10-12 minutes or until golden brown.

Nutrition Information

- Calories: 176 calories
- Total Fat: 10g
- Cholesterol: 22mg
- Sodium: 170mg
- Total Carbohydrate: 18g
- Protein: 3g
- Fiber: 1g

358. Whole Wheat Dog Biscuits

For a wholesome, healthy treat for your treasured family dog, try these easy biscuits. Your pup will be so excited when he tries these delicious treats!--Rose Crawford, Springfield, Illinois

Serving: about 2-1/2 dozen. | Prep: 15 m | Cook: 20 m | Ready in: 35 m

Ingredients

- 2-1/2 cups whole wheat flour
- 1/4 cup toasted wheat germ
- 1 garlic clove, crushed
- 4 tablespoons butter, cubed
- 1 egg, beaten
- 1/4 cup milk
- 1 tablespoon molasses
- Water

Direction

- Combine flour, wheat germ and garlic in a large bowl. Cut in butter. Stir in egg, milk and molasses. Add enough water so mixture can be shaped into a ball. Roll dough onto a floured surface to a thickness of 1/2 in. Cut into desired shapes and place on a greased baking sheet. Bake at 375 degrees for 20 minutes. Cool.

Nutrition Information

- Calories: 56 calories
- Total Fat: 2g
- Cholesterol: 7mg
- Sodium: 22mg
- Total Carbohydrate: 8g
- Protein: 2g
- Fiber: 1g

359. Whole Wheat Vegan Drop Biscuits

"*These vegan biscuits are quick, easy, and fluffy. They use all whole wheat flour. I couldn't find a biscuit recipe online that met all of these criteria - so I made one up!*"

Serving: 10 | Prep: 10 m | Cook: 10 m | Ready in: 20 m

Ingredients

- 2 cups whole wheat flour
- 4 teaspoons baking powder
- 1 teaspoon salt
- 2 tablespoons vegan butter
- 2 tablespoons coconut oil
- 1 cup almond milk

Direction

- Preheat an oven to 450 degrees F (230 degrees C).
- Mix flour, baking powder, and salt together in a bowl. Cut vegan butter and coconut oil into flour mixture using a fork until crumbly; stir in almond milk until just combined. Drop batter onto an ungreased baking sheet.
- Bake in the preheated oven until biscuits are soft and lightly browned, 10 to 12 minutes.

Nutrition Information

- Calories: 129 calories
- Total Fat: 5.3 g
- Cholesterol: 0 mg
- Sodium: 463 mg
- Total Carbohydrate: 18.8 g
- Protein: 3.4 g

360. Witches Hat Biscuits

These delicious biscuits have a delicious pumpkin flavor that appeals to everyone. The honey butter adds a bit of sweetness to every bite.

Serving: 1 dozen. | Prep: 20 m | Cook: 10 m | Ready in: 30 m

Ingredients

- 2 cups all-purpose flour
- 1/4 cup sugar
- 3 teaspoons baking powder
- 1-1/2 teaspoons ground cinnamon
- 1/2 teaspoon salt
- 1/4 teaspoon baking soda
- 1/4 teaspoon ground nutmeg
- 1/2 cup cold butter
- 3/4 cup canned pumpkin
- 1/2 cup buttermilk
- 1/2 cup chopped walnuts
- HONEY BUTTER:
- 1/2 cup butter, softened
- 1/2 cup honey
- 1/2 teaspoon grated orange zest

Direction

- In a large bowl, combine the flour, sugar, baking powder, cinnamon, salt, baking soda and nutmeg. Cut in butter until mixture resembles coarse crumbs. Stir in pumpkin and buttermilk just until moistened. Stir in walnuts.
- Turn dough onto a lightly floured surface; knead 8-10 times. Pat or roll out to 1/2-in. thickness; cut with a floured 3-1/4-in. witches' hat biscuit cutter. Place 1 in. apart on a greased baking sheet. Bake at 425 degrees for 8-12 minutes or until golden brown.
- Meanwhile, in a small bowl, combine the honey butter ingredients. Serve with warm biscuits.

Nutrition Information

- Calories: 311 calories
- Total Fat: 18g
- Cholesterol: 41mg

- Sodium: 391mg
- Total Carbohydrate: 34g
- Protein: 4g
- Fiber: 2g

- Cholesterol: 33 mg
- Sodium: 825 mg
- Total Carbohydrate: 35.4 g
- Protein: 12.1 g

361. Witchetty Grubs

"Bite-sized morsels perfect for kid's parties are made of creamed corn, flour, and cheese. And no, they don't taste like chicken."

Serving: 4 | Prep: 30 m | Cook: 15 m | Ready in: 45 m

Ingredients

- 1 cup shredded Cheddar cheese
- 1 cup cream-style corn
- 2 teaspoons olive oil
- 1 cup self-rising flour, or as needed
- 3 cocktail wieners
- 1 teaspoon blanched slivered almonds

Direction

- Preheat oven to 375 degrees F (190 degrees C). Grease a baking sheet.
- Mix together the Cheddar cheese, corn, olive oil, and self-rising flour to make a firm dough. Roll the dough out into a log shape, and cut into 16 equal pieces. Roll each piece into a ball. Cut the cocktail wieners into 6 slices each (there will be 2 extra slices). Pick out 8 almond slivers.
- To make the grubs, place 4 dough balls onto the baking sheet, and press them tightly together so they make a lumpy grub with 4 segments. Place a slice of cocktail wiener on top of each segment for markings. Stick 2 little almond slivers into an end ball to make eyes. Repeat for the other grubs.
- Bake in the preheated oven until the grubs are golden brown, about 15 minutes.

Nutrition Information

- Calories: 316 calories
- Total Fat: 14.5 g

362. Yeast Biscuits

Wonderful from-scratch yeast biscuits-golden and crusty outside and tender inside-were a staple Mom prepared regularly when I was growing up. They are perfect for sopping up gravy from bowls of beef stew and are also great for sandwiches.

Serving: about 2-1/2 dozen. | Prep: 30 m | Cook: 10 m | Ready in: 40 m

Ingredients

- 3-1/4 teaspoons active dry yeast
- 1/2 cup warm water (110 degrees to 115 degrees)
- 1/2 cup sugar
- 1/2 cup butter, softened
- 1 can (5 ounces) evaporated milk
- 2 eggs, lightly beaten
- 1-1/2 teaspoons salt
- 2 cups whole wheat flour
- 2 cups all-purpose flour

Direction

- In a large bowl, dissolve yeast in water. Add the sugar, butter, milk, eggs, salt and whole wheat flour; beat until smooth. Add enough all-purpose flour to form a soft dough.
- Turn onto a floured surface; knead until smooth and elastic, about 10 minutes. Place in a greased bowl, turning once to grease top. Cover and let rise in a warm place until doubled, about 1-1/2 hours.
- Punch dough down; divide into thirds. Let rest for 5 minutes. On a floured surface, roll out each portion to 1/2-in. thickness. Cut with a 2-1/2-in. biscuit cutter. Place on lightly greased baking sheets. Cover and let rise until doubled, about 30 minutes.

- Bake at 375 degrees for 10-12 minutes or until golden brown. Remove from pans to cool on wire racks. Serve warm.

Nutrition Information

- Calories: 110 calories
- Total Fat: 4g
- Cholesterol: 24mg
- Sodium: 159mg
- Total Carbohydrate: 16g
- Protein: 3g
- Fiber: 1g

363. Yogurt Biscuits

"Scoring the dough instead of cutting out individual pieces keeps these biscuits nice and moist," explains Rosemarie Kondrk of Old Bridge, New Jersey. "They have old-fashioned flavor that's very satisfying."

Serving: 6 biscuits. | Prep: 15 m | Cook: 15 m | Ready in: 30 m

Ingredients

- 1 cup plus 2 tablespoons all-purpose flour
- 1-1/2 teaspoons baking powder
- 1/2 teaspoon salt
- 1/4 teaspoon baking soda
- 2 tablespoons cold butter
- 1/2 cup fat-free plain yogurt
- 1 teaspoon sugar
- 1/2 teaspoon fat-free milk

Direction

- In a bowl, combine flour, baking powder, salt and baking soda; cut in butter until crumbly. Combine yogurt and sugar; stir into the dry ingredients just until moistened. Turn onto a floured surface; knead 4-5 times. Place on a baking sheet that has been coated with cooking spray; pat into a 6-in. x 4-in. rectangle. Cut into six square biscuits (do not separate biscuits). Brush tops with milk. Bake at 450

degrees for 12-15 minutes or until golden. Serve warm.

Nutrition Information

- Calories: 134 calories
- Total Fat: 4g
- Cholesterol: 0 mg
- Sodium: 429mg
- Total Carbohydrate: 21g
- Protein: 4g
- Fiber: 0 g

364. Zucchini Cheese Drop Biscuits

These colorful little drop biscuits are very easy to put together and yet are packed full of flavor. I serve them warm out of the oven. --Keith Mesch, Mt. Healthy, Ohio

Serving: 1 dozen. | Prep: 25 m | Cook: 25 m | Ready in: 50 m

Ingredients

- 3/4 cup shredded zucchini
- 1-1/4 teaspoons salt, divided
- 2-1/2 cups all-purpose flour
- 1 tablespoon baking powder
- 1/2 cup cold butter, cubed
- 1/2 cup shredded cheddar cheese
- 1/4 cup shredded part-skim mozzarella cheese
- 1/4 cup shredded Parmesan cheese
- 2 tablespoons finely chopped oil-packed sun-dried tomatoes, patted dry
- 2 tablespoons minced fresh basil or 2 teaspoons dried basil
- 1 cup 2% milk

Direction

- Preheat oven to 425 degrees. Place zucchini in a colander over a plate; sprinkle with 1/4 teaspoon salt and toss. Let stand 10 minutes. Rinse and drain well. Squeeze zucchini to remove excess liquid. Pat dry.

- In a large bowl, whisk flour, baking powder and remaining salt. Cut in butter until mixture resembles coarse crumbs. Stir in zucchini, cheeses, tomatoes and basil. Add milk; stir just until moistened.
- Drop by scant 1/3 cupfuls into a greased 13x9-in. baking pan. Bake 22-26 minutes or until golden brown. Serve warm.

Nutrition Information

- Calories: 205 calories
- Total Fat: 11g
- Cholesterol: 29mg
- Sodium: 482mg
- Total Carbohydrate: 22g
- Protein: 6g
- Fiber: 1g

biscuit mix, parsley, basil, thyme and onion mixture. In another bowl. Whisk eggs and milk. Stir into biscuit mixture just until combined. Fold in zucchini and cheese.
- Drop by 1/4 cupfuls 2 in. apart onto greased baking sheets. Bake at 400 degrees for 10-14 minutes or until golden brown. Serve warm. Refrigerate leftovers.

Nutrition Information

- Calories: 148 calories
- Total Fat: 9g
- Cholesterol: 55mg
- Sodium: 315mg
- Total Carbohydrate: 13g
- Protein: 4g
- Fiber: 1g

365. Zucchini Cheddar Biscuits

My husband grows a big garden, and our squash crop always seems to multiply! We give squash to everyone but still have plenty left over for making jelly, relish, pickles, breads, cakes and brownies. -- Jean Moore, Pliny, West Virginia

Serving: 16 biscuits. | Prep: 15 m | Cook: 10 m | Ready in: 25 m

Ingredients

- 1/4 cup butter, cubed
- 1 large onion, chopped
- 2-1/2 cups biscuit/baking mix
- 1 tablespoon minced fresh parsley
- 1/2 teaspoon dried basil
- 1/2 teaspoon dried thyme
- 3 eggs, lightly beaten
- 1/4 cup 2% milk
- 1-1/2 cups shredded zucchini
- 1 cup shredded cheddar cheese

Direction

- In a large skillet, melt butter. Add onion; sauté until tender. In a large bowl, combine the

Index

Evaporated milk, *68, 192*

F

Fat, *11–194*

Fish, *120, 142*

Flour, 12–15, 17–39, 41–56, 58–81, 83–117, 119–128, 130–142, 145–147, 149–152, 154–163,

166–194

Fruit, *14, 38, 52, 57, 66*

G

Garlic, 39–40, 44–50, 70, 76, 83, 91–94, 101–103, 109, 118, 125–126, 128–129, 131, 135, 142,

144–145, 149, 152–156, 159, 162–165, 177–178, 183, 190

Ginger, *66, 70, 94–95, 150, 174, 184*

Ginger ale, *70*

Grain, *173, 188*

Gravy, 11–13, 24, 70, 73–74, 108, 121, 162, 173, 178, 192

Ground ginger, *66, 95, 150, 174, 184*

H

Ham, 12, 22, 27, 52, 101–104, 125, 138, 148, 179–180

Heart, *105–106, 162*

Herbs, 56, 75, 83, 87, 91, 94, 149, 159, 164

Honey, 12, 15, 24, 34, 39, 43, 69, 78, 84–87, 90, 97, 103, 105–106, 112–114, 121–122, 139,

142, 146–147, 157, 159, 173, 175, 178–181,

184–185, 187, 191

I

Ice cream, *21, 66, 113, 121, 139*

Icing, *29–30, 58, 61, 115–116*

J

Jam, 38, 52, 65, 81–82, 86, 119, 122, 139, 173, 181

Jelly, 13, 15, 24, 58, 95, 119–120, 123, 175, 178, 186, 194

K

Kale, *122*

L

Lager, *149*

Lard, *22, 24, 32, 86, 89, 160*

Leek, *170*

Lemon, 11, 14, 21, 55, 66, 73, 78, 82, 123–124

Lemon juice, *14, 21, 66, 123–124*

Lime, *11, 73, 78, 82, 124–125*

Lime juice, *124*

Lobster, *125, 155–156*

M

Macadamia, *143*

Macaroni, *56, 142*

Mango, *61*

Y

Z

Conclusion

Thank you again for downloading this book!

I hope you enjoyed reading about my book!

If you enjoyed this book, please take the time to share your thoughts and post a review on Amazon. It'd be greatly appreciated!

Write me an honest review about the book – I truly value your opinion and thoughts and I will incorporate them into my next book, which is already underway.

Thank you!

If you have any questions, **feel free to contact at:** *chefemmakim@gmail.com*

Emma Kim
www.TheCookingMAP.com/Emma-Kim

Printed in Great Britain
by Amazon

61918639R00115